✠✠GERMANY✠✠ AND THE EAST

FRITZ T. EPSTEIN

✛✛✛✛✛✛✛✛✛✛✛✛✛✛✛✛✛✛✛✛✛✛✛✛✛✛

FRITZ T. EPSTEIN

GERMANY
AND THE EAST

SELECTED ESSAYS

✛✛✛✛✛✛✛✛✛✛✛✛✛✛✛✛✛✛✛✛✛✛✛✛

Edited, with an Introduction, by
ROBERT F. BYRNES

INDIANA UNIVERSITY PRESS
Bloomington & London

Published in Canada by Fitzhenry & Whiteside Limited,
Don Mills, Ontario
Library of Congress catalog card number: 72-85851
ISBN: 0-253-32580-3
Manufactured in the United States of America

To Fritz T. Epstein

*From those who have worked with him in
the Russian and East European Institute, Indiana University,
as a mark of their respect and affection
for him as a teacher-scholar, colleague, and human being*

Contents

This volume is a selection of some of the essays of Professor Fritz T. Epstein. They were written originally in German and published in Germany at various times between 1932 and 1966. A perfectionist, Professor Epstein introduced some new data and additional bibliography while the essays were being translated and prepared for publication in English. We are all grateful to him for this special effort.

Publication of this volume was made possible by a grant of Ford Foundation funds made available by the International Publications Advisory Committee of the Office of Research and Advanced Studies, Indiana University.

Mrs. Anna Strikis typed the manuscript, an especially demanding performance, with particular care and skill. We all thank her most warmly.

R.F.B.

RUSSIAN AND EAST EUROPEAN INSTITUTE
INDIANA UNIVERSITY
JUNE 1972

✤✤✤

Introduction:
FRITZ T. EPSTEIN

✤✤✤

by Robert F. Byrnes

This volume of essays continues one of the great traditions inherited by American scholarship from nineteenth-century Germany, that of honoring eminent and beloved colleagues by publishing a *Festschrift,* ordinarily a collection of essays written by former students as a token of gratitude and respect for their mentor. In the case of Dr. Fritz T. Epstein, Professor of History and Curator of the Slavic Collection at Indiana University from 1963 until 1969, and then again as a visiting professor in 1970 and 1971, his colleagues in the university's Russian and East European Institute decided to show their honor and affection, and that of hundreds of others throughout the United States and Western Europe, not by publishing a series of their essays, but by arranging the translation from German into English and the publication of some of Professor Epstein's essays which dealt with one of his central concerns as a scholar, relations between Germany and the Slavic world. As the depth and range of knowledge of these essays show, and as the list of his publications provided at the end of this volume demonstrates even more clearly, Professor Epstein had a remarkable number of scholarly interests. None was more pervasive or has received more penetrating attention than Germany and the East. The significance of this issue in international relations in 1973 is even greater than when it first attracted the attention of the young *gymnasium* student in 1916. Indeed, these essays should be studied because of their penetrating quality and the insight and perspective they provide concerning both historical and contemporary problems. No token of affection and esteem could therefore be more appropriate.

Fritz Epstein was born in Saargemünd in Alsace-Lorraine on August 20, 1898. His father was a mathematician (who failed to pass on to his son any special skills in mathematics), and his paternal grandfather was an astronomer and co-founder of the Mozarteum in Salzburg. He has remained "a child of the German West" throughout his life. Similarly, just as Alsace-Lorraine served for long as both a bridge and a battleground between France and Germany, Professor Epstein's career reflects a special relationship between Germany and the United States. "A wanderer between two worlds," as one of his German colleagues noted, he has helped to bring Germany and the United States together by his career as a teacher and scholar and by his activities in both countries on behalf of the larger, indeed universal, interests of learning.

Epstein's early education at the Protestantisches Gymnasium of the Thomasstift and the Kaiserliches Lyzeum (now the Lycée Fustel de Coulanges) in Strassburg from 1908 through 1916 created in him an interest in medieval history which has remained a powerful urge even during his long years of concern with *Zeitgeschichte*. His first year of university study at Heidelberg in 1916–1917 similarly created an interest in public law and in constitutional and administrative history, particularly through the courses of Professor Gerhard Anschütz, who inspired Professor Epstein as Epstein later did young Germans and Americans. After serving in the German army on the Lorraine front during the last year of the First World War, Epstein went to Jena University for one term, changing his interest then to history and political science. His formal education was completed at Frankfurt am Main and at Berlin, where he received his doctor's degree in 1924, with Professor Karl Stählin his *Promotionsvater*.

Epstein's interest in Russia began during his student days in Strassburg, when the wartime writings of Paul Rohrbach excited him to begin to learn Russian. While he was completing his graduate work in Berlin he attended the courses of such great scholars as Friedrich Meinecke, Hans Delbrück, Adolf von Harnack and Ernst Tröltsch, but his thesis was on Russian central administration before Peter the Great and reflected research directed by three German pioneers on Russian and East European history, Theodor Schiemann, Otto Hoetzsch, and Karl Stählin. In fact, he was the first Ph.D. candidate at the University of Berlin to substitute the history of Eastern Europe for medieval history in the oral examination.

After receiving his degree, Epstein devoted two years to editing *Minerva,* the Yearbook of the Learned World, and to using that journal to increase knowledge and understanding about the higher education and scholarship of Eastern Europe and the Balkans. He then spent 1926 through 1931 at the University of Hamburg Seminar for the History of Eastern Europe, where he had been invited to serve as research assistant to Professor Richard Salomon. It is clear from Professor Epstein's comments that these years were among the happiest of his life and that they laid the foundation for what would have been a productive and satisfying career in a major German university. During these years he also completed and Hamburg University published his first major work, the papers of Heinrich von Staden, a Westphalian adventurer who spent 1564 to 1575 in the Russia of Ivan the Terrible. This account of Ivan's court of the *oprichnina,* of Kazan and the Volga area, of the position of the foreigner in Russia, and of Russian life in general is among the most important Western sources on Russian history in the sixteenth century. Moreover, scholars everywhere recognize that the editing was superb. Indeed, Epstein's comments and bibliography made this work a model of its kind of scholarly publication. Epstein's connections with Hamburg have always remained strong. He served there as a visiting professor in the spring terms of 1966, 1967, and 1968, and the Philosophical Faculty of Hamburg University honored him, and itself, on his seventieth birthday by awarding him an honorary degree.

The early 1930s were not a comfortable time for most Germans, and German academic life in particular was tense and strained. Even so, Epstein was able to devote 1932 and 1933 to work on his *Habilitationschrift* as a Research Fellow of the Notgemeinschaft der deutschen Wissenschaft in Berlin and of the William Kerckhoff Stiftung in Bad Nauheim. This study ("Russland und die Weltpolitik 1917–1920. Studien zur Geschichte der Intervention in Russland") was, in a way, centuries removed from von Staden and yet closely related to Epstein's long-term interests, for it concentrated on the Versailles Peace Conference and Western intervention in Russia. It was completed, but the degree was never obtained, because Hitler's racial policies denied the position of lecturer or *Privatdozent* to a scholar of Jewish descent, and the Epsteins therefore went to England early in the Hitler regime. There, serving as a lecturer in German at the Institut Français in South Kensington and aided by a grant from the Academic Assistance Council, Epstein revised and enlarged the study from materials in the British Museum, the Royal Institute of International Affairs, and the library of the School of Slavonic Studies. This work was never published, but the extended German version and an abridged English translation are both available in typescript in the British Museum.

England in the 1930s, while generously hospitable to emigrants from Nazi Germany, was not able to provide adequate opportunities, so Epstein, always indomitable, traveled through the United States in the first eight months of 1937 on a lecture tour arranged by Professor Carl Friedrich of Harvard University and by Stephen Duggan of the Institute of International Education, both of whom recognized his abilities and were eager to aid German scholars. Epstein then began his American career at Harvard University, serving in 1937–1938 as research assistant in Russian constitutional and administrative history with Professors Friedrich and Michael Karpovich, and then until the United States entered the war, as a research assistant in the Bureau of Institutional Research at Harvard and Radcliffe. Until 1944, when he became an American citizen, he worked as librarian and bibliographer in Widener Library, helping to create its great collection for the study of contemporary history, in the Harvard School for Overseas Administration, in the Army Specialized Training Program, and in the Civil Affairs Training School. During the last year of the war, he served in the Latin American Division of the Office of Strategic Services. Immediately following the war he worked at the Central European Desk in the Department of State.

Professor Epstein's unique qualifications then brought participation in an Anglo-American-French study of the files of the German Foreign Ministry in Berlin, 1946–1948, the first systematic review of these important materials. After three years as Curator of the Central European and Slavic Collection and Research Associate of the Hoover Institute and Library at Stanford University, he served for three years as Director of Research of the Army-Navy-Air Force War Documentation Project in Alexandria, Virginia. There, along with Professor Philip E. Mosely of Columbia University, he helped organize and find staff for the immensely important job of cataloguing the captured German documents, a service for which scholars all over the world will be forever grateful. He was subsequently (1960–1963) invited by the Federal Republic of Germany to serve in Bonn as acting editor of the group for the *Akten zur deutschen auswärtigen Politik 1918–1945,* a signal honor for a scholar who had left Germany in 1933 and who was then an American citizen. Professor Epstein helped produce important volumes about these vast collections of materials. These include the German edition of the documents concerning Nazi-Soviet relations between 1939 and 1941 (with Professor E. Malcolm Carroll), a *Guide to Captured German Documents* (with Gerhard L. Weinberg), two volumes of the *Akten zur deutschen auswärtigen Politik 1918–1945* (with Professor Hans Rothfels as German editor-in-chief), and the on-going *Guides to German Records Microfilmed at Alexandria, Virginia.*

From 1952 until August 31, 1960, Professor Epstein was a member of the staff of the Slavic and East European (later Central European) Division of the Library of Congress, where his personal qualities and immense knowledge enabled him to help hundreds of scholars. His work at Indiana University Library has enabled that institution and its Russian and East European Institute to benefit from the accumulated experience and wisdom of his remarkable career. In addition, in 1968 Professor Epstein helped organize and served as the first director of the university's Institute of German Studies, demonstrating again that his career revolves always around Germany.

In the 1920s Professor Epstein of course hoped to have a career as a teacher-scholar in a German university and to carry on the pioneer work of his mentors in expanding and deepening knowledge and understanding of the Slavic world. The rise of Hitler and the course of international politics drove him instead into a career of service largely in great libraries and in preserving, organizing, and helping make widely available collections of important documents on international relations over the past century. At the same time, as the essays published in this volume and the bibliography at the end prove, he has been able to demonstrate creditable skills as a productive scholar, in German and in English, in his native land and in the United States as well.

He has also succeeded remarkably well in satisfying his other early hope, that of teaching and inspiring young scholars to continue the eternal quest for knowledge and understanding. Most of his effective teaching has in fact been the product of generous assistance to scholars of all ages and countries who have consulted him in the great libraries or document centers. But he has also enjoyed great success in the classroom and in seminars in both German and American universities.

He taught modern European history in the summer of 1941 at the College of the City of New York. Ten years later, he served as visiting professor of modern diplomatic history at the University of California at Berkeley. From 1952 through 1960, while he was at the Library of Congress, he served first as a Professor Lecturer and then as an Adjunct Professor in Russian and East European History at American University in Washington. I suspect he was even more pleased and honored by invitations to return to teaching in his native country: in the Free University of Berlin in 1950 (under the exchange program organized by the Department of State); at Bonn in 1954, and again on various occasions during the 1960s; and at his old university, Hamburg, in 1966, 1967, and 1968. He has lectured at universities throughout the United States and participated actively in national and international congresses here and throughout Western Europe. In 1963, he gave lectures in Brussels, Utrecht, Leyden, Amsterdam, Oxford, Graz, and Vienna. In 1966, as a Fulbright Professor, he lectured at a large number of German universities.

Professor Epstein has received many academic honors. The sweetest to him was no doubt the honorary degree from the University of Hamburg, where he had worked so happily with Professor Richard Salomon forty years earlier. This tribute was especially appreciated because it was based on a thorough knowledge and understanding of his achievements as a teacher, scholar, bibliographer, librarian, and editor, and as promoter of German-American cultural relations. Other honors from his native land have been showered upon him: the Cross of Merit, First Class, of the Federal Republic of Germany, in June 1959; corresponding membership in the Gesellschaft für deutsche Presseforschung, Bremen, in 1957; and dedication to him of the October 1968 issue of the *Jahrbücher für Geschichte Osteuropas* on the occasion of his seventieth birthday. In the United States, in addition to fellowships from the American Council of Learned Societies and from Indiana University, he was elected chairman for 1969–1970 of the Conference Group for Central European History of the American Historical Association, the highest honor the men and women in his field (or one of his fields!) could offer.

No brief account of the scholarly and other activities of Professor Epstein or of the honors he has received can constitute an effective account of his professional life or describe his career. For his colleagues at Indiana University and for all those with whom he has worked, Fritz Epstein's qualities emerge above the recital of his achievements, no matter how affectionately written. He has always been a truly dedicated teacher, no matter what his formal function might have been or where the location of his office. In the classroom he is transformed from a quiet and gentle scholar to a vital, penetrating, and forceful speaker. He possesses bottomless knowledge and matchless information concerning bibliography. Even these qualities, though, are less important than the care and attention he has always lavished on all who are interested in expanding knowledge. As those graduate students at Indiana University wrote when they asked that he be invited to return for a *second* year after the normal retirement age, he showed a desire to sacrifice his own time and work to aid them, which was an even greater inspiration than that provided by his lectures and his critical insights.

His scholarship can be judged on its own merits, because the evidence is readily available. I should only like to emphasize several of its characteristics which might escape one who reads only these impressive essays. First, one should note the violent wrench which 1933 introduced into his career. Before Hitler he had concentrated on Russian history in the sixteenth century, on Western policy toward Russia during and after the First World War, and on analysis of Soviet historical scholarship. After 1933 the first subject disappears almost entirely. Moreover, Epstein's career as a scholar was sacrificed to other more immediate and important concerns for almost another quarter century. Throughout that long period and after it as well, his research concerns reflect an amazing range of interests, from essays on National Socialism and French colonialism to studies of European military influence in South America. However, the main emphases are upon modern diplomatic history and its documentation, and upon the subject of the essays in this volume, Germany and the East.

One should note, too, the special qualities Professor Epstein has brought to his interest in Germany and the Slavic world. Elsewhere he has pointed out that Meinecke did not visit the eastern regions of the German Empire until the early years of the First World War, when he was fifty-one years old. Professor Epstein, himself a West German, has never been east of Berlin. Perhaps this physical detachment has helped him to counter the occasionally baleful influence which the "Baltic Germans" have so long exerted on German scholarship and on the German view of Russia and and Eastern Europe. In any case, both statesmen and the most learned scholars would profit from the immense learning and insight with which he has written concerning Germany's relations with Eastern Europe.

German and American scholars in particular, but Western scholars in general, have all been impressed by the infinite attention to detail, the meticulous accuracy, the rigorous impartiality, the independent critical judgment, and the sense of large historical perspectives evident in everything Professor Epstein has written. These qualities, and the services he has rendered others by his careful editing of vast masses of documents, have created the respect so deeply rooted among his colleagues.

Above all, Fritz Epstein is honored and loved as a person. Honorable in all his actions, compassionate in his dealings with others, relentless in his search for knowledge, modest about his knowledge and achievements, as stubborn as Molly Brown in defending his views, he reflects all the good qualities his parents must have hoped for when he was born more than seventy years ago on the west bank of the Rhine. But his crowning glories are his strength of character and courage. He has overcome the tragedy Hitler created for him, for Germany, and for the world. He has shown indomitable determination through all the large and small difficulties and disappointments life has placed in his way. He has even endured without complaint the tragic death of his highly gifted and beloved son, Klaus, whose most promising career as an historian was cut short on June 26, 1967 by an automobile accident in Bonn.

For Professor Epstein's friends and admirers, he serves also as a bridge between the United States and Germany. For Americans, he embodies the highest qualities of Germany in the nineteenth and twentieth centuries. In fact, he has been a kind of ambassador from Germany to the American academic world. At the same time, he has represented the United States in Germany. Like other distinguished scholars from Germany, such as Hajo Holborn, Dietrich Gerhard, Hans Baron, and Hans Rothfels, he has served as a bridge between our two communities and has helped to enlarge, enlighten, and unify the Western intellectual world. The way in which he is accepted in both countries is an honor and a tribute to him and his work. He is at home in Bonn as in Bloomington, in Harvard as in Hamburg, in Stanford as in Strassburg. We are proud that he has worked with us. We have been truly blessed by his presence and his work. We look forward to his golden years back "home" in Germany and to his completing two more great works, a study of German research on Eastern Europe and of relations between Germany and Russia between 1815 and 1917.

✠✠GERMANY✠✠
AND THE EAST

Political Education and Higher Educational Policy in the Soviet Union

IN THE SUMMER OF 1930, the Communist Academy in Moscow published a pamphlet entitled *Nauchnye kadry VKP(b)* (Scholarly Cadres of the Communist Party [Bolsheviks]), by G. Krovitskii and B. Revskii, which constituted an announcement and a warning to the Communist Party. The author of the preface, Zimin, pointed out that the Planning Commission estimated that the number of scholarly workers in the Soviet Union, which was given as approximately 20,000, would triple by the end of the Five-Year Plan (1932–33). Of these 60,000, he said that no less than 25 percent, i.e., about 13,000, would be Communists. Since 1928, the highest Party officials have repeatedly announced that the education of Communist specialists in all fields of scholarship and technology must be considered the Party's most pressing task. At the Congress of Marxist Agricultural Scientists in 1930, Stalin complained that Marxist theoretical thinking lagged behind practical accomplishments in the building of Socialism.

More accurately, at the time the pamphlet was written, only 2007 of the 25,286 registered scholarly workers in the entire Soviet Union (excluding Central Asia) were Communists. Over half (1054) of the Communists in scholarly work were employed in

This article was originally published in *Neue Blätter für den Sozialismus*, III, No. 11 (1932), 594–604.

Moscow. The rest were virtually swallowed up by the vastness of the Soviet Union. Thus, in Azerbaijan, for example, only twenty-two of 449 scholarly workers were Communists. In all Great Russia (the R.S.F.S.R.), only 117 Party members were employed in the exact sciences, in the Ukraine twenty-nine, in White Russia eight, and in Georgia only two. Of the wealth of statistical material available, the figures concerning the distribution of Communists in the various fields of knowledge are most relevant for providing a clear picture of Marxist influence in particular disciplines. By far the greatest number (541) of Communists with higher education were economists; then came historians (373) and, at considerable intervals, philosophers and psychologists (177), agricultural scientists, and jurists. The figures given for some disciplines (only twenty-nine Communist physicists and mathematicians, twenty-three chemists, sixteen geologists, two ethnographers) caused extreme surprise both in Party and in non-Communist circles as an admission of a weakness not previously suspected.

The official Party memorandum, as one may call the Communist Academy pamphlet, concluded by urging that the entire system for preparing scholarly cadres (The Institute of Red Professors, The Russian Association of Research Institutes in the Social Sciences,[1] The Communist Academy) be reorganized to ensure greater cooperation among all scholarly organizations. Moreover, the system required that the leadership of the Communist Academy be enhanced to make the academy the center of Marxist scientific thought. This has in fact happened. Ever since the Institute of Red Professors for Training Marxist Teachers for Soviet Institutions of Higher Learning was incorporated into the Communist Academy, the Communist Party has had a central institution of higher learning for training a Communist scholarly elite. The Institutes of the

---

1. Until 1930, this was the Russian Association of Scientific Research Institutes in the Social Sciences (abbreviated: RANION); now it is the Russian Association of Scientific Research Institutes for Material, Artistic, and Linguistic Culture (RANIMIRK). It comprises, in Moscow, the Institute for Languages and Literature, the Institute for Archaeology and Art, the State Institute for Musicology, and the Section for Theory and History of Music at the State Academy of Art; in Leningrad, the Institute for Comparative Study of Western and Eastern Languages and Literatures, the State Academy for History of Material Culture, and the State Institute for Art History.

Red Professors are nothing but high-level Communist professional schools. There are institutes for economics and agriculture, for world economy and world politics, for technology and technical policy, for Soviet political organization and law, for history, for philosophy, for literature, art, and language, and for natural sciences. And there is, as well, a "section for research into the problems of war." All institutes also provide introductory courses and special proseminars in dialectical and historical materialism and in theoretical and practical economics. The consolidation of the institutes in the Communist Academy is an obvious manifestation of the new synthesis of all areas of knowledge in the Marxist-Leninist system.

The mustering of scholarly manpower, its political education and intellectual disciplining in the service of the "building of Socialism," the Marxist view of the world, exclusive and supreme, propagated with fanatic zeal and arrogant intolerance, defended against "deviations" with extraordinary severity toward dissenters and "aberrations"—these are the hallmarks of institutions of higher learning and of scholarship in the Soviet Union. In the Communist state each field of knowledge derives its meaning and its justification for existence from political considerations, i.e., from its relation to Marxism. "Endocrinology in the Service of Building of Socialism," "The Contribution of Geophysics to the Socialist Industrialization of the Country," "The Role of Biochemistry in Industry," "Bourgeois Psychotechnology—a Science of Decaying Capitalism," "The Marxist-Leninist Treatment of Questions of Hygiene and Physiology of Work," and similar themes constitute a category of newspaper articles, in which representatives of the most disparate disciplines undertake to describe their specialties' relationship with and contribution to the "building of Socialism" in the country. The real (or pretended) conviction that one's field is not merely compatible with, but a necessary adjunct to Marxism, is today required of the Russian scholar. Years ago, when this development was just beginning, Trotsky had a foreboding of the extreme to which this tendency might be carried. He dared what seemed at the time the ridiculously bold "prophecy" that the day would come when Einstein's theory of relativity would have to be tested for its consistency with Marxism. "Marxism," a historian, Friedland, declared recently, ". . . is nothing other than the last and only word of real science. If something is not in harmony with Marxism, then it is not in harmony with the loftiest findings of science." [2]

The struggle for the new Marxist science has also to be included among Communist efforts toward autarchy. At the Sixteenth Congress of the Communist Party (1930), Pokrovskii, the leading Marxist historian and one of the most active and successful organizers of "collective" scholarly work, declared, "The task we assume—to make our Socialist State independent of the bourgeois states—will only be half accomplished or, more bluntly, will not be accomplished at all, if we do not create our own science."

As Klaus Mehnert pointed out in his excellent introduction to the 1930 reform in higher education in Russia,[3] a greater contrast than that between German and Russian institutions of higher learning can hardly be imagined. While the German university has not abandoned the claim that it embodies, at least in concept, the *universitas literarum,* despite the decline of the humanities, the Soviet Union has organized its institutions of higher learning by numerous individual scholarly disciplines or by organizing faculties into professional schools. Administration of the professional schools is decentralized to a large extent. As a rule, they have been placed under the state departments or, sometimes, public organizations most concerned. The Stalin Communist University for the Workers of the Orient, for example, is a Party institution of higher learning with the task of "training workers from the Oriental nationalities to be qualified Party workers capable of applying the methods of Marxism-Leninism in the revolutionary struggle and in the building of socialism." The Scientific Research Association for the Study of National and Colonial Questions administers this program. The Markhlevskii (Julius Baltazar Marchlewski) Communist University for the National Minorities of the West is the companion to the Stalin University, with "sectors" for Germans, Lithuanians, Latvians, Jews, Poles, White Russians, Moldavians, Bulgarians, and Greeks in Moscow, and for Estonians and Finns at the Leningrad branch. This "university" is similarly administered by an organiza-

---

2. *Istorik-Marksist,* No. 8 (1928), 126.
3. "Die russische Hochschulreform 1930," *Osteuropa,* VI (1930–31), No. 5 (1931), 258–270.

tion with the neutral designation, "Scientific Association for the Study of the Peoples of the West." These Party schools are no doubt also educating Communist propagandists for service in other countries.

An organization which is ostensibly not an agency of the Communist Party gives Communist work in education direction and intensity in still another area, on the "antireligious front." The previous theological schools have been supplanted by courses such as the two-year "Course for Opponents of Religion" at the Krupskaja Communist Institute in Leningrad. In this course, Party members (with at least three years' membership in the Party) are methodically trained "along the line of the League of Militant Atheists" to be leaders in antireligious work among the masses. This course also prepared antireligious inspectors of organs of public education. Even the applications for the Antireligious Section of the Department of History and Philosophy at Moscow State University had to be submitted in 1930 to the League of Militant Atheists.

Only someone who understands the most basic formal and educational conditions under which students and candidates ("aspirants") for further scholarly training at universities and scientific research institutes are accepted realizes how radically the Soviet state has broken with the requirements for admission and the educational traditions of the universities of the bourgeois world and of pre-Communist Russia. Some typical details, selected from the admissions requirements of universities and scientific institutes as published in the Russian press since 1929, deserve to be stressed. The terms of the announcements make plain in many ways that the application of one who is not a Party member is utterly pointless. For example, the Stalin All-Union Academy of Trade requires of its applicants no less than ten years' Party membership. The Narimanov Institute for Oriental Studies in Moscow requires five years' membership for workers and eight for employees. (For Party members from the Oriental nationalities with weaker Party organizations, the requirements are reduced to three and six years, as is often the case elsewhere.) The Institute for Soviet Political Organization and Law within the Institute of Red Professors requires at least five years for workers and at least eight for peasants from collective farms and employees. (For Communists who have belonged to the League of Communist Youth for at least six years, the minimum Party membership period can be reduced by two years.)

As a rule, the announcements indicate the total number of places available for distribution among Party organizations and state authorities, which then select candidates and assign them for study. Of the forty new admissions to the Institute for Economic Research of the State Planning Commission in 1930–31, the All-Union Planning Commission was given the right to select thirteen, that of the R.S.F.S.R. twelve, the Planning Commissions for White Russia, Transcaucasia, and Uzbekistan three each, and those of the Ukraine, Turkmenistan, and Tadzhikistan two each. Of the 160 new admissions to the Department of Literature and Art of the First Moscow State University in 1930, it was established that 75 percent be industrial and farm workers, 15 percent poor and middle peasants from collective farms, and 10 percent employees and children of scholarly workers. No less than 30 percent of the places were reserved for female industrial and farm workers. In the Section for Editing and Political Writing, all places in the course in editorial writing were reserved for Party members. In the course in criticism, the breakdown was 60 percent for members of the Party, 30 percent for members of the League of Communist Youth, and 10 percent for non-Party members (*Pravda,* May 27, 1930). It goes without saying that, other things being equal, applicants from the worker or peasant class are systematically preferred and that exceptions are often made in their favor. According to the announcement of the Moscow All-Union Museum of the Revolution, for instance, museum experience can compensate for educational deficiencies when such applicants apply for training as scholarly workers in musea of revolutionary history (*Izvestiia,* December 23, 1930).

The R.S.F.S.R. People's Commissariat for Education directives on the acceptance of candidates explicitly state that first choice be given to members of the Communist Party and the League of Communist Youth, workers (including farm laborers), peasants from collective farms, and poor peasants, in order to assure selection according to social class. Applicants of bourgeois origin are systematically excluded. Thus, the admissions requirements of the Association of Research Institutes prescribe, "From those who have successfully completed the oral examination, preference will be given in the selection of candidates to industrial and farm workers, participants in the Civil War, and members of workers' families" (*Pravda,* June 12, 1930). In many cases, however, Party membership is a condition. For instance, at least ten years' Party membership is required for the Section for Journalism and Editing at the Institute for Literature, Art, and Language, at least eight years for the Institute of Journalism, at least seven years for workers and ten years for employees at the Leningrad Research Institute for the History of the Communist Party.

The proletarization of institutions for higher learning and the fact that the students are on the average much older than in earlier years necessitate a unique system of stipends and other aid, for single as well as married students.

The requirement of membership in the Communist Party for acceptance to universities and research institutes and restricted enrollment (numerus clausus) safeguard, on the one hand, the homogeneous composition of the "scholarly proletariat," the term used here in the most positive sense to signify the emergence of a new class of intelligentsia, with firm ideological roots and unconditionally devoted to the Party and state. On the other hand, they guarantee the rationalized use according to economic plans of the new scholarly generation emerging from institutions of higher learning, especially of the "scholarly cadres" of the Party.

Admission to an institution of higher learning is contingent for all applicants on the demonstration of specific knowledge in the so-called socio-political disciplines as well as in areas of general education. In addition to mastery of spoken and written Russian and knowledge of elementary mathematics, the requirements of "General Education" apparently include knowledge of physical and economic geography, world economy, and political geography (the world before and after the war). Geography in its different manifestations thus appears to be the central area of general education. The socio-political disciplines add a certain minimum of political, historical, economic, and philosophical knowledge in the spirit of Marxism-Leninism, which neither acknowledges nor tolerates an intellectual sphere alien and impenetrable to its spirit. Thus, all scholarly work in Russia today assumes as an intellectual foundation a minimum Marxist political education, which the student or aspirant (insofar as he is not a graduate of particular courses or institutions of higher learning) must demonstrate by passing an oral examination on basic problems in dialectical and historical materialism, in general and applied economics, and frequently, in addition, in the history of the Russian Communist Party. A further requirement of the program cited at the outset, namely Marxist education for aspirants, has thus been recognized officially.

As early as 1929, the Department for Soviet Organization at the Communist University in Leningrad defined its requirements for the "politminimum" in the following fashion:

> Ability to orient oneself in current political events; correct [!] interpretation of the decisions of Party congresses and conferences, particularly in questions of Soviet political structure and economic organization, as well as knowledge of the most important resolutions of recent Congresses of Soviets of Great Russia (the R.S.F.S.R.) and of the Soviet Union; furthermore, specific knowledge of the history of the Party, of economic theory, and of the history of the class struggle.

Bolshevik "civics" (comparatively speaking) and Marxist "philosophical propaedeutics" are represented by the required mastery of a "literature minimum," which for years has been subject only to insignificant modification. Some announcements concerning places available identify a certain number of works required at a given time. In the summer of 1930, for instance, the publications marked with an asterisk in the list below were required reading for admission to the Institute for Literature, Art, and Language within the Institute of Red Professors; depending on whether admission was sought to the Sections for Literature, Art, or Journalism, additional knowledge of particular specialized literature was required.

The standard list of works introductory to Marxism-Leninism, a selection from which in any given case constitutes the required "literature minimum," looks somewhat like this: [4]

I. *Philosophy, i.e., Historical and Dialectical Materialism (in the official Russian abbreviations "Istmat" and "Diamat")*

*Marx, Critique of the Gotha Program (Zur Kritik des sozial-demokratischen Programms von Gotha. Kritika Gotskoi programmy).

*Marx and Engels, The Communist Manifesto, with Commentary by Riazanov [pseudonym for David B. Gol'dendakh].

*————, The German Ideology.

*————, Correspondence.

*Engels, Ludwig Feuerbach and the Outcome of Classical German Philosophy (Ludwig Feuerbach und der Ausgang der klassischen deutschen Philosophie. Liudvig Feierbakh i konets nemetskoi klassicheskoi filosofii).

*————, Herr Eugen Dühring's Revolution in Science (Anti-Dühring) (Herrn Eugen Dührings Umwälzung in der Wissenschaft. Perevorot v nauke, proizvedennyi gospodinom Evgeniem Diuringom).

*————, The Origin of the Family, Private Property and the State (Ursprung der Familie, des Privateigentums und des Staates. Proizkhozhdenie sem'i, chastnoi sobstvennosti i gosudarstva).

*————, The Dialectics of Nature (Dialektika prirody).

————, The Development of Socialism from Utopia to Science (Razvitie nauchnago sotsializma).

*Lenin, Materialism and Empirio-Criticism. Critical Comments on a Reactionary Philosophy (Materializm i empiriokrititsizm. Kriticheskie zametki ob odnoi reaktsionnoi filosofii).

*————, On the Question of Dialectics.

*————, What the "Friends of the People" are, and How They Fight the Social Democrats (Chto takoe druz'ia naroda i kak oni boiut protiv sotsial-demokratov).

*————, The Economic Content of the Narodnichestvo (Ekonomicheskoe soderzhanie narodnichestva i kritika ego v knige

---

4. This list provides original German titles and Russian original titles or translations in parentheses. Since many titles were often reprinted, places and dates of publication have been omitted.

g-na [P. B.] Struve, "Kriticheskie zametki k voprosu ob ekonomicheskom razvitii Rossii," 1894).

*———, The State and Revolution. Marxist Teaching on the State and the Task of the Proletariat in the Revolution (Staat und Revolution. Die Lehre der Marxisten vom Staat und die Aufgaben des Proletariats in der Revolution. Proekt platformy proletarskoi partii. Gosudarstvo i revoliutsiia. Uchenie marksizma o gosudarstve i zadachi proletariata v revoliutsii).

*———, The Proletarian Revolution and the Renegade Kautsky [in reply to Kautsky's Diktatur des Proletariats] (Proletarskaia revoliutsiia i renegat Kautsky).

*———, "Left Wing" Communism, an Infantile Disorder. A Popular Essay in Marxian Strategy and Tactics (Die Kinderkrankheit des "Radikalismus" im Kommunismus).

*———, Will the Bolsheviks Maintain Power?

*———, The Significance of Militant Materialism.

*———, Marx, Engels, Marxism.

*Leninskii Sbornik, Vols. I and II (Collection of Lenin Materials).

*Stalin, Questions of Leninism (Fragen des Leninismus. Voprosy leninizma).

*———, Political Report to the Sixteenth Party Congress of the Russian Communist Party (1930) as well as the Reports of Molotov, Kaganovich, Ordzhonikidze, and Iakovlev.

*Plekhanov, Fundamental Problems of Marxism (Osnovnye problemy marksizma).

*———, Essays in the History of Materialism (Ocherki po istorii materializma).

*———, In Defense of Materialism: The Development of the Monist View of History (K voprosu o razvitii monisticheskogo vzgliada na istoriiu) (Pseudonym "N. Bel'tov").

———, On the Sixtieth Anniversary of Hegel's Death.

———, From Idealism to Materialism.

———, Critique of Our Critics (Kritika nashikh kritikov) (Pseudonym "N. Bel'tov").

*Deborin, Introduction to the Philosophy of Dialectical Materialism (Vvedenie v filosofiiu dialekticheskogo materializma).

———, Sketches from the History of Materialism in the Seven-

teenth and Eighteenth Centuries (Ocherki po istorii materializma XVII–XVIII vv.).

———, Lenin as a Thinker (Lenin kak myslitel').

———, Essays on the Mechanists.

*Riazanov, Commentary on the Communist Manifesto (Marx and
Engels. The Communist Manifesto, D. B. Riazanov (editor),
with an Introduction and Explanatory Notes).

*Stoliarov, Dialectical Materialism and the Mechanists (Dialekti-
cheskii materializm i mekhanisty. Nashi filosofskie razno-
glasiia).

*Bukharin, Historical Materialism. A System of Sociology (Teoriia
istoricheskogo materializma).

*Resolution of the Cell of the Institute for Philosophy and Natural
Sciences within the Institute of Red Professors on a Decision
of the Party's Central Committee concerning the Journal,
Pod znamenem marksizma (Under the Banner of Marxism).
(*Pravda*, January 26, 1931.)

Pod znamenem marksizma, Nos. 10–12 (1930).

*Concerning a Turn on the Philosophical Front (A Discussion
in the Communist Academy, in *Vestnik* (Courier) of the
Communist Academy, Nos. 40–42.

In 1930–31, applicants to a research institute in the Lenin
All-Union Academy of Agricultural Science were expected to
be informed on the following issues for the entrance examination
in dialectical and historical materialism:

Materialism and idealism; fundamental concepts of dialectical
materialism (dialectic of nature and society, dialectic method);
French materialism of the eighteenth century; Hegel's dialectical
method; Ludwig Feuerbach; the dialectic in the interrelationship
between nature and society, i.e., means of production and the theory
of base and super-structure; the theory of social classes (their
nature, their development, and class struggle); the class struggle
under the dictatorship of the proletariat; Bukharin's errors [this
point would have been dropped subsequent to Bukharin's rehabilitation upon recanting his "errors"]; the theory of economic structures
and the dynamics of social development; the theory of social

revolution and of the dictatorship of classes; the theory of the state; social consciousness and the development of particular forms of ideology; the role of personality in history; the laws of history and teleology; Leninism and Marxism; the dialectic and the mechanistic "theory of equilibrium."

II. *Theory of Economics and History of the National Economy*
*Marx, Capital. Critique of Political Economy, Vols. I and III (Kapital. Kritika politicheskoi ekonomii).

*————, The Poverty of Philosophy. A Reply to "La philosophie de la misère" of M. Proudhon (Das Elend der Philosophie. Antwort auf Proudhon's "Philosophie des Elends." Nishcheta filosofii).

Engels, The Peasant Question in France and Germany (Krestianskii vopros vo Frantsii i Germanii).

*Lenin, Imperialism, the Highest Stage of Capitalism (Imperializm kak noveishii etap kapitalizma).

*————, Comments on Bukharin's Economics of the Transition Period; see below, Bukharin, Imperialism and World Economy.

*————, The Development of Capitalism in Russia (Razvitie kapitalizma v Rossii).

————, Articles and Speeches on Economic Policy.

*Stalin, Speech at the Conference of Communist Agrarian Workers (1930).

————, Speeches before the Central Committee of the Communist Party at the Fifteenth and Sixteenth Party Congresses (December 1927, and June 1930).

Bukharin, Imperialism and World Economy, with an Introduction by V. I. Ilyin [pseudonym for V. I. Lenin] (Mirovoe khoziaistvo i imperializm).

————, The Accumulation of Capital and Imperialism (Imperializm i nakoplenie kapitala).

*Miliutin and Borilin, Essay against Rubin, *Bolshevik,* No. 2 (1930).

Pokrovskii, Essays in the History of Russian Civilization (Ocherki istorii russkoi kul'tury).

Liashchenko, History of the National Economy of Russia (Istoriia narodnogo khoziaistva SSSR).

Kautsky, The Economic Doctrines of Karl Marx (Karl Marx's ökonomische Lehren. Ekonomicheskiia ucheniia Karla Marksa).

Hilferding, R., Finance Capital (Das Finanzkapital. Finansovyi kapital).

Rubin, I. I., History of Economic Thought (Istoriia ekonomicheskoi mysli).

Segal and Tal', Economic Policy of the Soviet Union.

Lapidus, I., and Ostrovitianov, K., An Outline of Political Economy. Political Economy and Soviet Economics (Politicheskaia ekonomiia v sviazi s teoriei sovetskogo khoziaistva).

Leont'ev, A. [pseudonym for Lev Abramovich], Political Economy. A Beginner's Course (Nachal'nyi kurs politicheskoi ekonomii).

Mikhalevskii, Course in Political Economy.

An announcement of the Institute for Economics within the Institute of Red Professors deemed "desirable" a familiarity with Lectures on the General Theory of Economics (Osnovy politicheskoi ekonomii) of the "bourgeois economist," Mikhail I. Tugan-Baranovskii (*Pravda,* September 28, 1930).

III. *General History of the Class Struggle and the International Revolutionary Movement*

Monosov, History of Revolutionary Movements (Istoriia revoliutsionnykh dvizhenii, 1789–1871).

*Pokrovskii, Brief History of Russia (Russkaia istoriia v samom szhatom ocherke).

Drozdov, History of the Class Struggle in the West and in Russia in the Nineteenth and Twentieth Centuries (Ocherki po istorii klassovoi bor'by v zapadnoi Evrope i v Rossii v XIX–XX vekakh).

Lenin, Articles on the Paris Commune and the Communist Internationale.

Stephanov, Ivan Ivanovich, The Paris Commune (Parizhskaia Kommuna 1871 goda i voprosy taktiki proletarskoi revoliutsii).

Arkan, Three Types of Workers' Movement.

Gurevich, A. I., Origin and Development of the Communist Internationale (Vozniknovenie i razvitie Kommunisticheskogo Internatsionala).

Theses and Resolutions of the Sixth Congress (July 1928) and of the Tenth Plenum of the Executive Committee of the Communist International.

*Lukin, Recent History of Western Europe (Noveishaia istoriia zapadnoi Evropy).

Rothstein (Theodore) [Rotshtein, Fedor], From Chartism to Labourism. Historical Sketches of the English Working Class Movement (Ocherki po istorii rabochego dvizheniia v Anglii).

IV.

A. *History of the Peoples of the Soviet Union*

*Pokrovskii, History of Russia from the Earliest Times to the Rise of Commercial Capitalism (Russkaia istoriia s drevneiskikh vremen).

————. Marxism and the Peculiarities of Russia's Historical Development (Marksizm i osobennosti razvitiia Rossii).

Piontkovskii, Essays in Russian History of the Nineteenth and Twentieth Centuries (Ocherki istorii S.S.S.R. XIX i XX vv.).

Drozdov, see III, above.

*Lenin, The Development of Capitalism in Russia, see II, above.

*————, The Agrarian Program of the Social Democrats, 1905–1907 (Agrarnaia programma sotsialdemokratii v pervoi russkoi revoliutsii 1905–7 godov).

*————, The Tasks of the Proletariat in Our Revolution.

*————, Essays on the Narodniki.

B. *History of the Russian Communist Party*

In addition to the official history of the Russian Communist Party (Ocherki po istorii VKP(b), edited by E. M. Iaroslavskii (pseudonym for M. I. Gubel'man), the shorter synopses by:

*Bubnov, A. S., A History of the Russian Communist Party (Osnovnye momenty v razvitii Russkoi Kommunisticheskoi Partii).

Popov, N. N., Outline History of the Communist Party of the Soviet Union (Ocherk istorii Vsesoiuznoi Kommunisticheskoi Partii).

Kerzhentsev, Platon M. [pseudonym for Platon Mikhailovich Leseden], and Leont'ev, A. [pseudonym for Lev Abramovich], ABC of Leninism (Azbuka leninizma).

C. *Leninism* (Theory of Classes and of the Class Struggle)
*Stalin, Problems of Leninism.

Major themes for the examination in Leninism are, e.g., the views of Marx, Engels, and Lenin on the theory of the party; the theory of the revolution of the proletariat and the dictatorship of the proletariat; the agrarian and peasant question; national and colonial questions; the tasks of the building of Socialism.

V. *General History*
*Marx, Capital (in particular, Volume I, Chapter 24).
*————, The Eighteenth Brumaire of Louis Bonaparte (Der achtzehnte Brumaire des Louis Bonaparte. Vosemnadtsatoe Briumera Lui Bonaparta).
*————, The Class Struggles in France, 1848–1850 (Die Klassenkämpfe in Frankreich 1848–1850. Klassovaia bor'ba vo Frantsii ot 1848 do 1850 g.).
*Engels, The Peasant War in Germany. Revolution and Counterrevolution (Der deutsche Bauernkrieg. Revolution und Kontrerevolution).
*Lenin, To Which Class Do the Cavaignacs Belong?
*————, Louis Blanc and His Thought (Lui Blankovshchina).
Fridliand, Boris Efimovich [pseudonym for B. Efimov], History of Western Europe.
*Lukin, see III, above.

As a rule, the professional schools require familiarity with several works of programmatic significance for the Marxist interpretation of the discipline concerned: for admission to an agricultural institute, perhaps familiarity with the works of Kautsky and Lenin on the agrarian question; for admission to a university program in "public law" (Soviet political structure), perhaps Lenin's *The State and Revolution* (see I, above) and Peter Ivanovich Stuchka's *State and Soviet Constitutional Theory* (Uchenie o gosudarstve i o konstitutsii R.S.F.S.R.). According to the text of the requirements, the "minimum" might often signify one-sided, but nonetheless considerable, philosophical, economic, historical, and political knowledge. However, as stressed before, a Party membership card may provide more certainty for admission than mastery even of a literature maximum.

In the study of social science, those fields which are clearly Marxist, and which already play such an important role in admission, occupy a central position. Thus, in the 1930–31 academic year, the Department of History and Philosophy at Moscow State University contained the following sections: History of Philosophy, Historical and Dialectical Materialism, History of the Epoch of Industrial Capitalism and Imperialism, Antireligious Indoctrination, and Archive and Museum Studies. At the All-Union Communist University in Leningrad, which, like the oldest Party university, the Sverdlov Communist University in Moscow, primarily produces teachers and research workers for Communist institutions of higher learning, a three-year program in the social sciences includes, for instance, the following areas:

> First Course: Economic Geography; History of the Revolutionary Movement in Western Europe and America; History of the Peoples of the Soviet Union.

> Second Course: History of the Communist Party (Bolsheviks); General Theory of Economics; History of Soviet Economy.

> Third Course: Leninism; History, Program, and Tactics of the Communist International; Dialectical Materialism; Foundations of the Natural Sciences.

These examples, which are confined to the so-called social sciences, should be sufficient to demonstrate the particular quality and singularity of the requirements in a Bolshevik experiment: the endeavor to fashion a new, politically and intellectually complete and self-sufficient type of individual, the "scholarly worker," to reform radically and to politicize the Russian system of higher education, and to point the way to teaching and research according to the Marxist compass.[5]

---

5. This article was written at the end of 1931. A resolution of the Central Committee of the Communist Party of August 30, 1932 makes qualification the decisive factor for admission to an institution of higher learning. The resolution develops the main lines of a school reform which can be viewed as the introduction of a new phase in Bolshevik educational policy. On the developmental tendencies of Soviet institutions of higher learning, see, most recently, Klaus Mehnert in *Osteuropa,* VIII, No. 1 (October 1932), 54–56.

II

Friedrich Meinecke
on Eastern Europe

ONE WHO HAS FOLLOWED with sympathy the growth and development of the Free University of Berlin from its daring beginnings in 1948 to its present consolidation cannot doubt Friedrich Meinecke's vital role. By declaring his solidarity with the new university, a university founded out of political necessity, he facilitated its recognition by older universities as an academic peer.

Friedrich Meinecke embodied in the work of his long life the ideal historian and the ideal political commentator. He was a political professor, a rare phenomenon in his day. The free world had to take notice when he resolutely put the weight of his name and achievement, his reputation for integrity, intellectual independence, and strength of character behind those who severed themselves from Humboldt University and opted uncompromisingly for the West.[1] In addition to bestowing upon Meinecke an honorary rectorship, the Free University, in a most appropriate expression of its enduring gratitude, linked his name with the Historical Seminar, calling it the Friedrich Meinecke Institute.

This article is an expanded version of a lecture given on July 7, 1954, at the East European Institute of the Free University of Berlin. It was originally published in *Jahrbuch für die Geschichte Mittel- und Ostdeutschlands,* III (1954), 119–144.
    1. Georg Kotowski, "Der Kampf um Berlins Universität," in *Veritas, Iustitia, Libertas. Festschrift der Freien Universität zur 200-Jahrfeier der Columbia University* (Berlin, 1954), 7–31.

Both the founding of the Free University and the establishment within it of an East European Institute, a center in West Berlin for teaching and research on Eastern Europe, were simultaneously of academic and historical significance. It was, therefore, particularly fitting that a guest lecturer, intended principally for the members of the East European Institute and the Friedrich Meinecke Institute, trace the role of the European East in Friedrich Meinecke's view of history and demonstrate the interest and open-mindedness—rarely found among nonspecialists—with which he approached the issues of Eastern Europe and the Slavic world.

Meinecke's own lifelong field of study was the unity of the Germanic and Latin nations as understood by Ranke: the history of the West, of the intellectual links between the Germanic and Latin spheres, and of their influence upon each other. It may thus seem strange at first that we should find in his historical works and journalistic efforts sufficient evidence of concern with questions of Eastern Europe to warrant careful assessment. In the course of our attempt to demonstrate Meinecke's contributions to a deeper understanding of contemporary history as manifested in current events, especially in questions concerning Eastern Europe, it will become evident, first, that we are indebted to him for essential contributions to the history of Germany's relationship to Eastern Europe, and, second, that his journalistic statements in this field deserve serious consideration for an analysis of German public opinion. Furthermore, as Eberhard Kessel emphasized in his perceptive tribute to Meinecke in the journal *Die Welt als Geschichte,* this is true "in spite of the fragility and relativity of the content of many of his statements and ideas." [2]

In the two volumes of his autobiography, Meinecke to a certain extent has put himself within the historical context of his time.[3] As an important part of his impressive list of publications, his memoirs provide an incomparable stimulus to analysis of his life and work. A considerable number of historians, for the most part former colleagues, friends, and students, have already traced with affection and perspicacity his intellectual development, and

---

2. *Die Welt als Geschichte,* XIV (1954), 8.
3. *Erlebtes 1862–1901* (Leipzig, 1941); *Strassburg, Freiburg, Berlin 1901–1919* (Stuttgart, 1949).

have described his place in the history of German historiography and in the intellectual history of Europe. In doing so, they took as their starting point his major works: *Weltbürgertum und Nationalstaat, Die Idee der Staatsräson in der neueren Geschichte,* and *Die Entstehung des Historismus,* those works which belong to the classics of German historical writing.

The aim of the following discussion is more modest.[4] Because of the theme, it is based to a great extent on Meinecke's shorter writings, his essays, reviews, and newspaper articles, although the major works are not neglected. It is based on expressions of opinion which, although written with great perspective, are more likely to become dated and be neglected than are the major works. Meinecke's views on Eastern Europe were principally the result of his reading and contemplation, for it was not until 1913, at the age of 51, that he paid his first visit to the eastern regions of Germany, the provinces of West Prussia and Posen, and Marienburg, Danzig, and Königsberg. His Freiburg students joked that he undertook this little tour to determine whether "the hens clucked in Prussian or Polish." [5] During the First World War he

---

4. I should like at this point to say a few words of personal reminiscence concerning Friedrich Meinecke. He was proud of his school in America, of his students, who, torn from their pursuits when the National Socialists seized power, had found asylum in America. It is sufficient to mention the names of Hajo Holborn, Hans Rothfels, Dietrich Gerhard, Gerhard Masur, and Hans Baron, men held in esteem on both sides of the ocean. Those named were associated with him personally or through their fields of study. Although I was a member of his Berlin seminar for several semesters in the early 1920s, I was, because of my major field, primarily a student of the historians of Eastern Europe in Berlin, Theodor Schiemann, Karl Stählin, and Otto Hoetzsch. It was not until the postwar period, when I was in Berlin as a member of the American research group of the Inter-Allied German War Documents Project for the preparation of the great German document publication (*Documents on German Foreign Policy, 1918–1945*), that a more personal relationship was established. It was then that his last major work appeared, *Die deutsche Katastrophe,* which has been called "the self-criticism of German bourgeoisie" (Heinz Holldack, *Hochland,* XXXIX, No. 2 [December 1946], 169–176). No public assessment gave him greater satisfaction than acknowledgment that that work had combined resoluteness of judgment with moderation. America conferred upon Meinecke the highest academic honors she could bestow on a historian, the Doctor of Letters degree of her oldest university, Harvard (Harvard Tercentenary Publications, *The Tercentenary of Harvard College. A Chronicle of the Tercentenary Year 1935–1936* [Cambridge, 1937], 221), and, as the first German historian since Mommsen, an honorary life membership in the American Historical Association (*American Historical Review,* LIII, No. 3 [April 1948], 695–696).

5. *Strassburg, Freiburg, Berlin,* 106.

gave lectures in several cities of the eastern regions, such as Posen, Frankfurt on the Oder, and Bromberg.[6]

Concentrating on three particular questions, we shall try to clarify Meinecke's contribution to an understanding of Eastern Europe. First, proceeding from his major works, we shall discuss his treatment of Herder's views on the peoples of Eastern Europe and his analysis of Russo-German relations in the nineteenth century. Then, taking his journalism as our point of departure, we shall discuss his handling of Eastern European problems during the First World War and in the interwar period. We are conscious of the fact that a well-rounded presentation of his views on Eastern Europe should also analyze his statements on Austria-Hungary and his position on questions concerning Germany's East.

In his *Entstehung des Historismus,* Meinecke could not neglect Herder's concern with the nationalities of northeastern Europe.[7] He accepted the supposition that the ancient dances and songs which Herder observed at the Latvian festival of the summer solstice on the Eve of St. John's Day in 1765 had persuaded him that he was witnessing the living remnants of a tradition and customs undefiled by modern habits. From that time forward, the Latvians embodied for him an existence that was close to nature and to the archetype of historical life. From this arose his question: How long would such a small ethnic group be able to maintain its original language, songs, and customs without succumbing to the onslaught of modern ways? It was Herder's conviction that individual national traits in Europe would soon be obliterated. Even so, as Meinecke pointed out, he expressed at the same time the hope that the Slavic peoples would one day be free to develop their nationhood. Whenever Herder bewailed the fact that the search for power of large, warlike peoples repressed the small nationalities, he was fond of citing the Latvians, Curonians, Prussians, Lithuanians, and Slavs as examples of the latter. It is well known that he and those German and Slavic professors and authors who came under his spell profoundly affected the intellectual life of the peoples of Eastern Europe by awakening

---

6. Ibid., 238.

7. Meinecke, *Die Entstehung des Historismus* (Munich, 1936), II, 395–398.

them to an awareness of their own nationality.[8] This intellectual current, whose breadth and depth has yet to be exhaustively explored, cannot be more precisely defined according to its origin and development than Meinecke has done: "Herder's idea of the nation was rooted in that very world of Eastern Europe in which it was to become most influential." [9]

Although Meinecke's statements in various contexts on themes of Russian history are numerous and concrete, he discussed medieval Russia only in his *Idee der Staatsräson*. In that work, he described Russia's progress from primitive to rational power politics and analyzed the development of Frederick the Great's views of Russia, especially Frederick's admiration for Peter the Great's achievement, as expressed in *Histoire de mon temps* (1746), and his attitude toward Russia in his political testaments of 1752 and 1768.[10]

Meinecke's views on Prussia's relations with its great eastern neighbors in the nineteenth century are to be found primarily in his *Zeitalter der deutschen Erhebung* and in his biographies of Boyen and Radowitz, that is, in the works on the two periods of German history in the last century to whose elucidation he has made definitive contributions. These were, on the one hand, the period of the great reforms in Prussia and the wars of liberation, and on the other, the period of the Revolution of 1848 and its aftermath in the early 1850s. The chapter on Boyen's involvement in the Polish campaign of 1794–95, which describes the struggle against Polish insurgents and robbers, provides an exciting picture of a prototype of the eastern partisan war as known from Russian military history for the year 1812 and the years 1941 to 1944.[11]

The exhaustive treatment of cooperation between the Prussian and the Russian armies in the Napoleonic period, particularly the wealth of information on the compaign of 1806–1807,

8. Hans Kohn, *Pan-Slavism, Its History and Ideology* (South Bend, 1953), 15–16.

9. Meinecke, *Die Entstehung des Historismus*, II, 396.

10. Meinecke, *Die Idee der Staatsräson in der neueren Geschichte* (Munich, Berlin, 1929), 3rd edition, 415–419.

11. Meinecke, *Das Leben des Generalfeldmarschalls Hermann von Boyen* (Stuttgart, 1896), I, ch. 3.

in Meinecke's biography of Boyen has long been an integral part of the history of the Prussian army. Turning to the field of political history, Meinecke then analyzed meticulously, principally in his *Zeitalter der deutschen Erhebung* and in his address, *Deutsche Jahrhundertfeier und Kaiserfeier,* Russia's relation to Prussia or, more exactly, Czar Alexander's attitudes toward Prussia. Prussia, he explained in 1919, in an essay on "The Historical Causes of the German Revolution," [12] was twice saved from total destruction by singular strokes of luck: during the Seven Years' War by the death of Czarina Elizabeth,[13] and at the time of the Peace of Tilsit by the consideration Napoleon had to show Alexander I. With regard to the Peace of Tilsit itself, Meinecke asserted that one ought not to forget the importance of the Czar, whose decisions determined Prussia's existence,[14] and who prevented Napoleon from diminishing Prussia any further by detaching Silesia. This, to use Meinecke's words, would have been "the most unfortunate thing" that could have happened to Prussia.[15]

Meinecke assessed positively the loss of the heterogeneous Polish provinces of South Prussia and New East Prussia, despite the fact that Prussia was weakened politically and her territory reduced by half in the Peace of Tilsit.[16] He saw therein the removal of dead weight that impeded Prussia in the fulfillment of her German mission. Those provinces that remained with Prussia, were, almost without exception, central provinces. Meinecke underscored sharply how in 1811, when Prussian patriots pressed for an alliance with Russia, the government gave careful consider-

---

12. "Die geschichtlichen Ursachen der deutschen Revolution," *Nach der Revolution* (Munich, Berlin, 1919), 18.

13. In his *Entstehung des Historismus,* Meinecke also reverted to the death of Czarina Elizabeth. In that work (II, 553), he said that Goethe and Voltaire, being realists, had always acknowledged the role of accident in history and that modern historians would do well to follow their example in this and acknowledge firmly and resolutely that the death of Czarina Elizabeth in 1762 was an accident without which the destiny of Germany and Prussia would have turned out much differently. See also *Aphorismen und Skizzen zur Geschichte* (Liepzig, 1942), 86; *Strassburg, Freiburg, Berlin* (1949), 223; *Werke,* 3 (1959), 512.

14. *Preussen und Deutschland im 19. und 20. Jahrhundert* (Munich, Berlin, 1918), 30; "Deutsche Jahrhundertfeier und Kaiserfeier" (1913).

15. Meinecke, *Das Zeitalter der deutschen Erhebung (1795–1815)* (1913; 6th ed., Göttingen, 1941), 111.

16. Ibid., 130.

ation not only to the Czar's notorious unreliability and weakness of character, but also to his plans for the restoration of Poland under Russian rule, which would pose a threat to Prussia's position on the Baltic.[17]

Meinecke's treatment of the personal relations between two central figures in Napoleon's defeat, Freiherr vom Stein and Czar Alexander, is particularly penetrating. He was especially interested in the internal tension between the objectives of Russian policy and Stein's hopes and aspirations for the nation, a conflict that was not resolved but rather intensified by Stein's appointment as the Russian delegate to the Central Administrative Council for the liberated German regions. To all appearances, it was Stein who prevailed upon the Czar to carry the war beyond Russia's borders and thus to transform a Russian war into a general European war of liberation. In Alexander's decision, "power and intellect, the world situation and the great individual were interwoven." [18] In *Weltbürgertum und Nationalstaat,* Meinecke sharply stressed the difference between Stein's idea of the nation and modern national sensibilities. He pointed out that at the turn of the year 1812 Stein's idea of the nation permitted a foreign dictatorship—with Russia, England, and Austria as Germany's overseers—in the liberated parts of Germany, since for Stein the liberation of Germany was neither a German nor a Russian but rather a European affair. By turning to the Czar for support and intervention in the matter of the German constitution, Stein burdened Germany with obligations that seem, to modern sensibilities, incompatible with national autonomy.[19] Further, Meinecke considered very carefully the respective interests of Prussia, Austria, and Russia during the Saxon crisis at the Congress of Vienna. He came to the conclusion that Prussia's aspirations could more readily come to nought than Russia's, and that a Russia whose ambitions in Poland had been satisfied would hardly have been a permanent ally of Prussia, if Prussia had taken recourse to the sword in order to realize her territorial claims.[20]

---

17. Ibid., 198.
18. Ibid., 205.
19. Meinecke, *Weltbürgertum und Nationalstaat* (1928), 7th edition, ch. 8: "Stein, Gneisenau und Wilhelm von Humboldt in den Jahren 1812–1815."
20. Meinecke, *Boyen,* II, 8.

Of particular interest to the historian of Eastern Europe is Meinecke's treatment of certain political and military ideas of Boyen's—Boyen was then Minister of War—concerning Eastern Europe. In an 1811 memorandum, Boyen recommended establishment of a system of small states dependent upon Russia in northern and eastern Europe. In this proposal Meinecke saw an underestimation of Russia's capability for expansion. Moreover, Russia would not have been content with a protective hegemony over Scandinavia and the tiny principalities to which the Polish state would have been reduced. Furthermore, Russia would not have been satisfied with these artificially created, unviable pygmy states.[21] Twenty years later, in 1830–1831, Boyen returned to the notion of erecting tiny, dwarf states in Russian Poland under Russian or Russo-Prussian domination, believing he could thereby acquire for Prussia the Vistula-Narev border. He did not surrender to the illusion that an independent Poland could at any time be Prussia's ally against Russia. What is more enticing to a ruler in Warsaw, he asked, Vilna or Danzig? By contributing to an independent Poland, Prussia would be digging her own grave; any other policy than aspiring for the seacoast would be unthinkable for Poland.[22]

Boyen's suggestions for improving the defense of Prussia's eastern border rested on firmer ground than his ideas concerning the political structuring of eastern Europe. He thought of renovating old castles and sturdy buildings along the border and equipping them for use as militia bases in a guerilla war. The forests, marshes, and lakes of East Prussia seemed to him natural for a small war. Owing to a lack of funds, virtually nothing had been done or planned for the erection of strong fortresses to defend the eastern border. In suggesting a multitude of lesser defense measures in 1818, Boyen hoped to compensate somewhat for previous oversights; his plan, however, was abandoned after his dismissal in 1820.[23]

As in his works on the age of the great reforms in Prussia and the wars of liberation, in his fundamental contribution to the

---

21. Ibid., I, 330.
22. Ibid., II, 438–439.
23. Ibid., II, 243–244.

history of the Revolution of 1848, the work on Radowitz, Meinecke again examined Russia's position in Germany and Russian views concerning Germany. He considered the arguments of greater-Germany advocates justified when they maintained that the "Small" German solution, which left Austria to herself, would have meant not only giving up parts of the German nation but sacrificing as well important material interests of the nation at large. The Danube route to the Black Sea would be endangered if a future Germany and a future Austria were to exist side by side as two autonomous states, if Slavs and Magyars in Austria were to advance, or if Russia were to become master of Austria and thus close the gateway to the Orient. The sole route for future extension of German ethnic strength that was still relatively open was toward the European Southeast.[24] This was an opinion expressed also by Friedrich List [25] and the young Moltke [26] at the same time. Here Meinecke saw a substantial political and historical relationship forming a connection between German colonization in an eastern and southeastern direction and the Near East policies of the German Empire.

Let us call attention only to what is most important in Meinecke's acute analysis of the policies of Nicholas I during the Revolution of 1848. From the old empirical law that the character and the intensity of a war depend primarily on its political aims, Meinecke concluded that Russia, should she have intervened militarily, would not have become Prussia's lifelong enemy, since the eradication of Prussia was by no means in Russia's interest. The Czar envisaged the restoration of the conservative Prussia of his father-in-law, Friedrich Wilhelm III. The Czar would have come to the aid of the Austrians against Prussia not in order to destroy Prussia, but to win Prussia back to the Holy Alliance and to maintain a dualism between the two German powers that served at the same time Russia's conservative and "realpolitische" interests.[27]

---

24. Meinecke, *Radowitz und die deutsche Revolution* (Berlin, 1913), 190–191.

25. Carl Brinkmann, *Friedrich List* (Berlin, Munich, 1949), 297.

26. Rudolf Stadelmann, *Moltke und der Staat* (Krefeld, 1950), ch. 2: "Die Orientfrage und die grossdeutsche Mission."

27. Meinecke, *Radowitz*, 253.

Thus, Nicholas could say that he would not allow Prussia to lose a single village if he were compelled to march against her in order to put down unchecked democratic elements.[28]

In this context, attention should be called to the fact that in his studies of historiography Meinecke attached great importance to an episode in the reign of Czar Nicholas I. A statement of Ranke's on the anti-Russian documents collection, the famous *Portfolio* published in 1835 by the Englishman David Urquhart, in Meinecke's opinion touched the heart of Ranke's concept of history and the state. While public opinion considered this collection of secret documents on contemporary history, which was intended to ridicule Russian policy, sensationalism and interpreted it as a sign that the Anglo-Russian split was widening, Ranke showed how the *Portfolio* should be viewed, and used, as a source of historical knowledge. Ranke concluded from the documents that the policies of the three conservative eastern powers were not as blindly reactionary with respect to the revolutionary movements in Western Europe as public opinion assumed. Moreover, the documents demonstrated to him that the distinction between reaction and revolution was for the internal political life of these nations secondary to questions of power politics and foreign relations, the real center of all politics.[29]

Most of Meinecke's statements on Eastern Europe are to be found in his political journalism, in which he sought to apply historical insights to the political questions of the day. Over and over again he sought a theoretical basis and justification for his concern with the history of his own time. Let us, therefore, examine his methodology for contemporary history.

Meinecke did not let himself be fooled by Ranke's skepticism, which held that history had not elevated politics, but had probably been dragged down by it. "The farthest-reaching, most ambitious, yet for one's personal reputation most dangerous, undertaking that an author concerned with the truth can dare," according to Ranke, is involved for the historian who is so bold as to approach themes of contemporary history. To Ranke, to explain the present genetically by its derivation from the past was not the main task of

---

28. Ibid., 516.
29. Meinecke, "Rankes politisches Gespräch," (1924), in *Vom geschichtlichen Sinn und vom Sinn der Geschichte*, 4th edition (Leipzig, 1939), 29–30.

historical scholarship. In such an objective, he saw rather "a danger and a temptation to the historian to appropriate from history what is useful in terms of the present, as though the past had meaning and worth only in reference to the present." [30]

It is the prerogative, but perhaps also the lot and the constant temptation of the historian to move all phenomena into the light of history, to view all phenomena from an historical perspective. Because Meinecke's concept of the historical encompassed in a very definite, realistic sense the present and future as well as the past, he was tempted to undertake the hazardous task of placing an interpretation on the present. Eduard Spranger, in his deeply felt tribute to Meinecke before the Peace Class of the Holders of the Pour le Mérite, expressed this idea as "the present's being charged with the past and pressing over into the future." [31]

Even though Meinecke had only limited accessibility to source materials, in his *Geschichte des deutsch-englischen Bündnisproblems 1890–1901,* published in 1927, he risked undertaking an interpretation of English policy that, though it might indeed be corroborated, might perhaps be modified or even refuted in a few years. For his assessment of German policy depended primarily on such an interpretation,[32] and he was of the opinion that without criteria for what should have happened, the most recent past could not be treated effectively.[33] Addressing himself to a critic of his *Geschichte des deutsch-englischen Bündnisproblems,* he was able to formulate a methodology for contemporary history that has universal validity:

> I do not proceed from ideals, but from an objective assessment of political situations according to the standard of "raison d'état," a standard which I try to apply to both German and English policy with the highest degree of objectivity. I acknowledge, particularly in the treatment of problems of contemporary history, that subjectivity and the ideal cannot be excluded from this method. I ask rather that they be controlled and held in check. For the deci-

---

30. Eberhard Kessel, "Friedrich Meinecke," *Welt als Geschichte,* **XIV** (1954), 3.

31. Public Session of the Orden Pour le Mérite für Wissenschaften und Künste in Bonn on May 31, 1954.

32. Meinecke, *Geschichte des deutsch-englischen Bündnisproblems 1890–1901* (Munich, Berlin, 1927), 6.

33. Ibid., 8.

sive factor is that with a method directed solely toward presenting the factual material, we shall attain not a deeper understanding of political events, but rather a more surface description. The political situations in which the persons involved found themselves have to be reexperienced. In this, however, we can never be successful if we limit ourselves solely to demonstrable facts.[34]

The publication (1927) of the first two volumes of the *British Documents on the Origins of the War* caused Meinecke to revise some of his views. In the Festschrift on the occasion of Hans Delbrück's eightieth birthday (November 11, 1928), he frankly admitted errors.

> Every intensive critical examination, even of incomplete and one-sided source material, is fruitful for research, even if it should lead to results which are modified or refuted by new sources. That error, too, which even the most meticulous research can commit, becomes instructive when its causes are revealed. One then becomes aware that the efficacy of even the best method, which consists in always combining criticism of the sources with objective political criticism, has its limits.[35]

From these and other statements, it is clear that Meinecke was not afraid to consider his own experience as source material and himself a valid witness for contemporary history. As Heinz Holldack explained, his work is to be considered simultaneously as a documentary source and as an interpretative statement on his time.[36]

The treatment of diplomatic negotiations belongs to the most difficult tasks of historiography.[37] It would be difficult to name a contribution to the diplomatic history of the modern period in which the conceptual nucleus has been extricated more perceptively than Meinecke's *Geschichte des deutsch-englischen Bündnisproblems*, which presents the idea that an alliance with Germany was

---

34. *Historische Zeitschrift,* CXLII (1930), 587.

35. *Am Webstuhl der Zeit,* Emil Daniels and Paul Rühlmann, eds. (Berlin, 1928), 82: "Zur Geschichte der deutsch-englischen Bündnisverhandlung von 1901."

36. Heinz Holldack, "Friedrich Meinecke," *Hochland,* XLVI (1954), 438.

37. Meinecke review of Bismarck's *Gedanken und Erinnerungen Historische Zeitschrift,* LXXXII (1899), 284.

not as necessary for England as an alliance with England was for Germany, and that this was the reason that the actual negotiations on alliance foundered.[38]

This brief examination of Meinecke's methodology for the study of recent history would be incomplete if there were no room for adducing his honest despair over the publication (on the ascendant again today) of murky source publications through which the historian has to wade. Of Poschinger's publications on German history of the nineteenth century, he said: "One has to take them as a force of nature which is simply there and to which one political great after another falls victim." [39] "One is torn between annoyance and gratitude." "Our readers know that we are not ungrateful for what Poschinger achieves when he falls not upon the waste basket of one of his victims, but gains access to his filing cabinet." For Meinecke, the infinitely conscientious researcher, any document that could contribute even a single additional nuance to our understanding of the life and thought of the men of the past was of intrinsic value; no one need fear that such a document would be made superfluous by new discoveries.[40] In view of the untamable flood of source material, one cannot ignore Meinecke's warning that the study of contemporary history always runs the risk of losing itself in the boundlessness of data in a quantitative, not qualitative, universalism.

During the First World War, Meinecke, then at the height of his creativity, became involved in political journalism. As an active publicist, he contributed much to a historically deepened understanding of the war period and of the founding of the Weimar Republic. Nevertheless, his efforts should not be construed as attempts to influence current events, directly and consciously. German historians at the time of the First World War, even as passionate observers of the events of the war, restricted themselves to statements of interpretation and hope, exhortation and reminder, challenge and rebuke, or restraint and admonition.

The Bonn historian Skalweit has spoken of the "infinitely fine, often hardly perceptible, threads" that went back and forth between

---

38. Meinecke, *Bündisproblem*, 15.
39. *Historische Zeitschrift*, LXXXVII (1901), 45f., 491, 503.
40. *Göttingische Gelehrte Anzeigen*, 1891, No. 21, 830–831.

historical thinking and personal experience in Ranke's contemplative, scholarly temperament.[41] This observation might hold as well for Meinecke. Basically a scholar, he put his knowledge at the disposal of German politics when the time demanded.[42] As Theodor Heuss put it, Meinecke, unlike Hans Delbrück or Ernst Troeltsch, did not feel a powerful urge to enter the battle of contemporary opinion as a speaker and writer.[43] It is true that Meinecke had conversations with Bethmann Hollweg, Prince Max von Baden, and Kühlmann. There is, however, no evidence of the extent to which his ideas influenced the policies of the German statesmen. How much he was aware of his responsibility as an historian in such conversations (one might call them private conversations of state) can be seen clearly in his practice of writing notes directly afterwards and submitting this record to his interlocutor for examination. Such self-control was a guarantee of the greatest possible degree of critical objectivity. Only he can claim judgments of enduring worth, Meinecke said, who has rid himself of feelings for or against Bülow, Bethmann, and Tirpitz, and has undertaken to assess with the greatest care the dynamic consequences of their deeds.[44] First of all, the historian has to try to transform himself into a politician of the highest order, that is, a politician who not only desires and wills, but also acts, responsibly. Thus this is an effort that places him in a certain opposition to Mommsen, who, according to his own confession, was not capable of "neutralizing" himself against his own times or against the past.[45] In the *raison d'état*, however, Meinecke saw the guide, the common lodestar, of the statesman and the political historian.

As a trained historian who had witnessed with acute concern German foreign policy since the turn of the century, Meinecke devoted himself continually after the outbreak of the war in 1914 to the question whether the developments which led to the war on two

---

41. Stephan Skalweit, "Ranke und Bismarck," *Historische Zeitschrift*, CLXXVI (1953), 281.

42. Walter Goetz, "Friedrich Meinecke," *Historische Zeitschrift*, CLXXIV (1952), 243.

43. Theodor Heuss, "Ein Grusswort," *Historische Zeitschrift*, CLXXIV (1952), 227.

44. *Historische Zeitschrift*, CXXI (1919–1920), 119.

45. *Historische Zeitschrift*, CLXXVII (1954), 656.

fronts had been unavoidable. In his review of Prince Bülow's *Deutsche Politik,* he criticized the former chancellor's treatment of foreign policy of the Wilhelminian period for glossing over the serious and difficult question concerning the wisdom of laying simultaneously the foundations for future English and Russian hostility by building a fleet and pursuing the Berlin-Baghdad railway. Subsequent developments showed that at the turn of the century Germany had set for herself tasks in world politics which were beyond her powers.[46] She needed, in Meinecke's phrase, "a bridled ambition, which recognized the limits of her own strength," a combination of self-restraint and drive for power, in order to enter the "international syndicate of the mightier." [47] According to him, German imperialism at the turn of the century should have decided in principle either for a western orientation, in which case it would have had to come to terms, by peaceful litigation, with England's predominance on the ocean, or for an eastern, continental orientation—Meinecke used the sharper word "Pointierung" (emphasis)—in which case it would have unavoidably come into conflict with Russia's interests in the Near East. Under the impact of the failure of German ideas concerning foreign policy in the Wilhelminian period and during Hitler's time, Ludwig Dehio demonstrated that Meinecke's alternative—either west or east— was overly optimistic, that German imperialism could at no time prevail in either an easterly or a westerly direction.[48] After the turn of the century Germany failed to apply successfully the imperialistic corollary of her idea of a national state, because her European power base was too narrow to allow her to enter world politics at such a late date. Over and over again, Meinecke returned to what was in his opinion the most obvious, the cardinal, error of German policy in the period before the First World War, namely that it pursued fleet construction and a Near Eastern policy at the same time. It was a policy which proceeded from the erroneous assumption that Russian and English interests were at odds, that

46. Meinecke, "Fürst Bülows *Deutsche Politik,*" *Historische Zeitschrift,* CXVII (1916), 80.
47. Meinecke, *Bündnisproblem,* 267.
48. Ludwig Dehio, "Gedanken über die deutsche Sendung 1900–1918," *Historische Zeitschrift,* CLXXIV (1952), 499–500.

hostility and hope for revenge on the part of France would evoke an irreconcilable enmity on the part of England and Russia.

The Berlin-Baghdad railroad policy, which strengthened Turkey economically and made her more resistant to Russian demands, created for Germany a "paltry" ("leidige") sphere of interest in Anatolia and Mesopotamia. Had Germany proceeded as Meinecke thought she should have, she would have sought the friendship of England with all the means at her disposal,[49] reached an understanding with England, and liquidated the eastern, Turkish, sphere of interest which resulted from the Berlin-Baghdad railroad. She could have sold her interests in Asia Minor and Mesopotamia for the highest possible price to England and Russia.[50] In other words, before 1914 Germany should have curtailed her efforts in the East, reduced the source of friction between herself and Russia, and removed her protective hand from Constantinople.[51] But Meinecke had to concede that what seemed logical was impossible psychologically. For what German statesman, in the Germany of that day, inflated with power and riding a wave of prosperity, would have dared to counsel the German public to retreat, rather than urge the government to go further and further? Such a policy could have been dared only by a statesman of Bismarck's stature; it was, as Meinecke put it, "too reasonable to be capable of implementation."

To be sure, Meinecke recognized certain dark sides of German militarism in prewar Germany. Yet it cannot be denied that in deriving militarism itself, at the beginning of the war, from threats posed to Germany from without by the "encircling powers," he moved conditions posed by the domestic situation to the background in a surprising manner. Otherwise, he could not have written:

> It [German militarism] is nothing but Germany's answer to the Thirty Years' War, to Louis XIV, to Napoleon I, and—as we may now add—to Edward VII and to all Czars named Nicholas.[52]

49. *Historische Zeitschrift,* CXL (1929), 405–406.

50. Meinecke, *Bündnisproblem,* 248.

51. "Ein Gespräch aus dem Herbste 1919," *Nach der Revolution* (1919), 129.

52. Meinecke, *Die deutsche Erhebung von 1914* (Stuttgart, Berlin, 1914),

The First World War gave rise to deep divisions and to unusually sharp, often personally bitter exchanges among German historians over the desirable course for German foreign and domestic policy, over war and peace aims. All the rancor of Meinecke's Berlin colleague Dietrich Schäfer, one of the founders of the Independent Committee for a German Peace and, later, of the Deutsche Vaterlandspartei, burst forth in a sentence in Schäfer's *Memoirs* in which he wrote, with bitterness, of the demand for immediate reform of voting laws in Prussia by Harnack, Delbrück, Meinecke, "and comrades"—a very friendly, "kollegial" expression indeed—in the summer of 1917, published, to be sure, "intentionally on the day of Koeniggrätz," July 3.[53] The necessity for internal reforms in time of war can hardly be expressed more pointedly than Meinecke did: "A state that has to wage war with a mass army of twelve percent of its population must also have a popular base for its internal politics." [54] Meinecke was among the champions of a policy that sought to offset through timely reforms the radicalization of the masses and their susceptibility to Bolshevism.

It is beyond the purview of this article to pursue further Meinecke's position on questions of domestic policy during the First World War. However, his involvement in discussion of some questions of foreign policy at that time, particularly those concerned with Germany's war aims, is of great interest. In an essay on "Bismarck and the New Germany" (1915), he pointed out that, in Bismarck's sense, the primary and most immediate task of the war was the preservation of Austria. In order to defend the Austrian state and its numerous nationalities against the onslaught of Pan-Slavism, Bismarck had been willing, when necessary, to place the full force of German power behind Austria in a struggle

---

30: "Die deutschen Erhebungen von 1813, 1848, 1870 und 1914." The similarity between this pronouncement and Ranke's famous statement during his meeting with Thiers in Vienna in October, 1870, that the war was aimed at the policy of Louis XIV, is unmistakable. See Hans F. Helmolt, *Leopold von Rankes Leben und Wirken* (Leipzig, 1921), 127f.

53. Dietrich Schäfer, *Mein Leben* (Berlin, 1926), 217.

54. Meinecke, "Vaterlandspartei und deutsche Politik," *Die Hilfe*, XXIII, No. 47 (1917), 702.

against Russia.[55] Here Meinecke adopted the reasoning of the Swedish political scientist and geopolitician, Rudolf Kjellén, whom he held in high regard: in the end, the Pan-Slavist racial idea served the geopolitical interest of Russia, Russia hoping to reach the Adriatic coast of the Mediterranean through Austrian territory inhabited by Slavs.[56] Thus, a kind of Russian corridor to the Adriatic would come into existence. This idea ought not to be overlooked in the discussion of corridor theories in the context of the First World War. Let us recall here, apart from the Polish corridor, only the plan for a territorial link between Lusatia and Czechoslovakia.

Bismarck considered the Russian threat to Austria, and to Central Europe in general, so great that after 1914 the Russian danger could actually become—to use Ludwig Dehio's expression —"the raison d'être" of German policy, the basis of the "German mission." [57] The First, and to a greater extent the Second, World War seemed to Meinecke to prove that the Russia that had threatened Austria and Constantinople between 1914 and 1916 was another, more national and hence more effective and dangerous, Russia than Bismarck had known and included in his calculations. From the Second World War he gained the impression that the Russian people met the German onslaught with an internal cohesiveness and national consciousness that was much greater than in the czarist period. We can agree in essence with Meinecke's assessment of Russia for the first two years of the First World War, while opinions of competent observers diverge widely respecting the first months of the Russo-German war in 1941.

When Russia foundered in the First World War because of the overextension of her resources, Meinecke, in an essay entitled "Basic Problems of German National Policy" in the *Neue Rundschau* in June 1918, after the Bolsheviks had established their rule, warned against underestimating the vitality of the Great Russians. Germany seemed to him at the time to be running the

55. "Bismarck und das neue Deutschland" (1915), *Preussen und Deutschland* (1918), 529.

56. "Probleme des Weltkrieges" (1916), *Probleme des Weltkrieges* (1917), 43.

57. "Gedanken über die deutsche Sendung," *Historische Zeitschrift,* CLXXIV (1952), 499.

risk of abandoning herself to what he called a "Baltocentric policy."
The decisive sentence reads:

> The Baltic-German writers, who exert an unusually strong influence
> on our journalism, are trying to convince us with their brilliant
> dialectic that the new Russia-Muscovy is a totally unviable state
> and therefore poses no threat, that Tartar-influenced Great Russia
> is not at all capable of constructing on her own an economically
> and politically efficient organism.[58]

Though Meinecke named no names, he doubtless had in
mind principally Paul Rohrbach, Axel Schmidt, and their followers, but perhaps he was also thinking of certain statements of
the Tübingen historian Johannes Haller, the Berlin theologian
Reinhold Seeberg, the Königsberg theologian Friedrich Lezius,
and even of statements by Hans Delbrück, who was strongly influenced by Rohrbach's reasoning and had even been convinced
by it.[59] With this statement Meinecke broached a very serious
problem concerning German information on Russia in the period
before 1914, a problem that still awaits comprehensive treatment: Germany's view of Russia at the time was conditioned to a
great extent by Germans from the Baltic provinces who immigrated
into the Reich. These men had an extremely critical, negative, if
not directly hostile attitude toward Russia. Many Baltic Germans
saw nothing but barbarism when they looked at Russia, a phenomenon that found its most ingenious expression in Victor Hehn's
book, *De moribus Ruthenorum* (1892). The underestimation of
Russia that prevailed in Germany at that time could be attributed
in great measure to Baltic Germans. Theodor Schiemann, who
achieved the admission of East European Studies as a special field
at German universities, is first among these influences.[60] Meinecke

58. Meinecke, "Grundfragen der deutschen Nationalpolitik," *Neue Rundschau*, XXIX (1918), 735.
59. See, e.g., Paul Rohrbach, "Der osteuropäische Frieden," *Deutsche
Politik*, 3rd year, No. 11 (March 15, 1918), 323–329; Johannes Haller, "Gedanken
eines Balten," *Süddeutsche Monatshefte*, September 1914, 812–816; Friedrich
Lezius, *Deutschland und der Osten* (Königsberg, 1918) (printed as manuscript;
confidential); Hans Delbrück, "Politische Korrespondenz," *Preussische Jahrbücher*,
CLXXII, No. 1 (April 1918), 135.
60. Hugo Freiherr von Freytag-Loringhoven, *Menschen und Dinge* (Berlin,
1923), 170.

considered his colleague Schiemann, who, as foreign policy contributor to the *Kreuzzeitung,* was an influential conservative publicist and who had the Kaiser's ear, the embodiment of the spirit of the Wilhelminian age.[61]

Though he was sensitive to the difficulties faced by the Germans in the Baltic provinces and concerned about their destiny, his healthy historical instinct kept Meinecke from equating the unmistakable *pro domo* plea of the Baltic Germans with German national interest. The correctness of his watch-and-wait attitude respecting the future of Great Russia, and of the Great Russians, needs no elaboration. His firm position on the Baltic Germans and their influence on journalism did not mean that he regarded the acquisition of territory in eastern Europe as outside German national interest. On the contrary, one can trace in his statements over the years 1915 to 1918 the development of a program for annexations in eastern Europe based on the strategic situation.

In 1915, in an essay on "The Social Democrats and Power Politics," in the collection *Die Arbeiterschaft im neuen Deutschland,*[62] Meinecke asked the Social Democrats whether their principle of not wishing to humiliate any nation also extended to Russia, in the sense that Russia would be allowed to maintain her complete, despotic domination over the nationalities in the zone between Russia and Germany. He answered the question himself in this way: "It is well known that the Social Democrats oppose that. What they desire for Russia is unquestionably . . . a humiliating . . . but nonetheless well-deserved reduction of her power." The principle of humiliating no nation was, he held, surely a lodestar not to lose sight of, but the path of German foreign policy should also be determined by both the wind and the weather. Nonetheless, this veiled mode of expressing himself allows only the interpretation that Meinecke did not dismiss a departure from the principle, that is, the humiliating demand that Russia relinquish her domination over the nationalities in the zone between Germany and Russia, if the strategic situation made such a policy possible.[63]

---

61. Meinecke, *Erlebtes,* 211.

62. Friedrich Timme and Carl Legien, eds. (Leipzig, 1915), 21–31.

63. In "Präliminarien der Kriegsziele," *Das grössere Deutschland,* 1915, No. 31 (July 31), 1001-14, Meinecke expressed Germany's war aim respecting

In the summer of 1916, Meinecke made a statement that we cannot regard without a certain amount of regret. He touched upon a policy then frequently accepted by Germans in theory, that of compulsory resettlement, and upon the prospects of well-defined, ethnically homogeneous areas of settlement which such enforced migration would create. Such a correction of ethnic conditions seemed to him desirable for Germany's eastern marches with their hodgepodge of nationalities, but he had reservations immediately. One had to guard against any excessive expectations, for the bond between man and soil was much firmer than German "politicians of evacuation" realized.[64] Even as late as the summer of 1917, he did not reject an "action to correct ethnic conditions" between Germany and Russia. The Russian peasant wanted the land of the German settlers in southern Russia; the Germans wanted these German settlers transplanted to Courland.[65] It cannot be over-stressed that the idea of involuntary migration and enforced resettlement of populations in eastern Europe has an intellectual history which reaches far back into the nineteenth century and has yet to be elucidated in detail.[66] It was, unfortunately, often German voices which demanded that large areas in the east be cleared of their indigenous populations in order to provide new land for German settlement.[67]

In the spring of 1916, in an essay on "Diplomacy and Pas-

Russia in the following way: "Our need in the East is to drive Russia back and obtain new land for the settlement of German peasants, above all those Germans of southern Russia who have been expelled from their plots by the Russian Government" (1013). This article should be added to the Friedrich Meinecke bibliography in *Historische Zeitschrift*, CLXXIV, No. 2 (October 1952).

64. *Probleme des Weltkrieges* (1917), 44: "Probleme des Weltkrieges" (1916).

65. "Kriegsziele hüben und drüben," *Deutsche Politik*, II, no. 25 (June 22, 1917), 790.

66. In the Festschrift for Hermann Aubin, *Geschichtliche Landeskunde und Universalgeschichte* (1950), Gotthold Rhode sheds light on the Russian practice of military or state-enforced resettlement of populations in the modern period: "Zwangsumsiedlungen in Osteuropa vor der Oktoberrevolution," 163–182.

67. Dietrich Schäfer, who had a sensitive understanding of regional attachments and the deprivations caused by displacement, wrestled with the same question as Meinecke. How he had a long time resisted the demands of his Pan-German associates and, finally, against his better judgment, allowed himself to be won over, can be read in the autobiography of Heinrich Class, president of the Alldeutsche Verband: *Wider den Strom* (Leipzig, 1932), 361–365.

sions" in the weekly *Die Hilfe*, edited by Friedrich Naumann and Gertrud Bäumer, Meinecke wrote, as if he had been visited by a dark foreboding, that the war could end with the defeat of Germany. He attempted to describe the situation that would result if the enemy were to persevere in the struggle and in two or three years actually defeat and destroy Germany. It is amazing that this hypothesis, which two years later became cruel reality, could be printed under war censorship. Meinecke prophesied that the defeat of Germany would prove "for the enemy a Pyrrhic victory in the worst sense," and he made the prognosis that Germany's enemies would then be themselves so exhausted that America and Japan, as the only two world powers still intact, would automatically gain ascendancy and place their influence on international affairs in a decisive manner. In this article Meinecke voiced his profound concern that passions on both sides seemed to delay indefinitely a diplomatic settlement of the war. With unwonted acerbity, he took to task the German "submarine monomaniacs and annexationists" who had completely lost touch with the time-honored and proven tradition of firm and prudent statesmanship. "They inherited Bismarck's cuirassier's boots, but not his head," reads Meinecke's condemnation of them.[68] Later, in his book on the Anglo-German alliance, one unexpectedly comes upon a sharp criticism of the German government for its failure to force "nationalistic loudmouths and population shifters" [69] to be quiet.

In the First World War few unofficial German statements on the course of the war found greater resonance in the enemy camp than an article by Meinecke entitled "The Rhythm of the World War" in the 1916 New Year's Eve edition of the *Frankfurter Zeitung*. This article, with its considered assessment of German successes and failures in the previous year, must have been a veritable sensation. It is still puzzling today why the censor did not object to the admission that the greatest display of German initiative and Germany's greatest effort in the western theater of war since the Battle of the Marne, the costly struggle for Verdun in

---

68. "Staatskunst und Leidenschaften," *Die Hilfe*, XXII, No. 39 (September 28, 1916), 636.
69. Meinecke, *Bündnisproblem*, 254.

1916, was merely an heroic episode. From the Verdun experience Meinecke thought he could conclude that certain limits were set to a strategy of annihilation ("Niederwerfung") in the struggle of the Great Powers with one another. "That means, however," he went on, "that a policy of annihilation, a policy aimed at radical change in the European power structure, is bad business and does not pay. . . . Not annihilation, but rather equilibrium, is the political watchword of the future." [70] The German successes in the eastern theater brought him then to the following conclusion: "We have achieved as much as we need in order to conclude a peace that realizes our war aims." [71]

But what were Germany's war aims in the East that Meinecke at that time hoped capable of realization? His political journalism of the years 1917 and 1918 provides the answer.

When the German victories in the East had shown Russia to be the weakest partner in the enemy coalition, all indications were that Germany should extend her Continental power base eastwards. After the conquest of Romania at the end of 1916, Meinecke believed that the Sereth Line in the southeast would be the likely future border between Russia and the states of Central Europe.[72] In 1917 the Russian Revolution seemed to him for a moment like the death of the Empress Elizabeth, "the miracle of the House of Brandenburg," which had once saved Frederick the Great.[73] Plans to demand the cession of Courland and to make it an area of settlement for German peasants still appeared realizable in the spring; the new German border was to include Kovno and Grodno.[74]

From the summer of 1917 on, however, when there was no longer any doubt concerning the infinitely superior strength of the enemy coalition, one can detect a marked change in Meinecke's views. He began to advocate a peace based on the *status quo ante,* i.e., on prewar boundaries, a "better peace of Hubertusburg," which he had considered an entirely successful result of the World War

---

70. *Probleme des Weltkrieges* (1917), 133–134.
71. Ibid., 135.
72. "Probleme des Weltkrieges," *Probleme des Weltkrieges,* 57.
73. See above, note 13.
74. See above, note 65.

for Germany.[75] Until then, at least as far as eastern Europe was concerned, he had clearly aligned himself with the annexationists, although as a moderate. It was only in the summer of 1917 that the objectives in Courland seemed to him "merely desirable, but not a vital necessity." [76] However, this does not mean that he entirely repudiated the "eastern orientation." Otherwise, he could not have written as late as November, 1917:

> The demand of the so-called eastern orientation has unquestionably a healthy core of policy based on reality, although to my way of thinking this demand is now being raised in the daily press with much too loud and insistent a cry.[77]

The disintegration of Russia following the November overthrow, the so-called October Revolution, opened up entirely new possibilities for territorial rearrangements in the East. In the summer of 1918 Meinecke wrote for the *Neue Rundschau* a comprehensive analysis of the strategic situation as he saw it after the Brest-Litovsk negotiations.[78] In its decisive points the essay must be regarded as a repeated warning against plans and appetites for major German annexations in the East.[79] "It is a matter of applying brakes to the vehicle," he wrote, "so that it does not hurtle down the new road to the East too quickly." He distinguished three concentric circles in Germany's new sphere of influence in the East: the first encompassing Poland and Lithuania; the second the Baltic provinces, Courland, Livonia, and Estonia; and the third and outermost, Finland and the Ukraine. The restoration of Poland by the proclamation of November 1916 Meinecke considered a hard and immutable fact. Germany's security needs could be satisfied by a permanent military convention under which she would have the right to occupy the fortresses on the Narev. He thought of Lithuania as a principality, nominally independent, yet allied with Germany

---

75. Meinecke, "Ein Gespräch aus dem Herbst 1919," *Nach der Revolution* (1919), 132.

76. Meinecke, *Strassburg, Freiburg, Berlin,* 229.

77. Meinecke, "Vaterlandspartei und deutsche Politik," *Die Hilfe,* XXIII, No. 47 (November 22, 1917), 701.

78. Meinecke, "Grundfragen deutscher Nationalpolitik," *Neue Rundschau,* XXIX, No. 6 (June 1918), 721–737.

79. Meinecke, *Strassburg, Freiburg, Berlin,* 281.

through perpetual military and economic agreements; the Niemen Line would be Germany's strategic line of defense in the east. In this way, he believed that the requirements of a German "Realpolitik" in the east would be met, especially with the solidification of Germany's military position on the Narev and Niemen. It is surprising that he did not discuss the psychological and substantial "realpolitische" difficulties involved in maintaining German garrisons in the midst of increasingly nationalistic Polish and Lithuanian populations. A thought in this direction would have made the projected close tie between Poland and Lithuania and postwar Germany appear questionable, if not downright utopian.

As far as the second circle, the Baltic region, was concerned, Meinecke advocated even at that time the retention of Courland; that constituted for him, however, the limit of German national policy. To cut off from Russia the whole Baltic region, including Livonia and Estonia, and thus to deprive Russia of most of her Baltic ports, seemed to him against the dictates of strict "Realpolitik," for a resurgent Russia would hardly be satisfied with free ports in Riga and Reval (Tallin), and any possibility of a future German alliance with Russia would thus be precluded. Russia would harbor the desire to become a Great Power once again. Similarly, the proclivity toward Baltic expansion would survive. As a possible future solution to the Baltic problem, Meinecke envisaged Courland's becoming a Prussian province after it had received a large influx of German peasants. Livonia and Estonia, on the other hand, would again become members of a Russian confederation of states, with a guarantee of internal autonomy. How correct this insight was has been confirmed by the secret agreement of August 1939, in which Hitler purchased Russian neutrality by recognizing that Finland and the border states lay in the Soviet sphere of influence and interest. Meinecke assumed that German troops would be withdrawn from Finland and the Ukraine when their missions were completed, and that close friendly ties would supersede the protection and aid then being rendered.

It is obvious that Meinecke was led to a gross overestimation of the opportunities and safeguards of peace in that area because he viewed the east too much in isolation. Only at the close of his article did he warn, for reasons of international politics (much as

Germany's position in international politics had been improved by the collapse of the Russian colossus), against viewing Germany's newly won influence in the east as either a political or economic substitute for those areas denied to Germany by her Western enemies. Open sea routes and a great colonial empire in Africa were and remained, he declared, German war aims of the first magnitude in the west. The admonition that aims in the west not be forgotten for territorial ambitions in the east—presented in an essay published four months before the collapse—indicates how much Meinecke still overestimated the military strength of Germany and her allies.

With respect to the Ukraine, the evacuation of which Meinecke had suggested in his analysis of the military situation in the summer of 1918, Meinecke knew that he and the former chancellor, Bethmann Hollweg, were in agreement. As early as the beginning of May 1918, in a conversation with Meinecke, the chancellor had written off the Ukraine, since he was firmly convinced that Russia would pull herself together once again.[80] Meinecke's view that from then on every German statesman had to consider a restored Poland as a "hard and immutable fact" by no means coincided with that of Kühlmann, then the responsible German statesman, as Meinecke discovered much later, when he prepared a memorandum on Kühlmann and the Papal peace move of 1917. Kühlmann's ideas form a stage in German eastern policy in the First World War before Germany was in part tempted and in part compelled by the development, which began with the Bolshevik Revolution on the former Empire's territory, to forge deeper and deeper into the east: thus far, however, this phase has not received the attention it merits.

In a memorandum of July 27, 1917, addressed to Chancellor Michaelis, Kühlmann wrote: [81]

> The establishment of the Kingdom of Poland was perhaps a tactical necessity due to circumstances; to make its maintenance an element of German policy would be suicidal to the highest degree. As soon as order has been somewhat restored in Russia and there is a

---

80. Ibid., 249.

81. "Kühlmann und die päpstliche Friedensaktion von 1917," *Sitzungsberichte der Preussischen Akademie der Wissenschaften,* Philos.-Histor. Klasse (1928), 192.

government capable of negotiating, German foreign policy should certainly have the opportunity at least to come to an agreement with Russia over Poland.[82] Such an arrangement will surely have to be made sooner or later. So better sooner than later! The Polish question might become the site on which Russo-German relations could be reestablished . . . .

Just as in the instance of the Baltic provinces, we can see that the events of August and September 1939, this time the partition of Poland arranged by Hitler and Stalin, were adumbrated in the First World War.

In the winter of 1918–1919, when his publicistic efforts were directed toward strengthening the narrow dike separating Germany from Bolshevism,[83] Meinecke wrote a memorandum at the request of the government on the question of the western border, that is, on Germany's historical claim to the left bank of the Rhine. Like Dietrich Schäfer's *Sprachenkarte der deutschen Ostmarken* [84] (published anonymously for reasons that are easy to guess), Meinecke's report remained unused and unnoticed as Germany's enemies pursued their own goals.

It would be worthwhile to analyze the role of professional historians as advisers to their governments in the preparation of the peace treaties after the First and Second World Wars. In 1919 Meinecke and Schäfer played an entirely peripheral role as consultants to the German government. The only historian among the four German experts called to Versailles to draft a response to the Allies' war guilt note was Hans Delbrück, whose greatness ought to be impressed upon the present generation. By way of contrast, in the last war, the levy of American historians for work in regular and war-improvised institutions was so large that one might have thought that the annual convention of American historians was sitting *sine die* in Washington.

Meinecke's published memoirs end with the year 1919. To trace his intellectual development during the last three decades of his life and assess his thoughts on contemporary history would

---

82. See Meinecke, *Bündnisproblem*, 254.
83. Meinecke, *Strassburg, Freiburg, Berlin*, 260; "Ein Gespräch aus dem Herbste 1919," *Nach der Revolution*, 113.
84. Dietrich Schäfer, *Mein Leben* (1926), 231.

require a special study.[85] Nevertheless, we should not proceed without mentioning his views on Russia in the *Deutsche Allgemeine Zeitung* in April 1922:

> It is true that they [the Russians] need years of peace now in order to restore to a certain extent, with Europe's assistance, the crushed organism, but then they could strike out again sooner than we expect to advance anew the boulder that Peter the Great began to roll up the mountain and that has now rolled into an abyss.[86]

So here again, as in Meinecke's criticism of Baltic political journalism of the summer of 1918, there appears the pensive admonition that one would do well to consider Russia—rather sooner than later—once again as a power factor.

Nine years later, on May 1, 1931, the *Vossische Zeitung* carried a review by Meinecke of Kühlmann's *Gedanken über Deutschland*. To what extent Meinecke's view of the world was influenced by his friendship with Kühlmann must be left to further research. Although Meinecke rarely used superlatives, he nonetheless designated Kühlmann as one of Germany's most gifted, perceptive, and at the same time best-educated diplomats. Kühlmann's rather colorless memoirs show little of such excellence. However, there is evidence in Meinecke's autobiography of his admiration of Kühlmann. His book reviews and newspaper articles are often introduced by phrases such as "the statement of a former statesman whose prudence is well known." [87] When Meinecke wrote this article, a Russia again capable of making alliances was beginning to take shape on the horizon. Meinecke agreed with Kühlmann's view of the French position on German-Polish questions: the Polish alliance was for France merely an expedient, although inevitable. Faced with the choice "Russia or Poland," France would one

---

85. Attention is called here to the trenchant discussion of Meinecke's ideas after the First World War by Hans Herzfeld in his article "Staat und Nation in der deutschen Geschichtsschreibung der Weimarer Zeit," pages 131–132, in the *Festschrift* cited in note 1, above.

86. "Geschichtliche Betrachtungen zur Weltlage" (April 12, 1922, morning edition).

87. See especially Kühlmann's statement on the construction of the German Navy, preserved by Meinecke, *Historische Zeitschrift*, CXXI (1919–1920), 120.

day have to opt again for Russia, as in fact happened a few years later.

In the center of the article under discussion, however, stands the problem of France and Germany. The closing sentences, written almost a quarter of a century ago, could have been written today:

> The French nation must be rid of its fear, not of the fettered Germany of today, but of the more potent Germany of the future. This is the most difficult problem ever to confront European diplomacy. Upon its solution rests the success or failure of all Western civilization.

After 1933 came the long years of enforced silence in public discussion of political questions. Meinecke's last work, *Die deutsche Katastrophe* (1946), the permanent and profound testimony of one who lived through, suffered, and reflected upon the years of Hitler's dictatorship, simultaneously crowns and concludes his historical and publicistic work. The book contains his last and most penetrating public statement on Russia and Bolshevism. In the chapter "Hitlerism and Bolshevism," he deals with the question, topical today more than ever, whether Hitler's struggle against Bolshevism should not be assessed positively and whether Hitler in this role did not thus show himself a more farsighted statesman than the leaders of the western democracies. All of Hitler's statements on Russia and Bolshevism, both published and unpublished, with which I have become acquainted since the publication of Meinecke's book, confirm Meinecke's view that Hitler never deviated from his ultimate aim, announced in *Mein Kampf,* of conquering Russia, Bolshevik or not. For it was Hitler's goal to make Russia up to the Urals a German colony and to exploit her territory for future German settlement. Hitler's proclamation of a crusade against expanding Bolshevism was only a pretext, a foil for his own will to conquer. In fact, Hitler's irrational strategy in the last months of the war seems to confirm Meinecke's suspicion that in the end Western democracy was more of an abomination to him than Bolshevism.

Among the felicitous observations in Karl Alexander von Müller's profile of Meinecke in his collection *Zwölf Historiker-*

profile is the insight that Meinecke's main works are in each instance personal attempts to come to terms with his own time.[88] How much more this holds true for his publicistic statements! That which is temporary, conditioned by the immediate situation, and that which is eternal, valid for all time, are almost inseparably intertwined in his view of the history of his times and of Eastern Europe. In growing old, indeed very old, he fulfilled Ranke's unique criterion for the historian: "I have always thought," Ranke wrote to Bismarck in 1877, "that the historian has to grow old. He must experience much and live through the entire development of an extended period in order to become for his part capable of judging past situations." [89]

Until the very end, Meinecke remained receptive in order to learn more, and open-minded in order to recast his views. Thus, he could in his last work review with exemplary lucidity the most difficult problems confronting German intellectual history in its effort to understand fully Hitler and the Hitler period. The chapter "Hitlerism and Bolshevism" represents Meinecke's legacy to the generation of young historians struggling to comprehend our times.[90]

---

88. "Friedrich Meinecke," *Zwölf Historikerprofile* (Stuttgart, 1935), 34–39.

89. *Bismarck-Jahrbuch*, II (Berlin, 1895), 256. See also Franz Schnabel, "Friedrich Meinecke und die deutsche Geschichtsschreibung," *Hochland*, XXXIV, No. 8 (May 1937), 159.

90. The attitudes of German historians concerning basic political problems of the First World War, especially those of Meinecke, Hans Delbrück, and Dietrich Schäfer, have been thoroughly analyzed by Klaus Schwabe, *Wissenschaft und Kriegsmoral. Die deutschen Hochschullehrer und die politischen Grundfragen des Ersten Weltkrieges* (Göttingen, Zürich, Frankfurt, 1969).

III

East Central Europe
as a Power Vacuum
between East and West
during the German Empire

AT THE END of the Second World War, the *Journal for Central European Affairs,* since 1941 America's representative journal for European *Zeitgeschichte,* was the appropriate periodical to offer two noted scholars of European origin, Hans Rothfels and Oscar Jászi, an opportunity to express their views on Russia's relation to Central Europe.[1] Neither historian confined himself solely to territorial conflicts. Rather, each emphasized in the context of his theme that discussion of fundamentally different forms of political and social organization and their principal contrasts was essential. Articles in the same journal by Paul Sweet and Felix Gilbert on the history of the *Mitteleuropa* idea after the First World War

---

This is an expanded version of a talk given on December 30, 1955, at the annual meeting of the American Historical Association in Washington, D.C., on the topic: "Ideas of Mitteleuropa and Ostmitteleuropa in the Period of the German Empire." It was published in *Die Welt als Geschichte,* XVI, No. 1 (1956), 64–75. The reader should remember that a topic in German history needs different treatment before an American audience than before German readers. The first case calls for a general outline; in the second case, when general knowledge of the subject matter can be assumed, the emphasis can be laid upon nuances.

1. Hans Rothfels, "The Baltic Provinces: Some Historical Aspects and Perspectives," *Journal of Central European Affairs,* IV, No. 2 (July 1944); Oscar Jászi, "Central Europe and Russia," ibid., V, No. 1 (April 1945).

may be considered a supplement.[2] Gilbert explained that Hitler was interested in the attainment of such a limited objective as Central Europe only as a step which brought him nearer to dominion over all Europe.

No work better documents American interest in the history of the *Mitteleuropa* idea than a study begun as a Yale dissertation and published in revised form after years of research at the end of 1955, Henry Cord Meyer's *Mitteleuropa in German Thought and Action, 1815–1945*.[3] The book, an important contribution to German and European history, to the history of political ideas, and to economic and diplomatic history, is nevertheless not a final treatment of the *Mitteleuropa* concept, of its evolution, its flowering, and its renunciation. Because Meyer's work confines itself to German and Austrian aspects of the *Mitteleuropa* idea, much room for further investigation remains. In particular, we still need a thorough analysis of German *Mitteleuropa* as it pertains to the East, namely to eastern and southeastern Europe and to the Near East. "Central Europe in Slavic Thought and Action," a companion piece to Meyer's exposition and a complement from the viewpoint of the East, would have to show how the *Mitteleuropa* idea is enmeshed in the history of East Central Europe and of eastern and southeastern Europe. Only a consideration of both the German and Slavic aspects of the problem will provide clear recognition of the significance of East Central Europe, for tendencies and forces from eastern-oriented German and western-oriented Slavic ideas of *Mitteleuropa*, both aiming at dominion over the belt of nationalities in the border regions, came into conflict. In other words, the history of the German *Mitteleuropa* idea as it pertains to East Central Europe, the area between the ethnic centers of the Germans and of the Great Russians, has to be supplemented and completed by an exposition of the Slavic claim to hegemony in East Central Europe.

The following observations [4] reflect studies in the intellectual-

---

2. Paul Sweet, "Recent German Literature on Mitteleuropa," ibid., III, No. 1 (April 1943; Felix Gilbert, "Mitteleuropa: The Final Stage," ibid., VII, No. 1 (April 1947).

3. *International Scholars Forum*, IV (The Hague). See Meyer's article " 'Mitteleuropa' als Symptom der gegenwärtigen europäischen Krise," *Die Welt als Geschichte*, XV (1955), 188–95.

4. In various respects, they are in agreement with Werner Conze's fundamental treatment, "Nationalstaat oder Mitteleuropa? Die Deutschen des Reichs

historical bases of German Eastern policy during the First World War, culminating in the Treaty of Brest-Litovsk, when the collapse of the Czar's empire opened up unlimited horizons for Germany in the East. The German *Grossmitteleuropa* idea, directed at control of the border regions between Germany and Russia proper, was pushed into the background and eclipsed by the idea of *Osteuropa,* i.e., by designs for German control and exploitation of the East, namely of Asiatic as well as European Russia.[5]

German colonization in the East, a phenomenon decisive for the history of East Central Europe in modern times and one also treated continuously and thoroughly in German and Slavic medieval studies, has frequently been characterized in popular and propagandistic literature as the peculiar German "Drang nach Osten." [6] This historical process is often acknowledged with pride by the Germans and extolled as the outstanding cultural achievement and the mission of the German people in the middle ages. From the Slavic and non-German Baltic viewpoint, however, it has met with vehement national hatred and rejection and has been condemned as annexationism and Pan-Germanism. But forces which worked on both sides in the opposite directions have often been either neglected or underestimated. Observers have failed to note, for example, that sociologists, historians, and geographers long ago established that a drive toward the East ought not be considered a singular and isolated phenomenon of German history. Thus, the geographers Eugeniusz Romer,[7] a Pole, and Hugo Hassinger,[8] a Swiss, described the "Drang nach Osten" of various West European countries. In particular, Hassinger pointed out the tendency in-

---

und die Nationalitätenfrage Ostmitteleuropas im Ersten Weltkrieg," *Deutschland und Europa: Festschrift für Hans Rothfels* (Düsseldorf, 1951).

5. Since the author of this article intends to discuss the present topic later in a different context, only a limited number of sources and studies are quoted.

6. Henry C. Meyer, in a lecture entitled "Drang nach Osten, 1860–1914: Myth or Mission?" at the International Congress of Historians in Rome in 1955, showed that the catchword originated in the nineteenth century and prompted political associations and reaction. Paradoxically, this occurred at a time when no signs can be discovered in Germany of such a movement with respect to the East. See Gotthold Rhode, "Deutschlands 'Drang nach Osten' und die internationale Geschichtswissenschaft," *Ostbrief: Mitteilungen der Ostdeutschen Akademie Lüneburg,* III, No. 5 (January 1956), 124–28.

7. E. Romer, "Problèmes territoriaux de la Pologne," *Scientia,* XXVIII (1920), 12–13.

8. H. Hassinger, *Die Tschechoslowakei* (Vienna, 1925), 207.

herent in each state toward expansion in the direction of decreasing civilization (*Kulturgefälle*) and of least resistance. If not the Germans, another nation in the same geographical situation and endowed with the same vitality, the same spirit of enterprise, and the same talent for organization, would have developed a similar "drive." Thomas Masaryk, whose political achievement in founding Czechoslovakia can be considered an attempt to establish a bulwark against further German expansion in the East, was nonetheless aware that Germany's eastern expansionist policy, as a historical phenomenon, was not unlike the policies of France with respect to Germany, Poland with respect to Russia, or Sweden with respect to Finland.[9] In this connection, however, we should remember that the ethnic frontiers of Germany and Poland have remained virtually unchanged for over half a millennium. The application of barbaric methods, in the wake of wars and revolutions which have raged over the nationalities of East Central Europe, has led to forced population movements which have wrought greater ethnographic change in this area in the four decades since 1914 than occurred in all the preceding centuries.

Any consideration of German-Slavic relations in the nineteenth century must revert to 1848, the year of the German National Assembly and of the first Congress of Slavs. The Revolution of 1848 not only exerted a great influence on the development of German political ideology, terminology, and mythology, in the nineteenth century but the German national movement of that fateful year, 1848, also inspired a parallel Slavic movement, which crystallized in the first Congress of Slavs in Prague and helped lead to Friedrich Naumann, the Anschluss movement of the 1920s, and the deepening interest in and understanding of the *Mitteleuropa* idea.

In the debates of the German National Assembly there developed a common Russophobe front, composed of such heterogeneous elements as Socialists, Democrats, Liberals, and Catholics. It represented an ideological joining of forces due to shared anti-Russian sentiments, which derived from very different sources and

---

9. Thomas G. Masaryk, *Das neue Europa. Der slavische Standpunkt* (Berlin, 1922), 22–23.

developed through seventy years of German parliamentary history, from 1848 to 1918. Since 1848 also witnessed the inception of the Marxist movement, with the publication of the *Communist Manifesto,* the fundamentally anti-Russian attitude of the founders of "scientific" socialism and their abhorrence of czarism as a barbarian Russian menace to Western civilization also played a role. Raised to dogma by its adherents in the First World War, the Russophobia of the German Social Democrats determined their attitude toward the financing of the war and their discussion of war aims, which went so far as to include the overthrow of czarism. Their war aims also included liberation of the nationalities oppressed by czarist Russia, particularly of the Poles and the Finns.[10]

Since the 1840s, ideas of a Greater Germany which met with an increasing Slavic opposition, consisted in a great number of individualistic and generally unrealistic proposals for the solution of the German problem. Some were founded on romantic and historical considerations, while others were based on purely practical, i.e., military and economic, reasoning. The conservative, anti-Bismarckian federalism of Constantin Frantz, who envisioned an Austrian Danubian Federation and a Prussian Baltic Federation, consisting of Prussia, Poland, Lithuania, Courland, and Livonia, contained a kernel of liberalism in that it recommended expansion against Russia without previously having provided for national security in the West. Critical reevaluation of Bismarck's policies led to a renaissance of the ideas of Frantz after the First World War, the offshoot of which was Friedrich Wilhelm Förster's suggestion during World War II of a Central European League of Nations. Through union of Germany and the western Slavic and the southeastern states, a German-Slavic symbiosis was to be realized.[11]

Between 1868 and 1871, the years when the German Reich was being founded, an anti-German attitude developed among the vast majority of Russian society, in contradistinction to the sentiments to be found at the Czar's court. At that time, General

---

10. Erich Matthias, *Die deutsche Sozialdemokratie und der Osten 1914–1945* (Tübingen, 1954), 3–10: "Kreuzzug gegen den Zarismus. Die Befreiungsideologie der Mehrheit."
    11. F. W. Förster, *Erlebte Weltgeschichte 1869–1953* (Nuremberg, 1953), 249.

Rostislav A. Fadeev and Nikolai I. Danilevskii propagated designs for Russia-centered federations which would penetrate deeply into Central Europe.[12] The publication of Danilevskii's *Rossiia i Evropa* was followed by numerous other Russian proposals for sweeping territorial changes of the map of Europe advantageous to the Slavs, from those of Miljutin to those of Kuropatkin, the neo-Pan-Slavists and propagandists of war aims in World War I. Fantasies of this sort proceeded from the assumption that all interests of the Russians were legitimate, as opposed to intrigues and unjustified territorial claims of the other side. The truth is that the viewpoint of each side comprised both concern for defense and expansionist tendencies. Those attitudes fostered in Germany by the fear of a Slavic (Russian or Polish) peril and in Russia by the vision of a German threat were basically defensive. Both attitudes, the defensive German fear of the Russians and the Poles, and Russian German-ophobia, as well as expansionist aspirations—of the Germans toward the east and of the Russians and Poles toward the west—influenced military thinking in both camps and resulted in military measures which were interpreted in turn as threats by the other side.

Bismarck's policies were based on the principle of the conservative solidarity of the three empires of the Hohenzollerns, the Habsburgs, and the Romanovs. The friendship between the Hohenzollerns and the Romanovs had its basis in shared monarchic and anti-Polish interests. Hans Rothfels has shown that Bismarck's achievement of a unified Germany shared certain traits with the national states of the West, but revealed at the same time unmistakable Eastern characteristics. The chancellor was aware that application of the principle of national self-determination to the "historical states," Germany, Austria-Hungary, and Russia, would have the effect of dynamite in East Central Europe, that is, in that area of Europe with the greatest national, social, and religious diversities. Thus, he dared to act "illogically" in that he declined to draw the inferences for the East of the idea of a national state of Western stamp, even when this meant disadvantages for German groups in

---

12. S. Harrison Thomson, "A Century of Phantom Panslavism and the Western Slavs," *Journal of Central European Affairs*, XI, No. 1 (January–April 1951), 67.

neighboring territories, i.e., for Austrian and Baltic Germans.[13] He saw the danger of Pan-Slavism not in Russian hegemony, but rather in the emergence of intractable Slavic nationalities from Poland to Illyria.

The harshest verdict that could be passed on Bismarck's foreign policy by his internal enemies was that it was dictated by fear of the Russians. Yet it cannot be denied that concern over unpredictable developments in Russia, veiled by an appeal to patriotism: "We Germans fear God, but nothing else in the world," was one of the most important factors which determined the chancellor's foreign policy.[14] Similarly, the conviction that Russia posed a threat to Europe influenced the foreign policies of his successors, Caprivi and Bethmann Hollweg.

In 1883, Bismarck declared that war with Russia would be a disaster, for Germany stood to gain nothing, not even the costs of the war. He would hear nothing of an effort to acquire the Baltic provinces, which were strategically so difficult to defend.[15] On January 13, 1887, he said in the Reichstag: "Russia wishes to conquer no German land and we desire to conquer no Russian land. It can only be a question of Polish provinces, and of these we already have more than is convenient for us." In a similar fashion, Moltke declared in 1878: "The Russians are disagreeable neighbors. They have absolutely nothing which could be taken from

---

13. The first volume of Rudolf Crämer's uncompleted work, *Deutschtum im Völkerraum* (Stuttgart, 1938)—in its execution, as compared with its orientation, a very commendable and valuable initial step toward an "Intellectual History of East German Ethnic Policy"—should be continued and completed for its treatment of a theme fundamental to the history of a transformed East Central Europe.

14. Ulrich Noack, reviving the ideologies of 1848 and of the Prussian Wochenblatt party in his book, *Bismarcks Friedenspolitik und das Problem des deutschen Machtverfalls* (1928), condemned the peace policy of the aged statesman as sterile, reactionary, and unconstructive. Bismarck, he held, failed to put an end to the Russian threat to Germany by crushing Russia. Moreover, he failed to organize East Central Europe to this end by creating an independent Finland (with Karelia), a Baltic state, a new Poland, consisting of Congress Poland plus Galicia, and, eventually, a rejuvenated, trialistic Austria-Hungary which would have incorporated all southern Slavs in the framework of the Habsburg state. For criticism of Noack's position, see Hans Rothfels, *Deutsche Literaturzeitung*, LI (3. Folge, 1st year), No. 44 (November 1, 1930), col. 2091–2101.

15. In 1872 Bismarck said he would not accept these provinces as a gift if Russia offered them. Helmut Muskat, *Bismarck und die Balten* (Berlin, 1934), 108.

them even after the most victorious war. They have no gold and we have no need of land." [16] His sober appraisal of the situation in the 1880s sounds unrealistic in the context of a transformed world, in which Soviet Russia is one of the largest gold producers, and which has twice witnessed a German push to the east.[17]

In the examination of Russo-German relations in the Bismarck period and under William II, insufficient consideration has been given to the military aspects, to wit, a comparison of German and Russian military plans and objectives. The German nightmare of feeling threatened by a Russian surprise attack, which was considered a possibility, stands in sharp contrast to the strictly defensive strategic plans of the Russians. Today there is no longer any doubt that almost up to the outbreak of the First World War the Russian General Staff preferred the defensive in the event of a European war and only under French pressure prepared to engage in a very cautious offensive with limited objectives.

As Russian enmity toward Germany increased in the 1880s, the idea of a preventive war against Russia gained ground in German military circles without receiving Bismarck's support.[18] The designs of the German general staff in the 1870s and 1880s for weakening Russia in a prospective war through support of separatist movements, particularly in Poland, Finland, and the Caucasus, have received less attention than have certain similar intentions of Bismarck's in the war against Austria in 1866. Responsible military plans based on doubts concerning the order and stability of the Czar's empire existed side by side with fantastic political demands of irresponsible German publicists. Bismarck made no secret of his utter disdain for the expectations of military circles that Russia

---

16. Robert Lucius von Ballhausen, *Bismarck-Erinnerungen* (Stuttgart, 1921), 139.

17. Count Ährenthal in 1909 and, during the First World War, Count Tisza, judged the annexation of Slavic territories by Austria-Hungary with a scepticism reminiscent of Moltke. They were convinced that the nationalities problem of the Monarchy would not be solved thereby, but rather further complicated, and that the Ausgleich of 1867 would be endangered. Nevertheless, important Austrian statements militate against underestimating Austria's so-called Drang nach Südosten, in the directions of the Black Sea and Salonica in the decades before World War I, as well as against making the generally conservative and defensive policies of Austrian statesmen an absolute.

18. See the penetrating chapter "Die russische Gefahr," in Rudolf Stadelmann, *Moltke und der Staat* (Krefeld, 1950), 297–323.

might be partitioned in the event of a successful campaign. He remained convinced that a policy of liberating the non-Russian nationalities from the czarist yoke, in particular, one of liberating the Russian Poles and making them independent, would create a serious threat to the Prussian monarchy, if not undermine its eastern foundation. Thus, it is surprising that in the event of a war with Russia or a Pan-Slavic revolution, Bismarck proposed the restoration of Poland, by no means free and independent, but rather under the rule of an Austrian archduke and thus in close association with the Habsburg monarchy.

Bismarck's successor, Caprivi, was firmly convinced that war with Russia was inevitable. His policy of reconciliation with the Prussian Poles can thus be explained as an effort to garner peacetime Polish sympathies for the coming war. Count Waldersee, chief of staff after Moltke's resignation, urged a policy which would bring the Poles to the side of Germany in the event of war. Critics of German *Weltpolitik* in the Wilhelminian period have maintained that colonial and naval concerns and the development of overseas trade pushed European problems into the background. Ernst Hasse, the theoretician of Pan-Germanism at the beginning of this century, called for a return from a colonial to a European policy.[19]

The intensification of the Russo-German conflict due to Russia's renewed interest in Europe and the Near East after the Russo-Japanese War, Russian sympathy with the Slavic movement in Austria, and Russia's efforts to emancipate the Balkans from the Turkish yoke strengthened the conviction of the Imperial Government that Austria-Hungary *must* be maintained under German and Hungarian leadership as a bulwark against the Slavs. The Imperial Government strongly discouraged speculation on the part of its representatives in Austria-Hungary as to probable German policy

---

19. Ernst Hasse, *Deutsche Politik* (Munich, 1908), II, "Weltpolitik," No. 1: "Weltpolitik, Imperialismus und Kolonialpolitik," 51: "We demand that, in preference to any sweeping world or colonial policy, policies for control over and settlement of those areas just outside the gates of the German Empire—areas where such policies have been in operation and have stood the test for a thousand years—be considered once again. . . . A German *Weltpolitik* must make the acquisition of areas suitable for emigration one of its primary tasks. The extension of the present, closed area of German settlement into Central Europe would probably be best."

in the event of the dissolution of the Habsburg monarchy. The maintenance of Austria-Hungary became the cardinal point of German foreign policy, for its dismemberment would have meant a victory for the Slavs, with untold consequences for the rest of Europe. Count Schlieffen, Waldersee's successor, was convinced that the alliance between France and Russia meant that Austria's fate would be decided not on the Bug but on the Seine.

In the first decade of this century, contributions to the theory of national minorities by Karl Renner ("Julius Springer"), Otto Bauer, and Aurel Popovici, inspired by the Austrian national crisis and directed at restructuring the monarchy, had effects which reached beyond the borders of the Empire. Renner's *Kampf der österreichischen Nationen um den Staat* (1902) influenced the national-democratic ideologies of the Poles, the Latvians, and the Estonians. His ideas also contributed to the radicalism developing among the intelligentsia of the national minorities in western Russia. His influence is perceptible in Dmowski's conception of Poland as a Western state dependent upon Russia and incorporating large parts of the German East. Similarly, Karel Kramář's wish for a Slavicized Austrian monarchy was influenced by Renner's ideas. Many details of Kramář's blueprint for a Slavic federation under Russian hegemony are paradoxically similar to the terms of German constitutions of the nineteenth century, i.e., the constitutions of the German Confederation and the Frankfurt Parliament, and the constitution of Bismarck's Empire.

Changes wrought on the map of southeastern Europe as a consequence of the Balkan wars increased the prestige of the Slavs. The Central Powers saw themselves placed on the defensive against the Slavic tide. The ethnic composition of Germany's Austro-Hungarian ally notwithstanding, Bethmann Hollweg allowed his foreign policy to be determined in a plainly fatalistic fashion by his conviction that a fundamental antagonism existed between Germans and Slavs. For him, the war of 1914 was principally a struggle between the civilizations of West and East. He "sought to discipline the war into one between Germany and Russia." [20]

---

20. Otto Westphal, *Feinde Bismarcks* (Munich, 1930), 231.

The test of the alliance of the Central Powers experienced its apotheosis in Friedrich Naumann's famous book, *Mitteleuropa*. Naumann gave the idea an unequivocally politico-geographical turn suitable for his purposes. He recast the *Mitteleuropa* idea into an idea of *Ostmitteleuropa*. His *Mitteleuropa* concept was an attempt to justify both emotionally and intellectually a *Mitteleuropa* created by the strategy of the Central Powers. He hoped for its consolidation in time of peace. Because of the wartime situation of 1915, which in the East was politically favorable to Germany, Naumann allowed considerations based on temporary military and economic conditions to play a decisive role. As the position of the Central Powers was enlarged and strengthened in the East and Southeast, he supplemented his basic conception with two studies, *Mitteleuropa und Bulgarien* and *Mitteleuropa und Polen*.

While the German Right (von Bülow) and Left (Kautsky and Hilferding) criticized Naumann sharply, Archibald Cary Coolidge, who pioneered East European studies at Harvard University, hailed the work as "one of the great general programmes in world politics to-day, not a program of Pan-Germanic conquest, but of arrangements that shall be mutually advantageous." [21] That is certainly a remarkably objective appraisal from the enemy's camp in the third year of the war. Masaryk, however, in his famous essay, *At the Eleventh Hour: A Memorandum on the Military Situation* (April 1916), attacked Naumann vehemently and exposed his *Mitteleuropa* idea as capitalistic and imperialistic, albeit democratic, Pan-Germanism.[22] Naumann's conception, he held, culminated in a plan to unite all Germans in an economic organization which would encompass all of Central Europe. The difference between the Germans' and the Slavs' views in proposals for the future of East Central Europe is unequivocal in Masaryk's polemic against Naumann. He saw Naumann's *Mitteleuropa* idea as a new form of Germany's familiar anti-Slavic "Drang nach Osten." In his inaugural lecture on "The Problem of Small Nations in the European

---

21. *The Military Historian and Economist,* II (1917), 350–51.
22. Robert William Seton-Watson, *Masaryk in England* (Cambridge, 1943), 153–202.

Crisis," [23] at King's College of the University of London on October 19, 1915, he emphasized the importance of the principle of self-determination for Central and Eastern Europe in the future.[24]

Under the influence of such able representatives and advocates of the Slavic cause as Masaryk, Beneš, and Dmowski, the First World War was increasingly interpreted in the Allies' camp as a war for Eastern Europe. The champions of the Slavic idea urged the creation of a Central Europe in opposition to Germany and were seconded by English and French sympathizers, such as R. W. Seton-Watson, Wickham Steed, Ernest Denis, and Anatole Leroy-Beaulieu. In 1916, Seton-Watson announced that the twentieth century was the century of the Slavs.[25] "It is one of the main tasks of the war," he wrote, "to emancipate the hitherto despised, unknown or forgotten Slavonic democracies of Central and Southern Europe." Reasoning which uses the expression "Slavonic democracies of Central and Southern Europe" and which points only to attempts to Germanize and Magyarize the Slavs while largely ignoring attempts at Russification and Polonization is open to historical criticism.

Masaryk's war aim and the war aims proclaimed by liberals and conservatives alike in Russia had in common the destruction and partition of Austria-Hungary. However, Masaryk sought to integrate Czechoslovakia into the broader framework of Western democratic development. His sympathy for the Russian people notwithstanding, throughout the prewar period he had uncompromisingly opposed granting Slavic leadership to Russia, the autocratic and orthodox Great Power. He assailed the Czech Russophiles under Kramář, who in 1914 were prepared to receive a Russian grand duke as viceroy as the first step toward the incorporation of Bohemia into a kind of Pan-Slavic confederation. In October 1914, during his secret meeting with Seton-Watson in the Netherlands, he advised against offering the throne of a future kingdom bordering directly on Russia to a grand duke, because the German minority

---

23. Ibid., 135–152.
24. Ibid., 152: "The Oriental Question is to be solved on the Rhine, Moldau, and Vistula, not only on the Danube, Vardar, or Maritza."
25. R. W. Seton-Watson, *German, Slav and Magyar* (London, 1916), 186.

in the new state, which he estimated would number some three to four million persons, would never become reconciled to a Russian prince.

A Bohemian secundogeniture in the House of Romanov would have increased Russia's influence among the western Slavs. Moreover, there was evidence in the same year of a prospective dynastic merger between Serbia and Russia. In February, 1914, the Serbian Prime Minister, Pašić, sounded out the Czar on the possibility of the marriage of one of his daughters to Crown Prince Alexander. On the horizon loomed the *fata morgana* of a grand duchess' becoming one day, as consort of the ruler of a unified Yugoslav nation, empress of a Greater Serbia, of a Yugoslavia in close alliance with mighty Russia.

The realization of Russia's territorial claims as recognized by her Western allies, the destruction of Austria-Hungary to the benefit of Russia and the Slavic states, and major annexations of German territory would have meant a revolution within the European system of states. All of Central Europe east of a line running from Stettin to Trieste would have come under direct Russian control or would have lain in an acknowledged sphere of Russian influence, a prospect which became a reality a generation later. During and since the Second World War, the continuity in Russia's foreign policy objectives has been rightly stressed in analyses of Soviet war aims.[26] The annihilation of Turkey would have brought Russia to the Mediterranean. The Russian program for expelling the Germans from the Danzig and Königsberg regions did not differ in the slightest from German plans to resettle the non-German populations of occupied areas in the East.

Only at the end of the Second World War did the German people come to realize how much they had been wronged by those propagandists who based the Germans' right to lay claim to Eastern Europe as their colonial domain in Europe on the theory that Western civilization diminished the further east one went.[27] The

---

26. David J. Dallin, *Russia and Post-war Europe* (New Haven, 1943), 168–73.

27. The "inferiority" of the Slavs as proclaimed by the leadership of the Third Reich led to massive forced recruitments in the occupied East, particularly

resettlement of Russian Germans, to a modest extent during the First World War and as forced resettlement of large numbers under Hitler, prompted an attitude which provided a basis for the theory of the right of the conquering nation to resettle forcibly, in the German interest, the allegedly "inferior" nationalities of Eastern Europe, to "expropriate" non-German elements by deporting them to the East, and to annex the territories thus opened up and settle them with German colonists, i.e., a theory which denied international obligations and restraints and totally disregarded the rights ("Heimatrecht") of native populations.

Lagarde, one of the early proponents of such a ruthless procedure, had conceded frankly that this method seemed somewhat "Assyrian," but he was convinced that Germany had no other choice. His disciples either felt no pangs of conscience or allowed their consciences to be assuaged, as illustrated by Dietrich Schäfer's yielding to the pleadings of Heinrich Class. Theories of German hunger for land in the East have rightly been characterized as a German neo-Darwinism which applied the theory of the struggle for existence and survival of the fittest to the struggle of the nationalities in the East.[28]

While Russian plans for annexation and resettlement remained on paper, German statesmen found themselves confronted in the course of the First World War with countless problems for the solution of which no preparations whatsoever had been made during peacetime. Improvisation, indecision, and lack of consistency were the hallmarks of German wartime policy in the East. The greatest weakness of German policy in the struggle with Russia lay in the absence of any plan for organizing politically the belt of nationalities on Russia's western border to the advantage of the Central

---

of Ukrainians. It was given expression by the director of the Ostministerium, Dr. Bräutigam, in a secret note of October 25, 1942, with a boldness which deserves to be remembered: "With a presumptuousness without equal, we disregard all matters of political wisdom and, to the joyful astonishment of the entire colored world, treat the peoples of the occupied Eastern regions as second-class whites, to whom Providence has ostensibly given no other task than that of serving Germany and Europe as slaves." *Trial of the Major War Criminals before the International Military Tribunal,* XXV (1947), 339.

28. Munro Smith, "German Landhunger," *Political Science Quarterly,* XXXII (1917), 460–61.

Powers. Bethmann Hollweg was incapable of mastering the difficulties and inner contradictions which stood in the way of creating a Polish state under German control.[29]

The reserve with which the German government set foreign policy objectives encouraged the emergence of militaristic propaganda, particularly from rightist circles claiming to be more patriotic than the government. The objectives of the latter in the East combined various viewpoints: military security against future attack, acquisition of land for colonization, and unrestricted access to the trade areas of the Near and Middle East. The annexationists sought to weaken Russia between the Baltic and Black Seas by cutting off the border regions, a process which Paul Rohrbach compared to peeling one leaf after another from the Russian artichoke. In a similar fashion, he later used the image of an orange to illustrate the federalization of western Russia, which he saw as a desirable possibility. First of all, Russia was to be expelled from Central Europe by separating the Ukraine from it.[30] Propagandists like Walter Schotte and Axel Schmidt explained without further ado that the Ukraine was part of Central Europe. A realistic consideration of the Ukrainian movement of the First World War must lead to the conclusion that establishment of a Ukrainian state was, politically, a utopian effort, explained by an overestimation of the differences between Great Russians and Ukrainians.

In the hope that separation of the Ukraine from Great Russia would endure, Rohrbach announced jubilantly in the days of the Brest-Litovsk treaty that "peace" and the end of the "Russian peril" were assured for all time. Germany's hegemony in the East seemed to him secured by an independent Finland in the North, an autonomous Ukraine in the South, and Baltic, Polish, and Lithuanian areas added to Central Europe in the center. The fundamental error of German leadership in the spring and summer of 1918 consisted in believing in the possibility of achieving long-range solutions in

---

29. Werner Conze, "Nationalstaat oder Mitteleuropa?" has analyzed them thoroughly.
30. See Eugen Lewizky, "Weltwirtschaftspolitik der Zentralmächte und der Krieg," *Osteuropäische Zukunft,* II (March 1916), 90: "If a viable and enduring enterprise is to be made of aspirations in Central Europe, Russia must first of all be forced back from the Black Sea and her impulses toward expansion must be directed away from the South toward the East."

the East as long as the outcome of the struggle in the West had not been determined. In a deeper sense, the fighting in the West in 1918 can be regarded as Germany's struggle to obtain recognition of the situation in the East, one favorable to the Central Powers, created by the peace treaties with the Ukraine, Great Russia, and Rumania. These treaties could at the same time be considered bourgeois-monarchic Central Europe's bulwark against the onrushing revolutionary wave from the East. In 1918, only a few Germans saw the incompatibility of the expansionist policies of Ludendorff's military dictatorship and a policy of balance of power in Europe.

Errors in appraising the Eastern situation made the stipulations for the East in the peace treaties of 1919 in many respects ineffectual and led to uninterrupted conflicts and tensions in the interwar period. The appearance of numerous delegations representing East European nationalities at the Peace Conference was the culmination of a development which could be defined as the insurrection of the nationalities against the historical centralist states and against the claims to authority and hegemony of the Germans, Magyars, and Great Russians. If the defeat of the Central Powers in the First World War was decisive for the ascendency of the Slavic nations, the outcome of the Second World War was a turning point in the history of relations between Germans and Slavs. The "Drang nach Westen" of the Slavs was given great impetus as the Russians advanced, with the approval of the Western Allies, in restrospect often repented and regretted, into the heart of Central Europe, and as they expelled virtually all Germans from East Central Europe, leaving only a culturally insignificant and economically impotent remnant.

These events are of enormous import—among the most decisive in modern European history. Those who refuse to come to terms with what has happened, though their pain and anger are understandable, show themselves blind to the irrevocability of these events, as do those who are unwilling to recognize the National Socialist precept of the "mission" of the German people in the East and the abortive attempt to realize it—in the fullest sense of the word—as a self-inflicted murderous attack on the life of the German people and one which led to the greatest setback in a thousand years of its history. So dramatically and extensively have the ethnological, political, and confessional maps of central and eastern Europe been changed since 1914 that it would require the mastery of a Gibbon or a Mommsen to do justice to this great upheaval and to the changes it has wrought in traditional conceptions. The struggle between Germans and Slavs is no longer, as it was before 1914, the dominant element in the history and politics of eastern and south-eastern Europe. It has been superseded by the cleavage of Europe into Communist and non-Communist camps.

In 1854, Bruno Bauer called Central Europe "a great territory of unanswered questions and unresolved contradictions, a region of half-demands which until now have enjoyed as little realization as proposals counter to them, and which seem products of visionary caprice because they aim at something whole, something new and enormous." [31]

Today the same holds true for Central Europe, East Central Europe, Eastern Europe, and Southeastern Europe. A peaceful future for the center, east, and southeast of Europe depends upon the degree to which the idea of non-Communist cultural autonomies and the principle of economic and political federalism can be combined and implemented successfully.

---

31. Bruno Bauer, *Russland und England* (Charlottenburg, 1854), 15–18.

IV

The Question of Polish
Reparation Claims, 1919-1922.
A Contribution to the Interpretation
of the Treaty of Versailles

1. THE LEGEND OF SOVIET RUSSIA'S CLAIM
TO GERMAN REPARATIONS

THE FOLLOWING DISCUSSION, which centers upon the paragraph concerning "Russia's" right to German reparations in Article 116 of the Treaty of Versailles, is closely connected with the author's studies on the Russian Question at the Paris Peace Conference: (1) "Russland und die Weltpolitik 1917–1920. Studien zur Geschichte der Interventionen in Russland," 6 parts, Frankfurt, 1933, a book-length study intended as a *Habilitationsschrift* in the Philosophische Fakultät of Frankfurt University in the winter of 1932–33, which had been completed before the author had to leave Germany. The unpublished manuscript has been deposited in the Library of the British Museum, where (according to the *General Catalogue of Printed Books,* LXVII [1960], col. 886) a reproduction is available under Call No. 20087.b.34. (2) "Studien zur Geschichte der Russischen Frage auf der Pariser Friedenskonferenz von 1919," *Jahrbücher für Geschichte Osteuropas,* VII (1959), 431–478.

This article was originally published in *Jahrbücher für Geschichte Osteuropas,* V (1957), No. 3, pp. 315–335. The introductory section has been revised to consider literature published through 1970.

These studies dealt especially with the Russian Political Conference and with the League of Nations' attitude in its early stages toward the Russian problem.

The main lines of the present article were presented in a paper delivered at the University of Göttingen on July 24, 1950, and were intended to show a German audience that during the Second World War and in the postwar period the study of the Paris Peace Conference and of the implementation of the peace treaties of 1919–20 had been placed on a new and comprehensive documentary basis.

In the first place, attention had to be called to the publication of the American documents on the Peace Conference in a special series of the Papers Relating to the Foreign Relations of the United States.[1] This series was supplemented by an annotated text of the peace treaty.[2] In addition, lithographs of protocols and documentary annexes of the Reparation Commission became accessible to scholars in American libraries, such as the library of the Harvard Law School.[3] Later, a large number of German war, armistice, and peace conference documents were filmed by the Inter-Allied German Foreign Ministry Documents Project, before the originals were restored to the Political Archive of the Bonn Foreign Ministry. So far relatively few of them have been published.[4] It was, indeed, possible to speak without exaggeration even five years after the end of the war of the beginning of a new era in the study of the Treaty of Versailles.[5]

---

1. United States, Department of State, *Papers Relating to the Foreign Relations of the United States, The Paris Peace Conference 1919* (Washington, D.C., 1942–1947), thirteen volumes. This magnificent edition has been neglected and not systematically used for almost a quarter of a century until Arno J. Mayer's basic work, *Politics and Diplomacy of Peacemaking. Containment and Counterrevolution at Versailles, 1918–1919* (London, 1968).

2. *The Treaty of Versailles and after, Annotations of the Text of the Treaty* (Department of State, Conference Series, No. 92).

3. Archive of the American "unofficial observer" to the Reparation Commission, Roland W. Boyden (1863–1931), deposited at the Harvard Law School Library.

4. André Scherer and Jacques Grunewald, eds., *L'Allemagne et les problèmes de la paix pendant la première guerre mondiale* [1914–1917] (Paris, 1962, 1966), two volumes.

5. The documentation published by the author of this essay in *Vierteljahrshefte für Zeitgeschichte*, III No. 4 (1955), 412–445 ("Zwischen Compiègne und Versailles. Geheime amerikanische Militärdiplomatie in der Periode des Waffenstillstands 1918–1919: Die Rolle des Obersten Arthur L. Conger") was one of the first attempts to show the interdependence of German and American documents on the topic.

This investigation is based primarily on documents of the Reparation Commission which reveal that a considerable body of diplomatic work in the years 1919–1922 centered upon Article 116, the paragraph of the Treaty of Versailles that refers to Russia.[6] The documents of the Reparation Commission clear the way for studies in history, international law, and political economy. The scholar will be required to work at all times in regions between his discipline and those bordering it. The historian, for instance, will find knowledge of international law and political economy indispensable. For the political historian, the documents of the Reparation Commission are of special importance, since they reveal the beginnings of the split between Great Britain and France over the question of the enforcement and enforcibility of the Treaty of Versailles.[7]

Germany's foreign policy in the period of the Weimar Republic can be reduced to the common denominator, "Locarno policy vs. Rapallo policy." In 1930, V. Kornev, a Russian political writer, criticized the argument that the results of Locarno were much more positive for Germany than the outcome of Rapallo. In his opinion, it was difficult to view Germany's political self-restraint as revealed in the Locarno treaties as more positive than her demonstration of an independent foreign policy at Rapallo. He agreed that the evacuation of the Rhineland based on the Locarno understanding merited a positive evaluation, but he argued that there was nothing

---

6. The Organization Committee of the Reparation Commission was succeeded by the Reparation Commission on January 10, 1920.

The following basic works are cited in the notes in abbreviated form:

Burnett = Philip M. Burnett. *Reparation at the Peace Conference from the Standpoint of the American Delegation* (New York, 1940), two volumes, in the series *The Paris Peace Conference, History and Documents,* published by the Carnegie Endowment for International Peace, Division of Economics and History.

Recueil des Actes, B 4.3 = *Conférence de la Paix 1919–1920. Recueil des Actes de la Conférence.* Partie IV: *Commissions de la Conférence (Procès-Verbaux, Rapports et Documents).* B. *Questions générales.* (3) *Commission des Réparations des Dommages* (Paris, 1927), "Confidentiel," now declassified.

La Documentation Internationale, IV = Albert Geouffre de Lapradelle, editor, *La Paix de Versailles* (Paris, 1932). *La Documentation internationale,* IV: *La Commission de réparation des dommages.*

7. About the significance of the reparation problem in Anglo-French relations, see Hans Schwüppe, "Grundlagen und Grundzüge britischer Aussenpolitik der Kabinette Lloyd George, Bonar Law, Baldwin und Macdonald 1919–1924," in Hellmut Rössler, ed., *Die Folgen von Versailles 1919–1924* (Göttingen, 1969), 100–105.

comparable the Russians could do: they were not occupying any part of Germany and, therefore, were not able to evacuate territory in exchange for billions in reparations. On the contrary, he asserted, the Russians had foregone the billions in reparations to which they were entitled by the Versailles treaty, long before the evacuation of the Rhineland, which Germany bought at such a high price, so that this positive fact automatically had its origins in Rapallo.[8]

Kornev's assertion or thesis that Bolshevik Russia had renounced billions in German reparations has not hitherto been subjected to close examination by historical criticism.

2. Origin and Meaning of Section 14 (Russia and Russian States), Articles 116 and 117 of the Treaty of Versailles

At first glance, it might seem strange that the Russia of Brest-Litovsk should at any time have been entitled to make a reparation claim against the Germany of Versailles. However, the manner with which Kornev presupposes a familiarity with the alleged Russian claim makes it worthwhile to pursue his assertion and prove that it is an historical legend, an absurdity. Allied relations with Soviet Russia in the period of the Paris Peace Conference would seem to militate against the suggestion that the drafters of the paragraphs in the Treaty of Versailles relating to Russia intended to provide the legal basis for reparation claims of Bolshevik Russia against Germany, and the interpretation of these paragraphs in the postwar period bears this out.[9] These paragraphs were drafted and inserted

---

8. V. Kornev, "Rapallokrise," *Zeitschrift für Politik*, XX, No. 4 (July 1930); "O krizise Rapallo," *Mezhdunarodnaia zhizn'*, No. 7–8 (1930), 78.

9. The character of Article 116 was completely misconstrued by Günter Rosenfeld, who in his essay, "Das Zustandekommen des Rapallovertrages," *Zeitschrift für Geschichtswissenschaft*, IV, No. 4 (1956), 687, wrote that Article 116 "held out to Soviet Russia the prospect of a claim against Germany for the payment of reparations." The same completely unfounded assertion was repeated as late as 1967 by Wolfgang Ruge, "Zur chauvinistischen Propaganda gegen den Versailler Vertrag 1919–1929," *Jahrbuch für Geschichte*, I, 79, note 1. Strangely enough, the Soviet treatment of the Paris Peace Conference in Boris E. Stein, *Die "Russische Frage" auf der Pariser Friedenskonferenz 1919–1920* (Leipzig, 1953), does not discuss Articles 116 and 117 relating to Russia in the Versailles treaty. Stein's study is primarily a contribution to the history of the idea of intervention, with an emphasis on charging the United States with chief responsibility.

in the Treaty of Versailles as stipulations in favor of a non-Bolshevik Russia; they were conceived and formulated with a view toward creating an abyss between Germany and, so it was hoped, a non-Bolshevik Russia, thus keeping Germany and Russia at loggerheads.

Section 14 of the Treaty of Versailles, "Russia and Russian States," reads: [10]

Article 116.

Germany acknowledges and agrees to respect as permanent and inalienable the independence of all the territories which were part of the former Russian Empire on August 1, 1914. In accordance with the provisions of Article 259 of Part IX (Financial clauses) and Article 292 of Part X (Economic clauses), Germany accepts definitely the abrogation of the Brest-Litovsk treaties and of all other treaties, conventions and agreements entered into by her with the Maximalist Government in Russia.

The Allied and Associated Powers formally reserve the rights of Russia to obtain from Germany restitution and reparation based on the principles of the present Treaty.

Article 117.

Germany undertakes to recognize the full force of all treaties or agreements which may be entered into by the Allied and Associated Powers with States now existing or coming into existence in the future in the whole or part of the former Empire of Russia as it existed on August 1, 1914, and to recognize the frontiers of any such States as determined therein.

The German peace delegation, in its summary position paper on the peace conditions, dated May 29, 1919, adopted the following position on the paragraphs relating to Russia:

The German Government claims for itself no territory which on August 1, 1914, belonged to the former Empire of Russia. The question of the constitutional structure, and therefore of the independence of individual territories formerly belonging to Russia, the German Government regards as an internal matter of those territories themselves, in which it has no intention of becoming involved.

The German Government has already renounced the peace treaties of Brest-Litovsk and supplementary treaties in Article 14 of the armistice agreement.[11]

---

10. *The Paris Peace Conference 1919*, XII, 272–273.
11. "Observations of the German Delegation on the Conditions of Peace," ibid., VI, 795–901.

Thereupon follows the sentence of crucial importance in our context:

A right of Russia to demand of Germany restitution and reparation cannot be recognized by the German Government.

The German Government repudiated as well the requirement of Article 117 that it make a blanket declaration on future treaties:

The German Government cannot recognize treaties and agreements between the Allied and Associated Powers and the states which have been formed or will in the future be formed on the territory of the former Empire of Russia, until it knows the content of such arrangements and has been convinced that recognition of such arrangements is not rendered impossible either by its previous relations with Russia or with individual parts of the former Empire of Russia or by its wish to live in peace and friendship with all its eastern neighbors. The same applies to recognition of the borders of these states.[12]

The German objections to Articles 116 and 117 of the draft treaty were dismissed in the Allies' response of June 16:

The Allied and Associated Powers are of the opinion that none of the reservations or the observations offered by the German Delegation as to Russia necessitate any change in the relevant articles of the Treaty.[13]

In the web of international entanglements in the years after the First World War, Article 116 is an unbroken thread with which the relations of both Germany and the Western Powers to Russia can be treated. Anti-Bolshevik Poland's attempt to derive for herself rights from Article 116, Paragraph 3, an effort of Polish diplomacy which has never been investigated in detail, sheds new light on Poland's position between Germany and Russia and her relation to the Western Powers. The position of the Powers in the period immediately following the war is reflected in the origins of Article 116 and in the disagreement over its interpretation.

---

12. Ibid., VI, 845; Friedrich Berber, ed., *Das Diktat von Versailles. Eine Darstellung in Dokumenten* (Essen, 1939), I, 934.
13. *The Paris Peace Conference 1919*, VI, 951.

All the arguments necessary to undermine the legal foundation of the clauses on Russia in the Treaty of Versailles were presented as early as 1920 by F. C. Zitelmann in his excellent commentary.[14] The genesis of these clauses, which at that time still lay in the dark, can now be presented in broad outline.

In the preparatory stage of the Peace Conference, the question of a claim to war indemnities by states formerly members of the Russian Empire was thrown open in a memorandum by the American financial expert, Frank L. Warrin, Jr., who considered it almost certain that no claim of any sort would be conceded to Great Russia and the Ukraine. The same would probably be true in respect to Finland, since "prior to the armistice the *de facto* government of Finland had acted more in harmony with the wishes of Berlin than with the hopes of the Allies." Warrin thus anticipated difficulties over whether Poland and states on the territory of the former Baltic provinces had a claim to indemnities. It was conceivable that the Western Powers would consider the role of these new states in the defense against Bolshevism so important that they would grant them indemnities. If, however, these states were overrun by Bolshevism and the Western Powers were compelled to take steps against the Bolsheviks and restore "law and order in the Slavic world," it would not be improper to insist that Poland and the Baltic state (or states) share in the costs of such an intervention on their behalf.[15]

On February 24, 1919, at the tenth meeting of the Organization Committee of the Reparation Commission, the Chairman, French Minister of Finance Klotz, proposed that the First Sub-Committee, charged with the determination of damages, include Russia in its work program and present an estimate of damages caused by Germany in Russia. As Russia's ally, the French Government then considered it a duty to support the claims of the Russian state against the common enemy.[16] No specific amounts were to be

---

14. Franz Carl Zitelmann, *Russland im Friedensvertrag von Versailles* (*Artikel 116, 117, 292 und 293 des Friedensvertrags*) (Berlin, 1920). See also Curt Menzel, *Das deutsche Vorkriegs-Vermögen in Russland und der deutsche Entschädigungsvorbehalt* (*Beiträge zum ausländischen öffentlichen Recht und Völkerrecht,* XVI) (Berlin, 1931).

15. "A Preliminary Memorandum upon Indemnities," January 3, 1919, Burnett, I, 487 (Document 75).

16. Burnett, II, 339 (Document 460); *La documentation internationale,* IV, 131–132.

assessed on behalf of Russia; rather it was for the time being simply a matter of upholding Russia's rights and registering Russia's claims.[17] At its twelfth meeting, on March 6, 1919,[18] the Reparation Commission answered an inquiry of the First Sub-Committee, which had requested instructions on what basis and to what extent it should assess Russian damages. Lord Sumner,[19] Chairman of the First Sub-Committee, explained that the Sub-Committee could not take up the question of damages sustained by Russia until it received more detailed instructions from the Reparation Commission, since Russia was not represented at the Peace Conference.

The Australian Prime Minister, William Morris Hughes, spoke as representative of Great Britain against the First Sub-Committee's concerning itself in any way whatsoever with Russia proper or with any parts of the former Russian Empire other than what were Russian Poland, Estonia, and Lithuania. The Reparation Commission, he pointed out, had received no instructions from the Peace Conference, that is, from the Committee of Ten, to include Russia in its work. The Russian Question was therefore a matter for the Committee of Ten.[20] Klotz angrily retorted that the mere fact that France had raised the question of Russia's right to indemnities should have been sufficient for the First Sub-Committee to begin an examination of the French proposal, even in the absence of a Russian representative. The First Sub-Committee should declare itself competent and submit to the Reparation Commission the result of its investigation of damages sustained by Russia.[21]

This French proposal spurred Poland into action.[22] A Polish

---

17. *Recueil des Actes*, B 4.3, 63.

18. Burnett, II, 347 (Document 460); *Recueil des Actes,* B 4.3, 71–72.

19. John Andrew Hamilton, Lord Sumner of Ibstone (1859–1934); biography in the *Times* (London), May 26, 1934.

20. Similarly, a French move in the Commission for the New States (meeting of June 10, 1919) to discuss a French proposal that part of the Russian debt should be assumed by Poland came to nought. The Commission decided that this question was beyond its competence: *Conférence de la Paix 1919–1920. Recueil des Actes de la Conférence,* Partie VII: *Préparation et signature des conventions et traités divers (Procès-verbaux des Commissions et textes des traités).* B. *Traités particuliers entre Alliés.* (1) *Commission des nouveaux états* (Paris, 1929) ("Confidentiel"), 96.

21. *Recueil des Actes,* B 4.3, 72.

22. The following Polish declarations are essential for an understanding of the Polish standpoint on the reparation question at the Paris Peace Conference: "Principes généraux concernant la réparation des dommages de guerre,"

delegate, Kazimierz Olszowski, director of the War Damages Department of the Polish Ministry of Finance, took an active part in the talks of the Organization Committee of the Reparation Committee.[23] When Lord Sumner mentioned that the Polish delegate could provide certain information on the Polish provinces of the former Russian Empire, Olszowski stated that he was in a position to supply statistics for the Lithuanian provinces and White Russia as well, since it was likely that these territories would form a common state with Poland in the future.[24] On April 11, he appeared before a special committee appointed by the First Sub-Committee for those states not represented on the First Sub-Committee and gave information on damages in Russian territories (comprising 40,000 square kilometers, exclusive of the Ukraine) east of the boundary claimed by Poland. His estimate of the damages inflicted by the Germans in this area, which he placed at 1,628,000,000 marks,

---

February 8, 1919: Recueil des Actes, B 4.3, 26; Burnett, II, 301–302 (Document 454).

"Catégories des dommages," February 20, 1919: *Recueil des Actes,* B 4.3, 146–147; Burnett, II, 402–404.

"Mode d'évaluation des dommages de guerre," March 2, 1919: *Recueil des Actes,* B 4.3, 201–202; Burnett, II, 464.

"Mémoire sur la répartition des navires de la marine marchande allemande (maritime et fluviale)," March 28, 1919: *Recueil des Actes,* B 4.3, 518, 529; Burnett, II, 715–716, 729.

"Déclarations faites par M. Olszowski au sujet des dommages causés en Russie, à l'est de la partie comprise dans le Mémoire des réclamations polonaises," April 11, 1919: *Recueil des Actes,* B 4.3, 386; Burnett, II, 582.

Materials published by the Polish delegation to the Peace Conference:

"Évaluation approximative des dommages de guerre causés à la Pologne" (Paris, 1919), 16 pp.

"La part de la Pologne dans les indemnités devant être paiées aux Alliés par l'Allemagne" (Paris, 1919), 16 pp.

"The economic situation of united Poland and the necessity of meeting her most urgent needs" (Paris, 1919), 52 pp.

The pamphlet by Tadeusz Szwaykowski on German reparation in the Treaty of Versailles ('Odszkodowanie niemieckie na tle Traktatu Wersalskiego" [Poznan, Instytut Zachodni, 1948], 65 pp.), adds nothing to our understanding of the present subject. The same can be said of a work caught up in Communist ideology, Bernhard Graefrath, *Zur Geschichte der Reparationen* (East Berlin, 1954), published by the Deutsches Institut für Rechtswissenschaft.

23. In addition to Olszowski, Zygmunt Chamiec, director of the National Loan Bank, and Etienne Markowski, a former director of the Russian Asiatic Bank in London and New York, were recognized as Polish delegates by the Reparation Commission.

24. *Recueil des Actes,* B 4.3, 71–72.

was a brilliant feat of calculation, but one so weakly founded on fact that it remained totally without influence on the course of events.[25]

The French proposal (avant-propos) of March 28, 1919, on the financial clauses of the Treaty of Versailles, submitted by Klotz to the Supreme Council,[26] is further proof of the French intention to represent and maintain Russia's interests. Paragraph 6 of the French proposal repeated the provision of Article 15 of the Armistice of Compiègne that Germany renounce advantages gained in the treaties of Brest-Litovsk. With slight modifications, this paragraph became Article 259 of the Versailles treaty. Article 7 of the French draft became Article 278.[27]

In Article 13, the French draft sought to extend the principle of German war indemnities to include Germany's new neighbors in the East. The draft read:

L'Allemagne reconnaît le droit pour les Etats compris dans l'ancien Empire russe, tel qu'il existait avant la guerre, de prétendre à réparation des dommages de guerre causés aux biens et aux personnes.

Nonobstant, les Gouvernements alliés et associés se réservent expressément le droit de comprendre dans leurs demandes de réparation les dommages, tels qu'ils sont définis à l'article 1er, causés aux biens de leurs ressortissants situés sur le territoire de l'ancien Empire russe.[28]

In its first sentence, this draft article came fairly close to Hughes's view referred to above, and it is surprising that the article remained a draft and was not incorporated into the treaty. If this article had been adopted, it would have provided a legal basis for claims to indemnities that the Polish Government failed to make

---

25. Burnett, II, 581–584 (Documents 496 and 497). The former finance agent of the Government of Imperial Russia in Paris, Artur G. Rafalovich, had submitted to the same special committee unofficial compilations containing estimates of the damages sustained by Russia. This is mentioned by Burnett, II, 592 (Document 507), published in *Recueil des Actes*, B 4.3, 372–385.

26. Louis Lucien Klotz, *De la guerre à la paix. Souvenirs et documents* (Paris, 1924), 213–249.

27. Ibid., 218.

28. Ibid., 219.

good only because they were not explicitly recognized in the peace treaty.

Only at a late stage of the Peace Conference, on May 4, did Clemenceau recommend to the Council of Four the paragraph on Russia's right to reparation. Upon its acceptance by the Committee of Four, the paragraph was brought before the Editorial Committee.[29]

3. The Interpretation of Article 116 of the Treaty of Versailles by the Reparation Commission until the Genoa Conference

The struggle for an interpretation favorable to Poland of the clauses on reparations in the Treaty of Versailles, which began in the spring of 1919 and dragged on for years, was further complicated by numerous questions it raised about the legal position of the Supreme Council, the Supreme Economic Council, and the Reparation Commission. These included: How far is a single Power entitled to give directives to the Reparation Commission? Are only the leading Allied and Associated Powers as a group entitled to this right? What is the competence of the Reparation Commission in general? Specifically, what is its relation to the Supreme Council in the interpretation of the peace treaties? How are rights to reparations and material restitution related? These are examples of questions whose origins can be traced to Poland's claim to reparations, but which later gained wider significance.

Since the new Poland sought primarily to obtain a share of the total war indemnities, Olszowski asked at the thirteenth meeting of the Organization Committee of the Reparation Commission on March 11, 1919 whether, on the principle of shared liability, the new states were to participate in the payment of damages by those

---

29. The original text, "The Allied and Associated Governments formally reserve all rights for Russia to obtain from Germany the restitutions and the satisfactions based on the principles of the present Treaty," was changed by the Editorial Committee into the final version cited on p. 74 above. See "Annotations on the discussions by the Council of Four and Council of Five of Articles 116 and 117 of the Treaty of Versailles," Nina Almond and Ralph H. Lutz, eds., *The Treaty of St. Germain, A Documentary History of its Territorial and Political Clauses with a Survey of the Documents of the Supreme Council of the Paris Peace Conference* (Stanford, 1935), 624–627.

states of which they were formerly part. He advanced the view that territories that had been freed from foreign domination, that had been estranged from the mother country and had now returned to it, could not in principle be called upon to pay indemnities to those states from which they had been separated. On the contrary, the successor states had themselves a right to indemnities! He explained eloquently:

> "The justice of this principle is an axiom which needs no proof. Poland, which has been the victim of German and Austrian policies for more than a century, cannot be chastised for the crime of her executioners." [30]

With this, Olszowski only reiterated a principle formulated in a memorandum of the Polish delegation of February 8:

> Territories torn by violence from the mother country and which are now returning to it shall not be liable to any reparation which shall be imposed on those countries from which they are separated by the re-establishment of their rights. On the contrary, they shall have a right to reparation.[31]

In the fall of 1919, the Supreme Council sought Poland's approval of the September 10 Agreement of St. Germain on sharing in the cost of liberating territories that had belonged to Austria-Hungary. The Polish Government interpreted as a recognition of Poland's claim to indemnities a declaration of the Supreme Council in connection with Article 3 of this Agreement and a communication from the chairman of the Organization Committee of the Reparation Commission to the Polish delegation stating that the commission would clarify Poland's right to indemnities when examining the compliance of Germany and her allies.[32]

At the end of the first year of Polish independence, the Polish Government considered the solution of the reparation problem so urgent, next to delineating the frontiers of the state, that the Foreign Ministry decided to press by diplomatic action for an interpretation of Article 116 in favor of Poland. A Polish memorandum to the

---

30. *Recueil des Actes,* B 4.3, 78; Burnett, II, 354 (Document 463).
31. Burnett, II, 301–302.
32. Reparation Commission, *Minutes,* No. 39, "Meeting of April 23, 1920," *Annex,* No. 205 b, 18–19.

French Government on December 5, 1919 set forth purely political arguments for satisfying the Polish demands, arguments that were certain to carry no weight with the Reparation Commission, a non-political body.[33] A second memorandum was announced, in which the legal basis of the Polish demands would be expounded. There is an unmistakable minatory undertone in the Polish memorandum of December 5, as in the remark that a refusal by the Powers to grant Poland reparation would have a serious effect on the pro-French and pro-Allied disposition of the Polish public. It would neither be understood nor taken lightly in Poland that Russia, whose territory suffered only little from the war, was granted advantages on the basis of Article 116, while Poland's claims were not honored, for Poland, as the principal theater of operations in the East, had suffered devastation no less than that suffered by Belgium and Serbia.

The Supreme Council gave this Polish note to the Organization Committee of the Reparation Commission on December 8 with the request that it review Poland's right to reparations.[34] On January 26, 1920, the Commission moved to have its Legal Service prepare a statement giving information on the time during the course of the war at which Poland found herself at war with Germany.[35] The majority of the Commission had no doubt about the right of restitution of objects that had been removed from Poland and could be identified.[36] On Poland's right to indemnities, however, views diverged. Albert Rathbone, who, as the American "observer," seldom took part in the deliberations of the Commission, declared that the question whether Poland was to be considered a belligerent Power was important for a judgment on indemnities: "reparation" was a question of law, "restitution" a question of moral right.

Thereupon, Poincaré explained that the French considered

---

33. Reparation Commission, *Minutes,* Nos. 1–10 ("January 24–February 11, 1920"); *Annex,* No. 6c, 100–101.
34. Reparation Commission, No. 1 c., *Annex,* No. 6b.
35. Reparation Commission, *Minutes,* Nos. 1–10, 19–20.
36. Meeting of March 1, 1920: Reparation Commission, *Minutes,* Nos. 11–20 ("February 11–March 3, 1920"), 98–99. It ought to be kept in mind that the First Sub-Committee of the Commission in its seventh meeting, on March 4, 1919, dismissed as beyond its competence a Polish proposal for immediate German restitution to Poland, such as Belgium and France had claimed for themselves in the Armistice: *Recueil des Actes,* B 4.3, 183; Burnett, II, 445 (Document 473).

Poland a belligerent Power from the day when he as president had conferred standards on the Polish regiments in the name of France [37] —that is, from June 22, 1918. Sir John Bradbury [38] contested the view that Poland be considered an Allied and Associated Power for the time she fought under the Russian flag, because the peace treaty did not name Russia as an Allied and Associated Power. He repeated this opinion with unusual severity at the meeting of December 10, 1920:

> For six months he had maintained that Poland had no right to reparation under the Treaty of Versailles, and the British Government was as clear as himself on this point.[39]

On March 19, 1920, a majority of the members of the Legal Service of the Commission declared themselves in favor of Poland's right to restitution.[40] The Legal Service was, however, unanimously of the opinion that Poland could derive indemnities for herself from the Treaty of Versailles only in the case of acts which had taken place in the period between Poland's recognition as an independent and belligerent Power and the date the treaty went into effect, January 10, 1920. For example, it was not until February 23, 1919, that France, in a letter from Foreign Minister Pichon to Paderewski, gave *de jure* recognition to Poland.[41] The Legal Service held that the Polish memorandum of December erred in assuming that Articles 116 and 117 of the Treaty of Versailles granted indemnities to those Polish citizens who were formerly Russian subjects. It stated that the articles of the section "Russia and Russian States" did not concern rights of Poland or Polish nationals. Article 116 only formally maintained the rights of Russia, indeed, of Russia alone, to claim restitution and reparation at some time in the future.

---

37. Stanislas Filasiewicz, ed., *La question polonaise pendant la guerre mondiale* (Paris, 1920). Bureau polonais d'études et de publications politiques. *Recueil des actes diplomatiques, traités et documents concernant la Pologne,* II, 477–479 (Document 228). Poincaré's allocution to the First Polish Division: Raymond Poincaré, *Au Service de la France* (Paris, 1933), XI, 242.

38. Lord John Swanwick Bradbury (1872–1950).

39. Reparation Commission, *Minutes,* No. 115 ("December 10, 1920"), 12.

40. Reparation Commission, *Annex,* No. 176 b: "The right of Poland to restitution," March 19, 1920.

41. J. T. Blociszewski, *La restauration de la Pologne et la diplomatie européenne* (Paris, 1927), 148; K. Smogorzewski, *L'union sacrée polonaise, le gouvernement de Varsovie et le "gouvernement" polonais de Paris 1918–1919* (Paris, 1929), 63.

The British member of the Legal Service, J. Fisher-Williams, returned a separate opinion unfavorable to Poland. He inclined, he said, toward the view that Poland's right to restitution stood or fell on her right to reparations.[42] On the question of the date Poland was to be considered an independent belligerent state on the side of the Allied and Associated Powers, the Legal Service had unanimously reached conclusions explicitly unfavorable to Poland: From the point of view of international law, at *no* time before November 11, 1918, the date of the Armistice Agreement of Compiègne, could Poland be considered an independent state at war with Germany. Neither the establishment of a Polish army in France under French command (decree of June 4, 1917) nor the recognition of this army as "belligerent" by the Great Powers in September, October, and November 1918 could be considered legally as recognition of an independent Polish state, an internationally recognized body corporate at war with Germany.[43]

This opinion of the Legal Service makes clear that the Reparation Commission was by no means an obliging tool of the victors, as has often been unfairly assumed in Germany. The Legal Service did not recognize and adopt Poland's reasoning and was not willing to interpret that the treaty confirmed the legality of Poland's claims to reparations.

On April 15, 1920, the Polish representative at the Commission, in his protest against the report of the Legal Service, cited a letter from the General Secretariat of the Supreme Council dated January 17, 1920, in which Polish rights to reparations were mentioned.[44] The letter represented an earnest warning to Poland not to maintain any longer her refusal to sign a declaration dated December 8, 1919 that modified the financial agreement of September 10, 1919 on the costs of liberating the Austro-Hungarian regions (see above, p. 80). This statement of the Supreme Council on Poland's right to reparations gave rise to a conflict over competence. The Legal Service of the Commission denied that the Supreme Council was entitled to hand down a decision on Poland's

---

42. Reparation Commission, *Annex,* No. 176 c, March 23, 1920, 39–40.
43. Reparation Commission, *Minutes,* No. 33 ("April 8 and 9, 1920"); *Annex,* No. 176 d, 40.
44. Reparation Commission, *Annex,* No. 205 b; *Minutes,* No. 39 ("April 23, 1920"), 18.

right to reparations. On April 23, 1920, the Commission discussed the question whether the Supreme Council was competent to interpret the peace treaty once it had been signed and whether the Supreme Council could represent all the treaty signatories on the side of the enemies of the Central Powers.[45] Pietro Bertolini, the Italian member of the Commission, declared that Poland's right was a purely "hypothetical right"; [46] he held that the Supreme Council was not authorized to make interpretations which modified the peace treaties once they had been signed. Only by common action of all the Allied and Associated Powers, as signatories of the Treaty of Versailles, could the Treaty be changed.[47]

Poincaré conceded that once the peace had been signed, the Reparation Commission, and no longer the Supreme Council, was entitled to speak in the name of the signatories to the treaty and to interpret the clauses on reparation. Thus, a decision of the Supreme Council was not binding on the Reparation Commission. On the other hand, however, it should not be forgotten that only provisions of the treaty and not decisions of the Supreme Council were to be interpreted by the Legal Service.

An agreement signed at Spa on July 16, 1920 by Great Britain, France, Italy, Japan, Belgium, and Portugal stipulated the manner in which German reparation payments were to be distributed.[48] Article 10 of this agreement stated explicitly:

The provisions of the present agreement do not apply to Poland. The right of Poland to reparation for damage suffered by her, as an

---

45. Reparation Commission, *Minutes,* No. 39, 5–7.
46. Ibid., 6.
47. In 1923, Poincaré placed himself wholly on the side of the Italian delegate on the matter of a revision of the Treaty of Versailles. He explained that it was a question of one of those documents that, by virtue of treaties in international law, had a binding force which could not be modified. The treaty had been formally placed on record in the chancelleries of all its signatories. For France, it was a law of the land. Modifications could be undertaken only after the signature of each European state had been obtained and ratified by its parliament. No conference could allow the alteration of even a single line of such an instrument. See Great Britain, Foreign Office, Miscellaneous, No. 3, 1923, "Inter-Allied Conference on Reparations and Inter-Allied Debts, held in London and Paris, December, 1922, and January, 1923. Reports and Secretaries' notes of conversations" (London, 1923), Cmd. 1812, 149.
48. United States, Department of State, *Papers Relating to the Foreign Relations of the United States, 1920* (Washington, 1936), II, 410–414; France,

integral part of the former Empire of Russia, is reserved in accordance with Article 116 of the Treaty of Versailles and Article
87 of the Treaty of St. Germain.

As set forth above, this assumption ran directly counter to the
view of the Legal Service of the Reparation Commission. At the
beginning of the year, the Legal Service had stated unequivocally
that the paragraphs of the Treaty of Versailles on Russia had no
connection with the rights of Poland or Polish nationals.

An exhaustive analysis of the Commission's extensive discussions of October 15 and December 10, 1920 [49] and of February 15,
1921,[50] on the significance of the Spa Agreement for Poland's right
to register claims to reparations is beyond the purview of this essay.
Suffice it to say that in a letter to the president of the Supreme
Council on October 21, 1920, Paderewski confirmed that the Polish
Government had taken notice of the Spa Agreement of July 16.[51]
Sir John Bradbury, who had contested from the outset the legality
of a Polish claim to reparations, on December 10, 1920 tri-
umphantly interpreted this letter as a formal renunciation of reparation payments on the part of Poland. Since Poland voiced no reser-
vations whatsoever, she was accepting the provisions of the Spa
Agreement.

Sir John asked the Polish delegate, Zoltowski, for a clear statement whether or not the Polish Government accepted the Supreme
Council's view that the Treaty of Versailles intended to reserve for
Poland a right to reparations, but at the moment did not allow the
realization of this right. The Polish delegate replied that there was
an absolute reciprocity between Poland's rights and obligations.
Since under the stipulations of the Treaty of Versailles, Poland had
to pay nothing, she would raise no claim to a share of the reparation payments. A Polish list of war damages sustained by Poland
therefore did not constitute a formal claim.[52]

Ministère des Affaires Étrangères, *Documents relatifs aux réparations* (Paris,
1922), I, 59.
    49. Reparation Commission, *Minutes,* Nos. 94, 115.
    50. Ibid., No. 138, 6.
    51. Reparation Commission, *Annex,* No. 522 b.
    52. At the meeting of October 15, 1920 (Reparation Commission, *Minutes,*
No. 94, 12), Sir John Bradbury remarked: "She [Poland] evidently had no
right to submit lists if her right to reparation were not recognized. The fact of

However, the Polish Government did all in its power to call attention to the acknowledgment contained in the Spa Agreement of its claim on the basis of Article 116. On February 12, 1921, it submitted to the Commission a provisional estimate of damages sustained by Poland.[53] The sum—21,913,269,740 gold francs plus one-half billion German marks (approximately)—was broken down as follows:

	GOLD FRANCS	DOLLARS
1. Material damages 4,312,743,000 gold rubles or	11,894,890,780 or	2,296,300,000
2. Damages sustained by individuals	9,818,830,960 or	1,895,500,000
3. Damages to railroads 72,300,000 gold rubles or	199,548,000 or	38,500,000
	21,913,269,740	4,230,300,000

	GERMAN MARKS	DOLLARS
4. Enforced payments (contributions)	500,000,000	119,050,000

This estimate deviated considerably from the claims presented in Paris by the Polish Delegation in April, 1919.[54]

On February 14, 1921, the Legal Service of the Commission clung to its opinion of March 19, 1920 that "Poland is not entitled to enforce a claim to reparation under the Treaty of Versailles." [55] But the rejection of the Polish claim was mitigated by the indication that a right to reparation might be maintained for the territory of Poland as constituted by the Congress of Vienna in 1815. It was proposed to inform the Polish Government that in handing over Poland's list of damages to the German Government, the Commission would abstain from any opinion concerning the legality of

---

accepting these lists would amount to a tacit recognition of this right." He therefore asked the Reparation Commission to specify that the fact of the receipt of lists from Poland would in no way prejudice the question of Poland's right to reparations. This was agreed to.

53. Reparation Commission, *Annex,* No. 878.
54. Burnett, I, 879–880 (Document 257).
55. Reparation Commission, *Annex,* No. 176 b: "Opinion of the Legal Service." See above, note 40.

Poland's claims.[56] At the meeting of the Commission on February 15, 1921, the Belgian delegate, Léon Delacroix, said that the question of Poland's rights was simply a matter of preserving for Poland, as a former part of the Russian Empire, the right to bring forward claims once a treaty between Germany and Russia had been concluded.[57] Sir John Bradbury interpreted the Spa Agreement to mean that Poland was to be allowed a moratorium in making payments called for under the treaties of Versailles or St. Germain, or under other agreements until such time as a final decision on Poland's right to reparation had been reached in a Russo-German treaty.[58]

In accordance with Article 232 of the Treaty of Versailles, the Commission, on April 28, 1921, informed Germany of the total reparations sum, 132 billion gold marks. In keeping with a recommendation of the Legal Service, it made explicit that sums claimed by Poland under Article 116 as a former part of the Russian Empire were not included in the total reparations sum.[59] In other words, the Commission acted only as a courier for Polish demands as far as the German government was concerned; it did not assume the role of intercessor on behalf of these claims, especially since it considered Article 116 to lie outside its competence.

In its official report on its work between 1920 and 1922, the Commission outlined its position on Poland's claims as follows: [60]

In the case of Poland, no doubt arose in the minds of the Commission that Poland could not have constituted an independent State during the war, and the Commission came to the conclusion that any claim which Poland might have must be limited to such claim

---

56. Reparation Commission, *Minutes,* No. 94, October 15, 1920, and note 60 below.

57. Reparation Commission, *Minutes,* No. 138, 6.

58. Ibid., 8.

59. The German Government, through the German War Debts Commission, inquired on June 16, 1921 which of the states signatory to the Treaty of Versailles were to be considered not entitled to reparation from Germany. The Commission replied on July 6 that Bolivia, Haiti, Peru, and Poland submitted claims which the Commission, acting under Article 232, was unable to recognize: Reparation Commission, No. 1017 a and b.

60. *Report on the Work of the Reparation Commission from 1920 to 1922* (London, 1923), 41; *The Paris Peace Conference 1919,* XIII, 274.

as could be sustained under Article 116 of the Treaty on the ground that part of Poland was during the war a part of Russia. It accordingly decided to transmit the claims received from the Polish Government with the following statement:

"The Reparation Commission transmit to the German Government, with a view to their examination and subsequent settlement in accordance with the terms of Article 116 of the Treaty of Versailles, the attached claims for damages received by it from the Polish Government." [61]

The Commission's view on Poland's claim to reparation was shared by the Permanent Court of International Justice in a decision of May 25, 1926, on certain German interests in Polish Upper Silesia.[62]

The announcement of Germany's total reparation debt was followed by correspondence between the Commission and the War Debts Commission, in the course of which a draft letter composed by the Legal Service and accepted by the Commission [63] defined the Commission's position to Poland's claim to reparations in the following fashion:

Poland is not entitled to share in the payment of the sum fixed by the Reparation Commission under the terms of Article 232. The amount thus determined does not include any sums which Poland may claim at any future date as a territory which formed part of the former Russian Empire under the terms of Article 116 of the Treaty of Versailles.[64]

---

61. In the fall of 1920, the Reparation Commission had discussed the kind of lists that were to be submitted by Rumania and, if the occasion arose, by Greece and Poland for restitution of livestock and materials. If Poland's right to reparation was not recognized, Poland apparently had no right to compile lists. The fact that such lists were accepted would be considered as tacit recognition of Poland's right to reparation. See above, note 52.

62. Publications of the Permanent Court of International Justice, Series A: Collection of Judgments, No. 7: "Case concerning certain German interests in Polish Upper Silesia (The merits)" (Leyden, 1926), 28.

63. Reparation Commission, *Annex*, No. 1017 b, 1. See above, note 59.

64. The copy of Roland W. Boyden of the papers of the Reparation Commission (see above, note 3) in the Harvard Law School Library has certain gaps for the summer of 1921, for instance in the correspondence of the Commission with the Kriegslasten-Kommission. This can be explained by a temporary interruption of Boyden's work as unofficial American representative on the Commission (See Boyden's obituary in the *New York Times* of October 26, 1931, 19). Boyden was later unable to obtain certain appendices to the protocols, for instance *Annex* 775 a and b.

4. The Annulment of Article 116 of the Treaty of Versailles by the Treaty of Rapallo

What has been said thus far sheds light on the conditions in which the Treaty of Rapallo in 1922 gave an unanticipated importance to the paragraphs in the Treaty of Versailles relating to Russia. The role of Article 116, both in the planning of the Genoa Conference on world economy and in the discussions during the conference, constitutes a theme in itself, and one that can be treated definitely only on the strength of additional documentary information.[65]

When Germany and the Soviet Republic, in compliance with Article 1 of the Treaty of Rapallo of April 16, 1922,[66] modeled after Article 5 of the Treaty with the Ukraine of February 9, 1918, and after Article 9 of the Treaty of Brest-Litovsk of March 3, 1918, reciprocally renounced repayment of war costs and payment of war indemnities, this was tantamount to an annulment of Article 116 of the Treaty of Versailles. The details known thus far of the Russo-German negotiations in the winter of 1921–1922 are contradictory. The possibility that in the altered world situation the Allies could interpret Article 116 in Soviet Russia's favor and use it to play the Russians against Germany and encourage them to reparation claims hung like a threatening cloud over the horizon and made German statesmen feel uneasy.[67]

---

65. New sources published by Günter Rosenfeld, "Das Zustandekommen des Rapallovertrags," *Zeitschrift für Geschichtswissenschaft,* IV, No. 4 (1956), supplement the picture of the Genoa Conference, but do not make it complete, as the author supposes. The latest special Polish study on Polish-Soviet relations at the Genoa Conference (Jerzy Kumaniecki, "Polska i Rosja Radziecka na konferencji w Genui," *Studia z dziejów ZSSR i Europy Środkowej,* No. 5 [1969], 103–114) makes no reference to the present article.

As far as documentary evidence on the German side goes, the newest and best account is Horst Günther Linke, *Deutsch-sowjetische Beziehungen bis Rapallo* (Abhandlungen des Bundesinstituts für ostwissenschaftliche und internationale Studien, XXII) (Cologne, 1970), 199–214. See also F. A. Krummacher and Helmut Lange, *Krieg und Frieden. Geschichte der deutsch-sowjetischen Beziehungen. Von Brest-Litowsk zum Unternehmen Barbarossa* (Munich, 1970), 126–135, 480–486.

66. Krummacher and Lange, 486–487; *Dokumenty vneshnei politiki SSSR,* V (1961), 223–224 (Document 121).

67. Advantages and disadvantages of Soviet Russia's participating in German reparations were discussed in an unusual fashion in a series of (soli-

Because of this reciprocal renunciation of reparations on the part of Germany and Russia, the Treaty of Rapallo was Germany's first open annulment of a paragraph of the Treaty of Versailles, her first formal act of disregard. Germany assumed for herself in Rapallo the right, vis-à-vis the Entente, to deviate in her foreign policy from the *Diktat* imposed by the Entente. The Treaty of Rapallo signified "the reciprocal recognition of Germany and the Soviet Union as fully independent agents in world politics." [68] "By the Treaty of Rapallo, Germany introduced [Soviet] Russia into the community of European Powers." [69]

No government was more surprised and incensed by this unprecedented and wholly unexpected move than that of Poland, which had been advised by the Allies after the Spa Conference to postpone its reparation claims against Germany until a Russo-German agreement had been concluded. Such an agreement had now become a reality, but it looked completely different from what the Poles had imagined. They recognized immediately that with

---

cited?) letters to *Izvestiia* at the beginning of 1922. An anonymous letter on putting forward Russian claims on the basis of the Treaty of Versailles ("Rossiiskii obyvatel'": "Svoja rubashka blizhe k telu," in *Izvestiia*, No. 17/1446, February 4) proposed fantastically that the Soviet Government should, through negotiations with the Entente, relieve the German capitalists of their millions and from this money provide the German proletariat with means for intensifying the class struggle. The Soviet Government was not to harbor sentimental feelings for the German bourgeoisie, which sought to overthrow the Soviet Power and was negotiating behind the scene with the Entente at the expense of the Russian people. It would be better if Russia herself negotiated with the Entente at Germany's expense. Russia's share of German reparations was set at 30 billion gold marks, a sum that would contribute greatly to combating hunger and rebuilding Russian industry. The close of the letter reads: "La charité bien ordonnée commence par soi-même. The shirt of the Russian working masses is closer to the Soviet body than the shirt of German bankers, industrialists, and speculators."

The editors of *Izvestiia* removed themselves diplomatically from the views of the letter writer. An editorial survey of rebuttals of the letter of "Rossiiskii obyvatel'" (to whom the editors opened their columns on February 10 for a similarly sensational statement on Soviet Russia's relations to the border states) mentioned, among other things, that Soviet Russia's consenting to receive reparations from Germany would be tantamount to signing the entire Treaty of Versailles and that Soviet Russia would then have to share with the Allies the hatred of the German proletariat (*Izvestiia*, No. 30/1469, February 8).

68. V. Kornev, "Rapallokrise?" *Zeitschrift für Politik*, XX, No. 4 (July 1930), 244.

69. Brockdorff-Rantzau to the Foreign Ministry, November 27, 1922. Auswärtiges Amt, Büro des Reichsministers, Akten betr. Russland. National Archives, Washington, Serial 2680, Fr. D 552703.

Russia's renunciation all eventual Polish claims against Germany collapsed, although the Poles had relied on the satisfaction of these claims within the framework and as part of reparations to Russia. This explains the tone of irritation in Polish statements in an exchange of notes with the Soviet Government after the Treaty of Rapallo.[70]

When the Polish Government joined the Powers that had called the Genoa Conference in their formal protest against the Treaty of Rapallo,[71] the leader of the Russian delegation, Chicherin, sharply rebuked the Poles.[72] On April 25, on instructions from its Government, the Polish delegation sent a declaration to the chairman of the First (Political) Commission of the Genoa conference, the leaders of the German and Russian delegations, and the Reparation Commission.[73] In it, the Polish Government announced its special reservations on Article 116, on which Poland's *right* to reparation rested, for Article 10 of the Spa Agreement on reparations had granted the Polish state a *right* in accordance with Article 116 to reparations for damages sustained by Poland as part of the former Russian Empire. The Polish note thus sought to limit the applicability of the Treaty of Rapallo to the territory of the Soviet Republic as of 1922. In other words, it denied the right of the Soviet

---

70. The Polish-Russian exchange of notes and letters was first printed in Rossiiskaia Sotsialisticheskaia Federativnaia Sovetskaia Respublika. Narodnyi Komissariat po inostrannym delam, *Materialy Genuezskoi konferentsii. Polnyi stenograficheskii otchet* (Moscow, 1922), 314–321; afterwards in Ministerstvo inostrannykh del SSSR, *Dokumenty vneshnei politiki SSSR*, V (January 1–November 19, 1922) (Moscow, 1961); and in Polska Akademia Nauk, Zaklad Historii Stosunków Polsko-Radzieckich, *Dokumenty i materialy do historii stosunków polsko-radzieckich (Dokumenty i materialy po istorii sovetsko-pol'skikh otnoshenii)*, IV (April 1921–May 1926) (Warsaw, 1965; Moscow, 1966). Chicherin to Skirmunt, April 24 and 30, 1922; see also Jane Degras, ed., *Soviet Documents on Foreign Policy*, I, 1917–1924 (London, 1951), 303–306.

For the relations between independent Poland and Soviet Russia, the exemplary diplomatic study of Piotr S. Wandycz, *Soviet-Polish Relations, 1917–1921* (Cambridge, Mass., 1969) should be consulted.

71. France, Ministère des Affaires Etrangères, *Documents diplomatiques, Conférence économique internationale de Gênes, 9 avril–19 mai 1922* (Paris, 1922), 53–54.

72. A. Giannini, *Les documents de la Conférence de Gênes* (Rome, 1922), 230–231.

73. Reparation Commission, *Annex*, No. 1417 c (to *Minutes*, No. 285a, "May 4, 1922"): "Declaration by the Polish Delegation with regard to the relation between the Treaty of Versailles and the Treaty of Rapallo"; *Materialy Genuezskoi konferentsii*, 321–322.

Government to come forward and act as successor to all the parts of former Imperial Russia. For herself, Poland demanded the right to advance claims on the basis of an article of the Treaty of Versailles that stipulated nothing to the effect that parts of the former czarist empire were to have the same right as "Russia" to make special reparation claims. On the contrary, it must rather be assumed that in the drafting of the Article 116, the second paragraph of which clearly betrays the hope of replacing the Bolshevik rule with another regime, the aim prevailed that the way be barred at the start to any separate claims of this sort.

The Polish note spoke of rights which were granted Poland by Article 116. On April 30 Chicherin gave an unequivocal reply to this note that nipped in the bud any Polish attempt to advance reparation claims against Russia indirectly. In his letter to the Polish delegation, he wrote:

> If claims of third states against Russia, which had to be satisfied by Russia through German mediation, were to be honored, then this right of third Powers should have to be known to Russia. The Russian Delegation, however, has no knowledge of such rights, and the Russian Government can therefore not recognize that such claims exist.[74]

5. The Reparation Commission's Investigation of the Relationship Between the Treaty of Rapallo and the Treaty of Versailles

Immediately after the announcement of the Treaty of Rapallo, Poincaré asked the Reparation Commission to examine its possible implications for the Treaty of Versailles. On April 20, the Commission instructed the Legal Service, which had always distinguished itself for remarkable independence in its advisory work, to honor Poincaré's request and give special consideration to the question whether, and, if so, to what extent, the Treaty of Rapallo infringed upon the rights and prerogatives of the Commission.[75] The Legal Service concluded that, unlike Articles 236, 248, and 260 of the Treaty of Versailles, which were possibly affected by the Treaty of

---

74. Giannini, *Les documents,* 234.
75. Reparation Commission, *Minutes,* No. 282 a ("April 20, 1922").

Rapallo, Article 116 did not come under the jurisdiction of the Commission. There was no question whatsoever of a decrease in German funds to satisfy reparation claims since Russia was renouncing financial rights that the Allies had explicitly reserved for her in Article 116.[76] In a separate opinion, the French jurist Jacques Lyon pointed out that in 1921 the Commission, the view of the Legal Service notwithstanding, had, in communications with the German Government,[77] twice mentioned Polish reparation claims which eventually might have to be satisfied, but without identifying itself with those claims. In the view of the French jurist, the Soviet Government had issued a renunciation on behalf of itself and its citizens, but the renunciation could not affect the rights to which Poland might be entitled under Article 116.[78] Thus, the French member of the Legal Service recognized, or rather maintained, the Polish thesis on reparation. The French thesis on the relation of the Treaty of Rapallo to Article 116 of the Treaty of Versailles was that Article 116 was only partially, if at all, annulled by the Treaty of Rapallo, that the Soviet Government could only speak and issue a renunciation on behalf of its *de facto* territory, and that the door thus remained open for Polish claims under Article 116.[79]

In the meeting of the Reparation Commission of May 2, 1922, Sir John Bradbury stated that the legal questions raised by com-

---

76. Reparation Commission, *Annex,* No. 1411 a: "Treaty of Rapallo; opinion of the Legal Service," 5.

Unlike the cool and measured stand taken by the Legal Service of the Reparation Commission, its Information Section was carried away by the new wave of anti-German hysteria which inundated public opinion in the countries of Germany's former enemies after the Rapallo Treaty had been announced. The *Weekly Summary of Documents* (No. 31, April 29, 1922, 7) said: "In order to justify the theater coup of Rapallo, the German Government uses the customary methods of the leaders of German policy, the same methods which the Imperial Government used for the declaration of war. It pronounces a judgment about the intentions of its opponents as proof that they forced its hand, in order to protect the interests of the fatherland."

77. In particular, in the Commission's letter of April 28, 1921; see above, note 59.

78. Reparation Commission, *Annex,* No. 1411 b: "Treaty of Rapallo; additional note by the French jurist," 8.

79. An editorial in *Le Temps* ("Annulation ou exclusion?" April 21, 1922) said: "le gouvernement soviétique, n'étant pas reconnu par les alliés, n'est pas qualifié pour renoncer aux droits que ceux-ci ont voulu assurer au peuple russe, et . . . n'est pas qualifié davantage pour renoncer aux droits que feraient valoir, en vertu de l'article 116, les États nouveaux dont le territoire a été ravagé par les armées allemandes, alors que ce territoire faisait encore partie de la Russie."

parison of the treaties of Versailles and Rapallo were "extremely obscure" and that they seemed entirely of subordinate importance when compared with the possible political implications of the Russo-German Agreement, which were the problem of the Allied governments rather than of the Commission.[80]

Because the Polish Government also had sent the Commission its interpretation of the relation between the Treaty of Versailles and the Treaty of Rapallo, the Commission was obliged to consider anew Poland's reparation claim, which step it took on May 4, 1922.[81] The outcome of this discussion in the Commission, however, did not satisfy at all Polish wishes and expectations. Sobolewski, the Polish delegate, developed in detail the theory which can be called the Franco-Polish thesis: namely, the Soviet Government could act only on its own behalf and on behalf of the population of its territory, and Poland, as a former integral part of the Russian Empire, could in addition independently derive for herself a separate right to indemnities from Article 116. In a brilliant declaration, Sir John Bradbury rejected Poland's argument. He explained that the claims referred to in Article 116 were claims by Russia, by which was to be understood the former Russian Empire that was at war with Germany as an Allied Power. According to international law, claims of this sort were necessarily transferred to the successor (or successors) of the former Russian Empire. The situation in Eastern Europe he regarded as so chaotic that it would require great boldness to venture which governments were to be considered "the legal and legitimate successors" of the former Empire. The matter of recognition of the Soviet Government by other Powers had not yet been settled, nor was it certain whether the Soviet Government itself asserted it was the sole and exclusive successor to the government of former Imperial Russia. Sir John said that he could only congratulate himself on the fact that it was not among the tasks of the Commission to form an opinion on these thorny questions. It was possible that the Soviet Government would never be recognized by other Powers to the extent that it could issue a renunciation that these other governments would consider legally binding for the claims of the Russian Empire.

---

80. Reparation Commission, *Minutes,* No. 285, "Decisions, 1918 to 1921."
81. Reparation Commission, *Minutes,* No. 285 a, "Decision 1921 a."

On May 4 the Commission informed the German Government of the possible points of conflict, as established by the Legal Service, between the Treaty of Rapallo and the Treaty of Versailles.[82] In its reply to the Commission five weeks later, on June 16, 1922, the German Government stressed that it did not intend to renounce rights that it was bound to transfer to the Commission under Article 260 of the Treaty of Versailles and that, furthermore, the view of the Commission was correct that the Treaty of Rapallo placed no further burden on the German budget. The German Government took note that the Commission held a positive view regarding German efforts to normalize Russo-German economic relations and asserted that the German Government did not intend to reduce its obligations under the Treaty of Versailles by these efforts.[83]

6. SUMMARY

In summarizing, the following can be said: After the Treaty of Rapallo, the Reparation Commission confined itself strictly to investigating the implications of the treaty for the fulfillment of the economic and financial provisions of the Treaty of Versailles. But it was inevitable that the Reparation Commission in its discussion of the Treaty of Rapallo raised questions which could not be disregarded in future discussions of the political significance of the treaty. The successful effort of the Commission, and of its Legal Service in particular, in steering clear of an emotional assessment of the Treaty of Rapallo and in not permitting itself to be influenced by the tense anti-German and anti-Russian atmosphere in Genoa and Paris attests to the intellectual freedom of that body. Its members were guided by the conviction that they were called upon to serve the law; they were conscious of serving the law rather than the politics of the day.

In the Legal Service, the French member alone sought to bring Article 116 to the fore and thus support Poland's claim. But the Reparation Commission, in spite of constant and unconcealed French support of the Polish claim, in fact upheld the Polish claim

---

82. Reparation Commission, *Minutes,* No. 285 a, "Decision 1921 bis"; *Annex,* No. 1426: "Draft letter from the Reparation Commission to the German Government concerning the Treaty of Rapallo, May 4, 1922."

83. Reparation Commission, *Annex,* No. 1490 a.

only hypothetically and theoretically. The Treaty of Rapallo and the ensuing discussions of the Commission practically marked the end of the Polish claims, the realization of which had always lain in the hazy distance.

Charles Seymour, one of the American experts in Paris and later president of Yale University, wrote in the *Virginia Quarterly Review* in 1945 that the leading statesmen of the victorious Powers were hampered in drawing up the peace treaties of 1919 by their inability, despite great personal prestige, to control public opinion at home, which was still in the grip of a war psychosis. Otherwise, a better Treaty of Versailles would have been written.[84] It remains a task for future research to show how far the "Reparation Commission," by means of a realistic attitude and an interpretation of the Treaty of Versailles independent of political vicissitudes, made amends for the errors of the governments.

It has been shown that the British took an increasingly firm stand against French intransigence on matters of reparation, as clearly manifested in constant French support of Poland's claims. It is noteworthy that only one week after the signing of the Treaty of Rapallo, John Maynard Keynes, whose scholarly views made him the first effective critic of the Treaty of Versailles on the Allied side, frankly declared that in his view none of the Great Powers was in any way harmed by the Russo-German Agreement.[85] He spoke out in favor of *de jure* recognition of Soviet Russia, while recognizing that Article 2 of the Treaty of Rapallo, Germany's renunciation of indemnification for expropriated private property, could make the settlement of British claims for liquidated property more difficult.[86]

The Reparation Commission at no time conceded to the Polish state a real and effectual right to war reparations, as understood by Part VIII of the Treaty of Versailles. Only restitution as understood by Article 238 was granted to Poland.[87] In the course of 1922,

84. Charles Seymour, "Policy and Personality at the Paris Peace Conference," *Virginia Quarterly Review,* XXI, No. 4 (Autumn 1945), 517–534.

85. J. M. Keynes, "Der russisch-deutsche Vertrag," *Berliner Tageblatt,* April 20, 1922.

86. See the secret letter dated April 16, 1922, from Chicherin to the German delegation regarding Article 2 of the Rapallo treaty: Krummacher and Lange, *Krieg und Frieden,* 488. See above, notes 14 and 65.

87. On a Polish proposal of March 1919 that Poland and the other eastern states be granted the same right to immediate restitution as enjoyed by Belgium and France under the Armistice Agreement, see above, note 36.

Poland and Germany concluded three separate agreements, on replacement of rolling stock (March 14), domestic animals (June 3), and industrial materials (August 1).[88] Under the Dawes Plan, Poland received payment in kind only on the basis of restitution claims for RM 1,100,000, and this consisted of horses exclusively. In the Young Plan, Poland was no longer allowed credits for payment in kind.[89] The Reparation Commission's refusal to recognize Poland's reparation claim was shared by the Permanent Court of International Justice in the decision cited above,[90] and confirmed by the Agent General for Reparation Payments under the Dawes Plan.[91]

It remains an irony of history that Article 116 of the Treaty of Versailles, which intended to make Germany and Russia perpetual enemies, contrary to the intentions of its framers became the bridge which brought the German and Soviet governments together. While the history of the Treaty of Versailles was otherwise one of attempted fulfillment and subsequent revision of the provisions of the Treaty, in the case of Article 116, implementation in the sense intended was dependent upon a prior revision of the course of history, namely the downfall of the Bolshevik Government and establishment of a regime acceptable to the Allied and Associated Powers. In 1922, Britain and France revised the attitudes they had assumed in the period of the intervention. They went so far as to offer, at least by way of suggestion, the advantages of Article 116 to the Soviet Government, a fear which had haunted the Germans for years. Thus, they helped the Bolsheviks gain a diplomatic victory which marked, as did the invitation to Genoa, the end of their diplomatic isolation.

---

88. The "Table of Restitution" in *Report on the Work of the Reparation Commission 1920 to 1922* (1923, see above, note 60) lists under restitutions made to Poland as of September 1, 1922, among other objects, 1450 freight cars and 12,408 horses.

89. Baptist Gradl, *Geschichte der Reparations-Sachleistungen* (Berlin, 1933), 101.

90. See above, note 62.

91. *The Execution of the Experts' Plan,* Second Annuity Year, September 1, 1925 to August 31, 1926. Reports of the Agent General for Reparation Payments and of the Commissioners and Trustees (Berlin [1926]), 11: "Interim Report of the Agent General for Reparation Payments," June 15, 1926.

V

Otto Hoetzsch as Commentator on Foreign Policy during the First World War

I T IS ONE OF THE ANOMALIES of the historiography of the First World War that a historian has written the history of the German war aims in the West, Germany's "Drang nach Westen," [1] while there has been no comprehensive treatment of the much more heated and dramatic discussions about the war aims and political decisions in the East, which culminated in the peace treaties of Brest-Litovsk and Bucharest.[2] The following sketch of the position taken by Otto Hoetzsch in the press with regard to questions concerning the East during the First World War is part of the preliminary work for study of the intellectual background of the policy of Brest-Litovsk.

1. OTTO HOETZSCH AS PUBLICIST

Otto Hoetzsch is one of the few German historians who played roles in German politics as members of parliament and as publicists during the German Reich and the Weimar Republic. Following his

---

This article was originally published in *Russland-Studien. Gedenkschrift für Otto Hoetzsch* (Stuttgart, 1957), 9–28.
1. Hans W. Gatzke, *Germany's Drive to the West* (Baltimore, 1950).
2. For a very concise but precise characterization of the Russophobe and Russophile tendencies of German policy in the East in the First World War, see Immanuel Birnbaum, "Deutsche Ostpolitik, alt und neu," *Forum* (Vienna), No. 22 (October 1955), 348 f.

firm conviction "that foreign policy should take precedence over domestic policy," [3] he commented on international political affairs in the *Kreuzzeitung* for almost ten years, starting in November 1914, in weekly articles on foreign policy. Unquestionably, we shall always remain greatly indebted to the *Kreuzzeitung* for putting at his disposal many columns of the Wednesday morning edition and permitting him to expound a coherent view of world politics over a period of several years.

Although this article was originally planned as a comprehensive analysis of Hoetzsch's work as a publicist during the First World War, the abundance of material and the limited space available have caused the author to limit himself primarily to an examination of the issues of the *Kreuzzeitung* in the Library of Congress from the last year of the war. The articles from the years 1914–1917,[4] which had been published in book form during the war, will be consulted only when they increase historical understanding. The fact that the articles from the year 1918 are not collected and are not readily accessible is all the more regrettable, because foreign policy in the East was in the foreground in the year of the peace treaties of Brest-Litovsk and Bucharest. However, it is understandable that Hoetzsch (and his publisher) had no inclination to turn attention to the graveyard of his hopes, exhortations, and warnings after the unfortunate outcome of the war.

Hoetzsch made his most comprehensive contribution to the education of his readers in political thought by his writings on current events. Teaching the German educated classes to think about foreign policy, and the question of disseminating basic information for making judgments about foreign affairs occupied him a great deal. In 1928, he received a number of suggestions while he was visiting the United States, where the treatment of con-

---

3. Otto Hoetzsch, Autobiographie, in *Deutscher Aufstieg. Bilder aus der Vergangenheit und Gegenwart der rechtsstehenden Parteien.* Hans von Arnim and Georg von Below, ed., (Berlin, 1925), 491.

4. *Der Krieg und die Grosse Politik. I. Bis zum Anschluss Bulgariens an die Zentralmächte,* II. *Bis zum Eintritt Rumäniens in den Krieg,* III. *Bis zum russischen Waffenstillstand* (Leipzig, 1917–1918). Hereafter, volume, page, and date of each article used are cited. For the year 1918 of the *Kreuzzeitung,* the number of the respective edition and the date of publication are given in each case.

temporary political affairs had figured prominently for some time in the curricula of colleges and universities.[5] Whoever studies him as a publicist and tries to understand him is astonished by the range of his vision, his careful observation of the work of foreign publicists, his sense of justice, his persistence in the clarification of facts and fundamental principles, and his adherence to certain basic positions.

The object of Hoetzsch's articles under the title "The War and High Politics," in which he almost always took a position with regard to daily events, was, he said, to serve "politics in the World War," to create the political understanding of the war only possible within a historical framework. His articles were supposed to help form a political will. He was anxious to direct this will to quite specific German international war aims (Foreword, I, 2). Nowhere in German journalistic treatment of the war is there a parallel to Hoetzsch's way of viewing the world in objectivity, wealth of information, and accuracy of views expressed, particularly concerning questions of the East.

By his unerring objectivity, which rarely led him into positions which later had to be corrected, by his logical reasoning, by always giving careful consideration to serious opinions which differed from his own, and by never stooping to personal attacks in his polemical writing, Hoetzsch must be recognized as the most unyielding and best advocate of a German "Eastern orientation" in the First World War. He advocated this orientation consistently, of course not in the sense and in the service of the cliché of a "German drive to the East," or extensive German expansion toward the East, but rather in the opposite spirit. Hoetzsch, the prudent advocate of an understanding between Germany and Russia, had visions of a great concentration of Continental interests against England and the United States (III, 476, August 8, 1917). He wanted to oppose the Anglo-Saxon idea of the League of Nations with the unification of central, eastern, and southeastern Europe and with cooperation with Japan. This seemed possible to him, however, only

---

5. See his two essays, "Aussenpolitische Bildung und aussenpolitische Erziehung," in *Politik als Wissenschaft. Zehn Jahre Deutscher Hochschule für Politik,* Ernst Jaeckh, ed. (Berlin, 1930), 13–19; and "Aussenpolitische Bildungsarbeit an den Universitäten Nordamerikas und Deutschlands," in *Aussenpolitische Studien. Festgabe für Otto Koebner* (Stuttgart, 1930), 7–29.

through an understanding with the Slavic peoples in Austria-Hungary, as well as with those living in the territory of the former Russian Empire (No. 411, August 14, 1918).

This view, which led some to denounce Hoetzsch during the First World War with the spiteful phrase "the Russian threat to Germany at home" [6] and others to ostracize him under National Socialism for being pro-Soviet, was the conviction of a genuine scholar of conservative persuasion. Particularly because of the absence of German official and semi-official publications, he saw it as his patriotic duty to have a broad effect, beyond the university lecture halls, and to use his knowledge to improve the political education of his people.[7] Deep resignation is revealed in a remark he made on February 16, 1916: "We have become resigned to the fact that the makers of our foreign policy do not as a matter of principle seek support in public opinion" (II, 280).

He was embittered because discussion of the Polish issue had not been permitted before the monumental decision of the Central Powers to proclaim Poland an independent state was made (III, No. 90, November 8, 1916).

The war years 1914–1918 mark the high point in Hoetzsch's work as a publicist permeated with a lofty national responsibility. In a sense, his articles represent a political history of the war. They have the flavor of the period in which they were written, with all of the limitations which one associates with procuring source material and expressing one's opinion in wartime. Hoetzsch also followed the stipulations of the censor conscientiously. Thus far, the study of

---

6. In the discussion of war aims during the First World War, aside from the case of Below and Valentin, there was probably no sharper clash than that between Hoetzsch and the temperamental and sarcastic Johannes Haller. The latter attacked Hoetzsch mercilessly in an article entitled "Die russische Gefahr im deutschen Hause" (No. 6 of the series *Die russische Gefahr. Beiträge und Urkunden zur Zeitgeschichte* [Paul Rohrbach, ed.; Stuttgart, 1917]). Hoetzsch answered this attack in a short essay under the title, "Russische Probleme" (Berlin, 1917). One is almost grateful to Haller for having elicited this answer from Hoetzsch. In the larger view of the course of Russian history, as well as in the discussions concerning opposing evaluations of certain events, most experts, almost without reservation, now as then probably agree with Hoetzsch.

7. See the disgraceful pamphlet by Hermann Greife, "Sowjetforschung. Versuch einer nationalsozialistischen Grundlegung der Erforschung des Marxismus und der Sowjetunion," *Schriften des Instituts zur wissenschaftlichen Erforschung der Sowjetunion* (Berlin, 1936), 58–62.

newspapers in Germany has shown little interest in analyzing journalism in the First World War. This is understandable if one proceeds on the assumption that the censor and the so-called "Burgfrieden" limited the acquisition of information necessary for the formation of informed opinion and also limited public expression of opinion to such an extent that war reporting can be spoken of as a mirror, a standard, and a leader of public opinion only with great reservations. This alone explains why contemporary commentaries, in which Hans Delbrück in the *Preussische Jahrbücher* and Hoetzsch in the *Kreuzzeitung* followed the events of the war, have still not received the critical attention they deserve, although the greater part of their remarks have been collected and are available in book form.

In spite of the difficulties and limitations to which the work of a publicist in a country at war is subject, Hoetzsch's remarks have a significance which extends beyond the moment of their conception as a coherently conceived explanation of political events by a publicist of academic objectivity. The characterization "applied history" is quite appropriate for many of his observations, especially his initial analyses of the Polish question. His hundreds of articles contain no ingenious, daring speculations or questionable prophecies.[8] His work of clarification was an unceasing struggle against political illusions prominent everywhere during the war, especially in the treatment of eastern and southeastern Europe, in part as a result of the neglect by German scholars and by German writing in the years preceding the war. As one of the few experts in the area of eastern European history, Hoetzsch vigorously opposed these illusions.

Hoetzsch fought uncompromisingly from the beginning against

---

8. Like Eberhard Gothein, "Die Veränderungen des Wirtschaftslebens im Kriege und nach dem Kriege," *Der Kampf des deutschen Geistes im Weltkrieg*, K. Hoenn, ed. (Gotha, 1915), Hoetzsch could have said of himself: "In looking into the future, I have purposely kept my eye only on immediate concerns and probable circumstances, because imagining remote possibilities and fantastic programs at this time seems a foolish and questionable game."

The seriousness of Hoetzsch's way of viewing the world, without illusion, becomes apparent in his detailed discussion of Friedrich Naumann's *Mitteleuropa*. It began with the following sentence: "This wise book also reflects the apodictic, constructive and therefore also doctrinaire trait which is characteristic of Naumann" (II, 121, January 5, 1916).

two closely related ideologies of the war against Russia, which were derived from Social Democratic and liberal anti-Russian traditions. He resisted on the one hand the view that the war was being conducted against "Czarism" and "the Russian Reaction," and on the other, the idea that the war in the East should be seen as the liberation of the non-Russian peoples from the yoke of the Czar.[9] He rejected the "condemnation of Czarism, which with regard to foreign policy was wrong," and which he thought Karl Marx had imparted to the Social Democratic movement (III, 75, October 25, 1916), and he fought against the slogan "Fight Czarism":

> The form of government of another country is none of our business; in any case, it cannot be the cause for a world conflict.

Conservative, he said, must not be equated with Russophile. Instead, the relationship between Germany and Russia must be viewed like that between Germany and any other great power, with no dependency upon the political philosophies of the parties (I, 168, April 21, 1915). Hoetzsch urged that the overthrow of Czarism and the question of the internal organization of Russia were in no way German war aims (II, 8, October 16, 1915; III, 31, September 20, 1916; III, 302, April 4, 1917). The longer the war lasted the less significant was the role played by the doctrines of the political parties in determining future Russo-German relations (III, 308, April 4, 1917). The German war aims in the East which Hoetzsch envisioned were, briefly stated, successfully to defend Austria-Hungary as a great power in Central Europe, to secure Germany's position of power in the heart of Europe, and to secure its territory east of the Elbe against repetition of an attack such as that of 1914. He clung tenaciously to the thoroughly defensive character of German goals toward the East.

Hoetzsch was not one of those who at the outbreak of the

---

9. See Erich Matthias, "Die deutsche Sozialdemokratie und der Osten 1914–1945," *Arbeitsgemeinschaft für Osteuropaforschung. Forschungsberichte und Untersuchungen zur Zeitgeschichte,* No. 11 (Tübingen, 1954), 7: "A 'liberation' of the eastern nationalities suppressed by Russia, primarily the Poles, was quite in line with the struggle against Russian despotism as the main enemy which was proclaimed by the party on August 4, 1914."

war had a low opinion of the internal strength of the Russian government and daringly predicted secession of the non-Russian nationalities and revolutionary unrest within the country. The course of the war confirmed his conviction that Russia entered the war in 1914 better armed than ever and prepared splendidly from a political, economic, and military point of view. He wrote in October 1915 that no one familiar with Russia who wished to make a precise judgment could make a general statement about the gloomy mood of the masses (II, 10, October 6, 1915). However, with regard to the Russian revolutionary movement Hoetzsch was misled to underestimate the situation, as opposed to the dominant overestimation of wishful thinking. On January 5, 1916, he wrote that revolutionary socialism in Russia was dead (II, 127), and on May 10, 1916, he characterized the Mensheviks as "those who want less" and the Bolsheviks as "those who want more" (II, 313), a mistake difficult to understand because he was always so conscientious.

But even where Hoetzsch's judgment reveals weaknesses, his analyses of events in Russia still have value today as a primary source for research, as do those of Theodor Schiemann, his predecessor as foreign policy expert of the *Kreuzzeitung* between 1902 and 1914, because they were based on careful reading and evaluation of Russian publications and often cite verbatim statements of the press which cannot be found elsewhere. It is remarkable how quickly he gained access to the most varied Russian sources immediately after their appearance. He followed the often-neglected rightist organs, such as *Zemshchina, Kolokol,* and *Moskovskaia vedomosti,* no less carefully than the liberal ones and the emigré press which appeared outside Russia.

At least *one* quotation from the appeal of the *Rech* of September 24, 1915 to Czar Ferdinand of Bulgaria should be mentioned in this connection, because it bears a remarkable similarity to Stalin's oft-repeated order of the day for February 23, 1942 about "Hitlers who come and go" and "the German people, the German state, which endure":

Monarchs come and go, but people endure. At the moment, when those in control of Bulgaria want to lead it to war against Russia, the Bulgarian people should remember that in the course of their existence it will still occasionally be its fate to come into contact with the great Russian people. [II, 22, October 6, 1915.] [10]

2. HOETZSCH AS A CRITIC OF GERMAN FOREIGN POLICY

Study of Hoetzsch as a critic of German foreign policy shows that he passed judgment mercilessly on German policy of the most recent past in the area of political history, judgments which in nearly every case were harsh condemnations. He gave unqualified approval only to the outstanding work of the experts on law and economics in the Foreign Office, for the German-Turkish Agreements of January 1917 (III, 357, May 9, 1917), for the Ukraine Treaties (No. 105, February 27, 1918), for the Bucharest Peace Treaty (No. 244, May 15, 1918), and for the treaties supplementary to the Treaty of Brest-Litovsk. Without overestimating their significance, he found these last treaties "excellent, frequently a masterful formulation" (No. 476, September 18, 1918). He saw in them models for future peace agreements.

In the course of the war, Hoetzsch was sharply opposed to Bethmann Hollweg. The main points of his criticism were aimed at the chancellor's attempted understanding with England, at his Polish policy, and at his refraining from strengthening and extending Germany's alliances before and during the war. In opposing the Bethmann-Jagov-Lichnowski view of the relationship between Germany and England, he stated that Bethmann Hollweg, with his idea of an understanding with England and a "Western orientation" of German foreign policy, was chasing a *fata morgana*. Unless Bethmann were willing to abandon the German navy, he thought, his attempt to opt for England was doomed from the very beginning (No. 167, April 3, 1918). He did not believe in a compromise with England. At the beginning of July 1918, he wrote that England had

10. Bruno Siemers, "Die Vereinigten Staaten und die deutsche Einheitsbewegung," *Geschichtliche Kräfte und Entscheidungen. Festschrift für Otto Becker* (Wiesbaden, 1954) quotes (p. 182) a statement of Marx's in the *New York Tribune,* November 23, 1853: "We said: Germany's end has arrived but that is not so. Dynasties and governments end but not a great nation." The issue of the *New York Tribune* cited has no trace of the quotation; probably the date is incorrect.

no intention of permitting Germany an extension of its power in the East in exchange for renouncing it in the West (No. 333, July 3, 1918). He considered wrong-headed the optimistic view of Vice-Chancellor von Payer in early autumn that peace in the West was possible without annexations and reparations, if the Entente recognized the Treaty of Brest (No. 489, September 25, 1918). He mercilessly criticized Bethmann Hollweg's policy in the Polish question, and he accused him of serious dereliction in neglecting to strengthen Germany's relations with her allies and to work toward a coherent, uniform program of war aims according to the principle that common prosecution of war must lead to common liquidation of the war (No. 255, May 22, 1918). At the end of the war, his criticism of Germany's dissolved alliances hit the nail on the head and deserves to be quoted verbatim:

We look for the blame primarily and above all on our side. Never did those in positions of responsibility in Germany heed the advice that Austria-Hungary and Turkey should not be judged by our standard of performance, that our leaders always had to keep in mind the moment at which our allies would not be able to continue. Essentially the collapse . . . is also a consequence of the incorrect evaluation of these alliances by those in positions of responsibility, a consequence of the mixture of weakness and arrogance which we call the policy of alliances. Nowhere were we able to win new sympathy, nowhere create a broader basis for relations within the alliances. An organic policy of alliances, which we called for in this column unceasingly for four years, was rejected as if on purpose by our leaders, and rendered impossible . . . .

The Peace of Bucharest was in large measure responsible for the withdrawal of Bulgaria, and the supplementary treaties to the Peace of Brest-Litovsk, which Germany signed without her allies, forced Austria and Turkey to what was really a separate policy. [No. 567, November 8, 1918.]

If one summarizes Hoetzsch's criticism of German foreign policy before and during the war (in each case the more detailed reasoning can be read in his critical remarks referred to below), German policy after Bismarck appears almost as a single chain of mistaken judgments and incorrect decisions that had to lead unavoidably to the catastrophe of 1918. Insofar as the problems of eastern and southeastern Europe were concerned, the war years especially seemed to him a chain of mistakes, self-deception, or missed opportunities. The policy of the so-called eastern orientation, according to which the war in the East had to be ended as quickly as possible by a separate peace of compromise and understanding in order to free all of Germany's energy for the decisive struggle against England, was an axiom for him (No. 643, December 18, 1918). Again and again, he reiterated to his readers that the war "in its essence" (III, 174) was an English-German war and that England would make every sacrifice to defeat Germany as a world power.

Hoetzsch, who saw the Eastern European questions in their larger context, was deeply disturbed by the war policy which he characterized a month before the end of the war as "a conglomerate of unconnected and minor decisions, of indefinite and ambiguous statements" (No. 502, October 2, 1918). In September he had listed gigantic problems which awaited solution in the East: an understanding between Germany, Turkey, the Ukraine, and Russia; definition of the war aims on the Balkan Peninsula; clear solution of the Polish question; elimination of the differences between Bulgaria and Turkey; regulation of the controversy between the Ukraine and Turkey; and an agreement between Germany, Turkey, Russia, and Persia about the Black Sea and the Caucasus (No. 463, September 11, 1918). He also was doubtful as to whether German policy was sufficiently aware of these issues and adequate to resolve them.

In part, he blamed shortcomings in organization for the failure of diplomacy. His suggestions for reform of the Foreign Service envisioned primarily creation of a central section and regional subsections, with an Anglo-Saxon Section and a Near East Section for matters relating to the Balkans and the Orient (II, 33, September 27, 1916; II, 123, November 11, 1916; No. 294, June 12, 1918; No. 617, December 25, 1918). After the revolution, he considered it necessary to end the "chaos of the old days" in the Foreign Office and to introduce a new concept of the Foreign Service and its operations.

3. Hoetzsch's Advocacy of an Understanding with Russia

Crowning the military victory in the East with the establishment of permanent friendly relations with Russia seemed to Hoetzsch the greatest prize and highest commandment of German diplomacy.[11] Relentlessly he stressed the notion that merging the vital interests of the Eastern powers was possible within the framework of the mutual interests of Germany, Austria-Hungary, and Turkey (I, 171, April 21, 1915; III, 76, October 25, 1916). He felt Bismarck had proved that. He considered the Russo-German Treaty of Potsdam in November 1910 one of the few positive accomplishments of German foreign policy during the Wilhelminian era. He felt that no other German treaty of the prewar period was more significant than this agreement, through which Germany and Russia coordinated their interests in Asia Minor and thereby proved that the alignment of the Triple Alliance and the Triple Entente could still be adjusted. The treaty formulated "one of the most significant and original ideas of German foreign policy" (II, 274, April 12, 1916). In the spirit of the Potsdam treaty, he thought it quite possible to find an accommodation between Russia's "drive to the South" and Germany's plans for Asia Minor (II, 318, May 10, 1916). Even in the question of the straits, he saw no absolute barrier to an understanding with Russia. Germany, he felt, had to recognize as justified the demand that the Russian economy needed free exit through the straits to the ocean and world markets (II, 351, June 7, 1916). She could not object if Turkey agreed that freedom of transit through the straits were guaranteed for merchant ships (III, 78, October 25, 1916). With a polemic severity which otherwise was unusual, he accused Paul Rohrbach and his followers of publishing Russophobe articles which had the effect of telling Russia, "more emphatically than Russian politicians could," that an irreconcilable struggle with Germany for possession of Constantinople was a vital interest of Russia.

---

11. Otto Hoetzsch, "Russland im Weltkrieg." Lecture given in the Industrie-Club, Düsseldorf, May 6, 1916, 24: "There are no areas of friction between Germany and Russia."

As a vigorous advocate of a policy which would have gone far toward accommodating the Russians, Hoetzsch stands completely alone among those who wrote about the war who are to be taken seriously. He struggled "against the current" in the most literal sense of the word when he stated again and again that an understanding between Russia and Germany and her allies was possible in all questions, "from the Baltic Sea to the Black Sea and the relationship to Asia"; that Germany would have to side with Russia and Japan in a future constellation of world powers; and that the Eastern orientation would therefore be proper and necessary for Germany's future interests (III, 382, May 23, 1917). The crucial thing about the Brest negotiations, its truly international significance for German foreign policy, lay in the dissolution of the Anglo-Russian alliance (No. 15, January 9, 1918). Here there arose for Germany the prospect of dissolving the enemy coalition, of bringing about an understanding between Germany and Russia about all of Eastern Europe and a large part of Asia, and of making contact with the Japanese (III, 649, December 12, 1917). He maintained that Germany could not live without good relationships with the East as the land bridge to the Far East (No. 450, September 4, 1918). After the cataclysm, he saw in a Greater Germany (through the legal unification of Germany and German Austria) "the proper way to the Slavs," to the Russians, to the Czechs, to the bridge to the Balkan Peninsula, even to central and eastern Asia (No. 617, November 4, 1918; No. 643, December 18, 1918).

Hoetzsch saw no opposition between the "essential and lasting" interests of Germany and Russia if they were to succeed in solving satisfactorily the question of a harbor for Russia on the Baltic Sea (III, 635, November 28, 1917; No. 15, January 9, 1918). While one of his Berlin colleagues from the Baltic area, Reinhold Seeberg, made fun of the "window theory" (the notion that Russia needed a "window" to the sea), Hoetzsch took very seriously the provisions of the supplementary treaties of August 27, 1918 concerning Livonia and Estonia, which proclaimed the independence of these areas from Russia and thereby deprived Russia of very important harbors on the Baltic Sea. He reminded his readers that the question of a harbor was crucial for future Russo-German relations and demanded that the gate to the Baltic Sea be kept open "for all time" for the Russian economy by safeguarding the commercial routes and granting free ports (No. 476, September 18, 1918).

It is quite a different matter with Hoetzsch's position with regard to the Brest negotiations, the armistice negotiations as well as the peace negotiations, and the summer discussions with regard to the execution of the peace treaty, very little news of which reached the public. He commented in great detail in many articles on all phases of these negotiations. His basic position is perhaps best expressed in the following sentence of January 1, 1918:

> Germany entered unfirm and uncertain ground when it took the peace proposals of the Bolsheviks as the basis for her negotiations with Russia, but also on this unfirm ground it must be possible to attain the highest goals of these negotiations, namely the military protection of our border and the possibility of permanent good relations between Russia and Germany.

Hoetzsch sharply criticized the tactics of the German peace delegation at Brest-Litovsk. While he was decidedly in favor of strategically necessary improvements of the eastern border (III, 381, May 23, 1917; III, 411, June 20, 1917), he opposed annexations, even disguised annexations, "incorporations and detachments" (No. 15, January 9, 1918). He did not consider as annexations border adjustments made with mutual agreement for strategic security reasons, such as those on the border of Silesia and Posen opposite Poland and on the border of West Prussia and East Prussia opposite territories which had been Russian. However, all territorial demands on Russia which went beyond strategic security he considered foolish. By using at Brest the right of self-determination of nationalities for all practical purposes for her own goals, Germany separated from the former Russian Empire more than it needed and gave the impression of being more interested in annexation than military and strategic considerations in the East justified (No. 28, January 16, 1918). As a worthwhile war aim in the East for Germany, he envisioned primarily reestablishment of the status quo of the prewar period. He disassociated himself completely from the excesses and fantasies of the annexation fanatics, who were otherwise politically often close to him. The one time he mentions "justified demands for land to be used for settlement" (III, 303, April 4, 1917) appears therefore almost as a *lapsus calami*.

4. HOETZSCH'S POSITION WITH REGARD TO THE PROBLEMS OF NATIONALITY IN THE EAST, ESPECIALLY WITH REGARD TO THE FUTURE OF POLAND, LITHUANIA, AND THE UKRAINE

Hoetzsch recognized quite early the danger represented for Germany by "liberation of the non-Russian nationalities," the formula of the right of self-determination of the nationalities applied to the former Russian Empire. The conviction that an understanding could and must be reached between Germany and Russia determined his basic attitude toward the Russian nationalities problem and his rejection of German policy toward nationalities in the occupied East, especially in the Baltic provinces, Poland, and the Ukraine. On the future of the non-Russian nationalities, he dismissed Paul Rohrbach and his following completely. He mercilessly criticized their war aim of "breaking up the Russian colossus," dissolving Russia into its allegedly natural components, which he called a new edition of the ideas of the "Wochenblatt" party in the Crimean War (III, 480, August 4, 1917).[12] He fought stubbornly against falsification of history by Rohrbach and his followers and against their demands for a German policy in the East based on false assumptions. He insisted upon carrying the Rohrbach theory of disintegration through to its logical conclusion:

If one begins to consider this theory of disintegration, one must follow it through to the point where the position of power of Moscow and of Great Russia is eliminated. If they remain, according to the experience of 600 years of Russian history, there will begin anew the process of accumulation of Russian lands, which in Russian history is what the work of the Grand Princes of Moscow is called, a process in which until now the Great Russians have proved to be superior politically as well as militarily to the other nationalities in the Russian Empire. [III, 480, August 4, 1917.]

---

12. See Otto von Bismarck, *Erinnerung und Gedanke* (*Die gesammelten Werke*) (Berlin, 1924–1935), XV, 80 f.

Again and again he pointed out that none of the peoples along the border of Russia, not even in the areas occupied by Germany, desired to be annexed to Germany and that the desired combination of a German protectorate in these areas on the one hand and a partnership of common interests based on a feeling of affinity on the other was wishful thinking on the part of the Germans.

With the eyes of a trained historian, Hoetzsch saw clearly the threat posed for Germany's Austrian and Turkish allies by the war aim calling for liberation of the non-Russian nationalities (III, 446, July 18, 1917). The proclamation of the right of self-determination of the nationalities of eastern Europe threatened to bring about a disintegration which could not be regulated nor controlled nor influenced by German policy. To stem such an immense development, he demanded that the right of self-determination of the nationalities be limited by the power interests of the large states and be subject to them (III, 652, December 12, 1917). It seemed to him a fundamental mistake that German foreign policy approached the liquidation of the war with Russia with the long-standing determination to separate Courland, Lithuania, and Poland from Russia, instead of seeking an understanding with Russia about these areas (No. 15, January 9, 1918). He maintained that Germany and Russia should agree about the western areas, taking into consideration granting autonomy to the nationalities, however, primarily in accordance with their interests as great powers (III, 615, November 4, 1917). He warned against forming powerless "buffer states and partial states," which politically and economically would gravitate for the most part toward Russia and would represent a heavy burden for future German-Russian relations (III, 511, August 29, 1917):

> We do not want economic relations between Germany and Russia, which are necessary for our main task after the war, namely for the reconstruction of our economy, to be endangered and harmed by experiments with small states and buffer states. [III, 636, November 28, 1917.] [13]

---

13. After a speech by Hoetzsch, the resolution of the second general plenary session of the Russo-German Economic Committee on February 3, 1918 insisted that a separation of parts of Russia must not lead to complicating Russo-German trade (No. 63, February 4, 1918).

On May 23, 1917, Hoetzsch set as a "cardinal demand" that Germany and Russia should border on each other directly all along the line:

> Germany cannot be interested in partially sovereign and powerless border states at its eastern border which seriously complicate the political and especially the economic relations between her and Russia . . . .
>
> All . . . questions can be settled in mutual agreement with Russia. There is no longer any war aim in the East that cannot be worked out in this way. (III, 381.)

Hoetzsch welcomed the supplementary treaties to the Peace of Brest-Litovsk insofar as German foreign policy in them set itself limits with regard to border states, in accordance with its interests and power. He correctly saw in the treaties a confirmation of Germany's lack of interest in the question of White Russia. With reference to the buffer states (Poland and Lithuania), however, the treaties did not please him. He considered utopian the view of the majority in the Reichstag and of Vice-Chancellor von Payer that the liberated border states, in recognition of their own interests and in free understanding with Germany, would provide protection against the Russian Empire. He insisted upon a realistic recognition of the fact that setting hopes in completely or partially sovereign and powerless buffer states was not what Germany needed. He entreated German diplomats not to carry out the policy with regard to border states, which had been continued by means of the treaties, in such a way as to weaken rather than strengthen Germany's eastern border in comparison with the prewar period. He felt that it was extremely difficult, even impossible, to reconcile real protection of Germany's eastern border with recognition of the right of self-determination; thus, real protection was virtually unattainable (III, 520–522, September 5, 1917; III, 551, September 26, 1917).

Hoetzsch's position with regard to the Polish question before the war, during the war (especially his arguments in opposition to the Austro-Polish solution), and after the war (when he was one of the first German politicians to warn emphatically against the illusion of seeing in the new Polish government only a "seasonal state" about which Germany and Russia would soon and easily agree) is worthy of special study. Here we wish to say only that he had turned his attention to the struggle of the nationalities in the eastern provinces of Prussia even before he was called to the Academy in Posen. In academic circles, along with Ludwig Bernhard, Waldemar Mitscherlich, and Max Sering, he was one of the authorities on the subject. Because of his specialization in Russian and Polish history, his statements about the Polish question are particularly important. On the basis of the experience of the last forty years, it is easy to criticize his position, which did not do justice to the dynamics of historical events in revolutionary times, such as those that began with the First World War. Nevertheless, it contains a full measure of objectively established results of historical science and irrefutable insights into the psychology of nations:

A state that makes the Poles in Warsaw free and independent [cannot] continue the Poland policy of Bismarck and Bülow in Posen and Oppeln. There will never again be an independent Poland on a permanent basis, because this is only possible in the framework of historical Poland . . . . Only in combination with parts of German, Latvian, Lithuanian, White and Little Russian territory can a Polish state be created which could really maintain itself as a state in the East. Such a state is impossible. It assumes, as Bismarck said as early as 1867, the destruction not only of Russia but also of Germany and Austria-Hungary, and all of these nationalities, Germans, Latvians, Lithuanians, Little and White Russians, want today less than ever to become part of such a state. We just want to remind you of the struggle for Vilna and Cholm, not to mention Danzig.

The only thing that would be in our interest would be the union of Poland with a federal Russia, with strategic border adjustments in favor of our eastern border . . . . [No. 53, January 30, 1918; similarly, No. 617, December 14, 1918.]

Bethmann Hollweg's Polish policy, which either did not clearly think through or underestimated the connection between the Prussian Polish policy and any solution of the extra-Prussian Polish question (III, 473, August 1, 1917), seemed to Hoetzsch to disregard completely the national and political interests of Germany.[14] He accused the chancellor of "dangerous and injurious anticipation of the results of the war in the East" (III, 560, October 3, 1917). He maintained that Bethmann, since in principle he considered Russia the main enemy, had destroyed the possibility for an understanding with Russia by doctrinaire partisan support of the Poles against the Russians (No. 53, January 30, 1918). The policy of the Central Powers, he said, had been "prejudiced against Russia" by the Polish decision (III, 218, January 31, 1917), and the "fateful decision" had made impossible a separate peace with Russia before the revolution (III, 184, January 10, 1917; No. 53, January 30, 1918). As late as January 1918, he refused to accept the Polish policy of the Central Powers as inevitable. He felt that a balance would have to be found between Germany's interests as a great power and the justified expectations of the Poles. In his opinion, the Belgian question, i.e., the Flemish coast demanded by Germany, involved Germany's position in the *world;* the Polish question in his opinion involved Germany's position as a *great power* (III, 542, September 26, 1917).

Hoetzsch never formulated his position with reference to the Polish question, which he considered basically a Russo-German problem (III, 534, September 12, 1917), more sharply than on September 26, 1917:

> Three-fourths of the people of the earth can be in favor of a free and independent Poland; we in Prussia and Germany cannot . . . . The national goals of the Germans and the Poles are irreconcilable. [III, 548.]

He considered Lithuania's future to be inseparably connected with the Polish question. The Lithuanian question strengthened him in his fundamental conviction that small ethnic fragments had to yield to the large perspectives of power. He did not consider the independence of this border state a German war aim, especially since a firm and secure land bridge to Courland was necessary.

---

14. About Bethmann Hollweg and Poland, see Fritz Hartung, "Deutschland und Polen während des Weltkriegs," *Deutschland und Polen. Beiträge zu ihren geschichtlichen Beziehungen,* Albert Brackmann, ed. (Munich and Berlin, 1933), 250 f.

Only ethnographic Lithuania, preferably without Vilna, which was to revert to Russia, should be permitted to become a state. The uniformity of German policy in the East, particularly German Polish policy, seemed secure only by joining Lithuania to the Empire or to Prussia, which was the only way to protect Lithuania from Polonization. A Greater Lithuania, he thought, would be united with Poland in two generations, and East Prussia would thereby be threatened with Polonization (No. 424, August 21, 1918). With these observations, he moved far into the area of conjectural policy, contrary to his usual restraint.

While in their Polish policy the Central Powers had originally joined forces with the enemies of the Ukrainians, their policy was reversed by concluding the Ukrainian separate peace and the promise to separate the area of Cholm from Poland and give it to the Ukraine. Hoetzsch, who wanted to restrict the Poles and the Lithuanians strictly to their ethnographic borders, welcomed this change. The "Cholm Crisis" seemed to him the point at which the incoherence and indecisiveness of German Polish policy were mercilessly revealed, a policy which later caused him to speak with bitterness of the "fateful, basically false" German policy in the East (No. 92, February 20, 1918):

> Our Polish policy faces today total collapse and bankruptcy such as was not anticipated even by the sharpest critics of the November Proclamation. [No. 604, November 27, 1918.]

By underestimating the impetus which the idea of a Polish national state and Polish expectations and demands had received from the proclamation of the Kingdom of Poland, he still believed that the Act of November 5 could be revoked at least in part and that it would be possible to reduce Poland again to an occupied area, such as Courland and Lithuania (III, 475, August 1, 1917; No. 193, April 17, 1918).

Hoetzsch welcomed the separate peace of the Central Powers with the Ukraine as a step toward breaking the ring of the enemies, but not without a clear warning:

> One should remember, however, that with this we are launched on an absolutely uncertain venture and no one in Germany today can say how it will turn out. [No. 66, February 6, 1918.]

He was prepared to attribute real political value to the Ukraine peace only as a bridge to a lasting peace with Great Russia (No. 79, February 13, 1918; No. 232, May 8, 1918), and he relentlessly stressed that economically the Ukraine was an integral part of Russia. The central point in the East for him was not the Ukraine, but rather what should become of the greatest homogeneous mass of people in eastern Europe, who were of the utmost importance, the 80 million Great Russians, that is, what would become of Moscow "in an historical and political perspective" (No. 459, September 4, 1918). He struggled desperately against a policy which, influenced by Rohrbach's agitation, proceeded on the assumption that Russia could no longer be considered a great power and which tried to build Germany's future in the East upon her relationship with the border states, which included the Ukraine.[15] Such a policy was a thoroughly uncertain venture as long as it was unknown how long Great Russia would remain powerless, whether the political separation of Moscow and Kiev would endure, and whether the border states would become oriented toward Germany out of a feeling of affinity. The course of events has fully proved how justified were Hoetzsch's objections to German policy in the East in the last year of the war. His demand that the questions of the East required a policy which would be of "broad vision and long term" was more farsighted than the Brest-Litovsk policy, which was based on illusions.

On February 13, 1918, he offered an impressive formulation of his objections to the exaggeration of the differences between Kiev and Moscow.

When one says to us that Kiev and Moscow are two totally different political and historical factors, that has always seemed as if Bavaria and Prussia were competing with each other for the kingdom of the Carolingians, which is a common historical past for both of them. One best appreciates the difference between Great Russians and Ukrainians if one compares it to that between the North and the South in the German Empire, or, still better, to that between the

15. "It is pure fantasy that the Ukraine should be and continue to be oriented geographically and economically toward 'Central Europe'" (No. 53, January 30, 1918).

old motherland in the West and the younger colonial area in the East of the German Empire, except for the common religion in Russia, an additional factor that is lacking in Germany.

When Skoropadsky came to power with German help, Hoetzsch could point out correctly that, after the original over-estimate of the Ukrainian national movement, those like him who from the beginning had expressed doubts about whether the Ukraine and Great Russia would remain enemies in the long run were proving right (No. 372, July 24, 1918).

5. HOETZSCH'S POSITION WITH REGARD TO GERMAN POLICY IN THE BALKANS AND THE ORIENT

As Hoetzsch pointed out in January 1915, the "primary areas of decision" during the war lay militarily in the East, but politically the decisive direction which determined the future of Austria-Hungary pointed toward the Southeast, toward the Balkan Peninsula and Turkey (I, 62, January 20, 1915). Again and again, he demanded a German policy for the Balkans which had been well thought through (III, 82, November 1, 1916) because only the common policy of the Central Powers in the Balkans and the Orient, he thought, would make their alliance an active factor in world politics and would last (III, 534, September 12, 1917). In the attitude of the Imperial Government toward Balkan questions, he criticized the same vagueness of German goals as in the East. There was no recognition, he said, of their intimate connection, and a single direction and firm position were therefore lacking. After the summer campaign of 1915, he showed that the primary war aims did not lie in the East, especially for Austria-Hungary, but rather that the demands to be made on Russia there should be limited to defense and permanent security. On the other hand, the victories in the East were the absolutely necessary prerequisites for the prospects and plans of the Central Powers for the Southeast. The victorious campaign in the East had made it possible to proceed from a defensive war to realization of the positive goals for the future in the Southeast (I, 392, September 29, 1915). He demanded that Austro-Hungarian foreign policy be oriented toward the Southeast, since Serbia belonged in the system of states of the Danubian monarchy geographically as well as economically (III, 529, September 12, 1917; No. 219, May 1, 1918). When he wrote the epitaph for German war policy in the Southeast (No. 515, October 9, 1918): "We will not be involved in the future developments in the Balkans," he complained above all that every opportunity for making peace with Serbia at the right time and with a view for the future had been missed. A German overall orientation in Balkan questions should have been based on the German connection with a Great Bulgaria and Turkey, which determined this orientation from the very beginning, in opposition to Rumania, Serbia, and Greece (No. 219, May 1, 1918). The stronger Austro-Hungarian interests in the Balkans and the stronger Imperial German interests in Turkey merged for Hoetzsch into a higher unity, with Bulgaria as the third member (I, 391, September 29, 1915).

The subjugation of Montenegro seemed to open up for Austria-Hungary the possibility of a Gibraltar on the Adriatic Sea (II, 147, January 19, 1916), and he thought Albania's association with the Central Powers should result analogously in the demand for a German base on the Adriatic Sea, the Bay of Valona (III, 530, September 12, 1917).

The preceding remarks about Hoetzsch's general position with regard to Balkan questions and the Orient require some supplementation for Bulgaria, Rumania, and Turkey.

He supported "unconditionally and without limitation" the Bulgarian war aims, annexation of Macedonia, the Morava region, and northern Dobruja (III, 530, September 12, 1917). It is Germany's will, he said, that a Great Bulgaria should arise in the Balkans and become dominant there (No. 105, February 17, 1918). By viewing Bulgaria as a state on the mouth of the Danube, he spoke curiously of German "foreign trade bases," which were not clearly defined (No. 219, May 1, 1918). In the North and in the South, in the question of the Aland Islands (No. 131, March 13, 1918), and in the Danube question, he envisaged a readjustment of the settlements under international law with the complete exclusion of the Western powers. He was aware of the deterioration in relations between Germany and Bulgaria in the summer of 1918. He considered the so-called Rumanophile aspect of German policy responsible for Bulgarian discontent; this avoided definite support for the Bulgarian claim to northern Dobruja, helped establish a condominium there, and "either brought about" the annexation of Bessarabia by Rumania or "permitted it to happen" (No. 320, June 26, 1918). However, he specifically expressed his agreement with the expansion of Rumania by addition of the Rumanian part of Bessarabia (No. 219, May 1, 1918). In addition, Germany maintained a reserved posture on revising the treaty of the spring of 1915 between Bulgaria and Turkey. Bulgaria's withdrawal from the war came as a shock for him. "This is a danger to our Empire greater than any other we have yet had to face in this war." With these words, he began his article of October 2, 1918 (No. 502), after receiving the melancholy news from the Balkans. He felt that Bulgaria's "betrayal" could change the whole world situation in favor of the Entente. A week later, on October 9 (No. 515), he confessed with resignation, "The turning point in the war has occurred. As a world war, the war has been decided against us."

Hoetzsch accused German diplomacy of failing to recognize Rumania's importance in international affairs before the war (III, 5, September 6, 1916). Keeping in mind that German economic interests in Rumania were greater than those of Austria, he felt that German policy during the decades of King Carol's Government should have had greater influence in Bucharest (III, 65, October 18, 1916). He felt that one of the greatest mistakes of German policy was its failure to clarify in any case the alliance relationship between the Triple Alliance and Rumania. In 1914, when King Carol's wish to take up arms against Russia was not realized, Hoetzsch felt that most of the blame lay with the Central Powers (II, 397, July 12, 1916). If the Central Powers had succeeded in bringing about Rumania's entry into the war against Russia in 1915, after the breakthrough battle of Gorlice, or at the latest after the victories of the summer (III, 1, September 6, 1916), then it is probable that the Russian army would have suffered a complete collapse at that time (No. 643, December 18, 1918). In this way, however, the brilliant German victories in the East fizzled and remained without any political influence. Hoetzsch wanted a Rumania capable of maintaining itself. An attempt should be made by means of common economic interest with the Central Powers to lead it back to the ideas of King Carol (No. 219, May 1, 1918). King Ferdinand would have to make the way free for this, after having opposed Germany, by abdicating (No. 105, February 27, 1918).

In the early part of 1918 and in the summer, Hoetzsch followed with great concern the policy and the conduct of the war by Turkey. The direction of Turkish expansion toward the East and the Northeast and the enlargement of the Turkish sphere of interest through a "very extensive interpretation" of the Treaty of Brest (No. 281, June 5, 1918) seemed an obvious overextension of Turkish military power and organizational ability. As early as March he expressed the hope that Turkey would not fall prey to the fantastic temptations of Pan-Turkism, which would lead to extravagances (No. 144, March 20, 1918). He favored complete re-establishment of Turkish state territory and greater Turkish border security in the Caucasus by federal annexation by Turkey of all of an autonomous Armenia. On the other hand, he considered it unwise for Germany and Turkey to oppose the reassociation with Russia of Georgia and the Tartar region with a guarantee of their internal freedom (No. 463, September 11, 1918).

On October 2, 1918, the Soviet government had annulled the peace with Turkey. Hoetzsch wrote at the end of his remarks then about the Turkish policy of expansion, which he had always opposed. He noted that Turkish statesmen should now realize the error of their Caucasus policy, which had been introduced by the Treaty of Brest, and that German policy had made a serious mistake when it permitted and supported this policy (No. 515, October 9, 1918). Hoetzsch called "quite correct" the decision in the supplementary treaties to the Brest-Litovsk Treaty which expressly recognized the Russian claim to Baku and thereby put the German-Turkish alliance to its greatest test (No. 476, September 18, 1918).

6. HOETZSCH AND THE COUNTERREVOLUTION IN RUSSIA

Immediately after Brest-Litovsk, Hoetzsch expressed his hopes for the counterrevolution in Russia by speaking of a snowball which started moving with the conclusion of peace in the East and which "hopefully" would become a landslide in the not too distant future. He saw the significance of the peace in that Germany had thereby erected for Europe a wall against the wave of Bolshevik Revolution (No. 118, March 6, 1918). When the situation in Russia in the summer of 1918 became more and more chaotic, he concluded that the Entente was already counting on "the Russia of the future." He therefore warned the Imperial Government with regard to its policy "in and with Russia, in and with the Ukraine" against counting in like fashion on "the Russia of the future" (No. 320, June 26, 1918). Under no circumstances, he felt, should any final decisions be made in the East which bound Germany: "all premature decisions should be avoided" (No. 281, June 5, 1918). Obviously, he believed that Germany should take up relations in time with the forces that were apparently replacing the Bolsheviks in order to be prepared for all eventualities:

> We must . . . be prepared if the Bolsheviks should fall, if the conditions in Russia should be consolidated, so that a fateful change of course in the foreign policy of a new Russia not be introduced for us. [No. 346, July 10, 1918.]

Shortly thereafter he wrote even more clearly that Germany had to create a situation in which any Russian government would find an association with the Central Powers most advantageous (No. 372, July 24, 1918). When the supplementary treaties to the Peace of Brest showed that the Imperial Government, in spite of the assassinations of Count Mirbach and of Fieldmarshal von Eichhorn, continued to adhere unswervingly to the Peace of Brest-Litovsk and paid no attention to warnings not to bind itself irrevocably, Hoetzsch wrote that it was necessary to convince "Russia" that Germany, while maintaining its own security interests, did not want to withhold from Russia the things necessary for its survival (No. 450, September 4, 1918). Here again we have an example of his conviction that the vital interests of Russia and Germany were not incompatible.

Modification of the relations between Soviet Russia and Germany at the end of the summer of 1918 by the supplementary treaties of August 27 and the secret correspondence between Secretary of

State von Hintze and Ambassador Joffe,[16] which did not become known until much later, introduced a short episode in the history of Russo-German relations between Brest-Litovsk and Compiègne. Until now the political, economic, and military significance of this has not been sufficiently studied by either German or Russian historians.[17] But no study of the treaty can neglect Hoetzsch's article of September 18, 1918 (No. 476), which stated that the treaties, although formally designated as supplementary treaties, essentially created a new foundation and amounted to a revision of the Peace of Brest. Looking back, he remarked at the end of November that, "inhibited by a curious mistake," German policy makers had believed that questions in the East could be solved in isolation and without considering the outcome of the war (No. 604, November 27, 1918).

The idea which he first expressed on October 30, 1918, "It is in our interest, and at the same time we act in the interests of the whole of civilized humanity, if Germany remains the shield against Bolshevism" (No. 554), he elaborated upon a week later, still before the armistice in the West determined that German troops would remain in the Baltic states. He envisioned a common anti-Bolshevik front and action by Germany and the Entente (No. 567, November 6, 1918). At the end of November he thought that the iron ring around the Bolsheviks was being drawn tighter and tighter. For internal reasons, the threatening Bolshevization of Germany, and for external reasons, the endangered peace negotiations with the Allies, he spoke sharply in opposition to any further connection with the Bolsheviks (No. 604, November 27, 1918).

The preceding sketchy remarks, limited to Hoetzsch's thoughts about policy in the East, are far from a complete presentation of his views of the war and the world in the area of foreign policy. We still need to study him as a conservative politician and publicist of

---

16. *Europäische Gespräche*, III (1926).
17. See now: Winfried Baumgart, *Deutsche Ostpolitik 1918. Von Brest-Litowsk bis zum Ende des Ersten Weltkrieges* (Vienna, Munich, 1966).
Fritz Klein's partisan study, *Die diplomatischen Beziehungen Deutschlands zur Sowjetunion 1917–1932* (Berlin, 1952), quotes Stalin 36 times on 183 pages, touches on the agreements of August 27, 1918 with a single uninformative sentence, and does not mention the secret agreements.

the waning Imperial era and the period of the Weimar Republic, to pay proper attention, especially in his reporting of the war, to the war aims in the West which he advocated, to his position with regard to German policy in the Far East and German colonial policy, to the neutral powers, to the financing of the war, etc. Hoetzsch interpreted the end of the war as the victory of the Anglo-Saxon political idea, in which the right of self-determination of nationalities played a central role (No. 592, November 20, 1918). This right of self-determination was for him identical with the idea of the nation in the nineteenth century. If fate had permitted him to analyze international developments of the last decade, we may assume that he would have seen in the formation of new national states above all the parallelism and the connection between the efforts and movements for independence in Asia and Africa and the European national movements in the nineteenth and twentieth centuries, and he would have been fascinated.

VI

Russia and
the League of Nations

I N THE SAME YEAR, 1919, there appeared "two nuclei of world organization," the League of Nations in Paris and the Third International in Moscow.[1] Perhaps the main purpose of the initiators of the Congress which established the Third International was to create a counterweight to the League of Nations.[2] The relationship of the idea of the League of Nations to Bolshevism and of the League of Nations in its early stage to the Russian question are hitherto neglected fields. It was the obligation of mutual protection of their territories by the members of the League of Nations, an obligation resting on the Covenant, which made the new organization appear to the newly established states an important instrument for the defense of their rights. And the system of mandates offered the possibility of protectorates over territories which in their development toward independence were still in an infant stage, especially formations on the territory of the former Russian Empire.

In this connection, the criticism of the League of Nations by Elihu Root must be adduced. The famous statesman declared that Article 10 of the Covenant, which guaranteed the territorial integrity

This article was originally published in *Jahrbücher für Geschichte Osteuropas,* VII (1959–60), 460–478 as Part 4 of "Studien zur Geschichte der 'Russischen Frage' auf der Pariser Friedenskonferenz von 1919," 431–478.
    1. Lt. Colonel Malone: *Parliamentary Debates,* House of Commons, Series 5, CXXI, Col. 735 (November 17, 1919).
    2. *Times* (London), March 31, 1919: "The Conference and the Bolsheviks."

of all members of the League, was "an independent and indefinite alliance for the preservation of the status quo." [3] Between 1918 and 1920, the League of Nations was frequently regarded as a power for peace, as protector of the status quo of new states in the East after the abandonment of the idea that it could be used as a war alliance against Soviet Russia. In the judgment of Sir Alfred Zimmern, if the Great Powers had accepted responsibility for governing eastern Europe, western Asia, and Asiatic Russia, this would have been a scheme to change the system of mandates from a plan for the betterment of conditions within underdeveloped countries into an organization which could have been regarded as the Holy Alliance of the 20th Century.[4]

Prominent German publicists were among the advocates of intervention against Russia by the League of Nations at the beginning of 1919. Hans Delbrück, for instance, wrote in the *Preussische Jahrbücher* that it would be the most natural thing for the League of Nations to start its activities by uniting all Powers for defense against the danger of Bolshevism.[5] Other protagonists in the fight against Bolshevism, men such as Eduard Stadtler [6] and Paul Rohrbach,[7] pleaded for military intervention by the League of Nations as the sole way to peace. If the German troops in the East had not been demoralized and receptive to Bolshevist propaganda, then cooperation in the East could have been established between the Entente and Germany, the occupying Power on the East, in order to build together a wall for protection of the Ukraine, the Baltic Provinces, and Poland against the Red flood. Such common measures could have immunized Central Europe against Bolshevism.[8]

Sir Samuel Hoare regarded Bolshevism as "the antithesis of every principle for which the League of Nations stands." [9] Thus,

---

3. Elihu Root, *Men and Policies* (Cambridge, Mass., 1924), 219; Philip C. Jessup, *Elihu Root* (New York, 1938), II, 400.

4. Alfred Zimmern, *The League of Nations and the Rule of Law, 1918–1935* (London, [1936]), 212.

5. Hans Delbrück, "Der zu erwartende Friede," *Preussische Jahrbücher*, CLXXV (1919), 145.

6. Eduard Stadtler, *Als Antibolschewist 1918–1919* (Düsseldorf, 1935), 151.

7. *Der deutsche Gedanke*, April 25, 1919.

8. Prince Max von Baden, "Völkerbund und Rechtsfrieden," *Preussische Jahrbücher*, CLXXV (1919), 307.

9. *National Review*, LXXIII (April, 1919), 227.

he came close to James Garvin's opinion that the tremendous Russian question was the riddle of the Sphinx for the Paris Congress and the League of Nations.[10] From the sentiments and demands expressed in the letter of War Minister Lord Milner to the London *Times* on December 19, 1918, that the Powers as "the trustee of European order" could not tolerate aggressive measures of a government against its neighbor, it was only a short step to proposals to entrust the League of Nations with the task of fighting against the revolutionary government,[11] i.e., to make the League of Nations "an alliance of the nations against Russia." [12]

Garvin, who was convinced that it was necessary for the peace and security of the world to restore Russia by effective intervention, declared intervention by the League of Nations a "great and crucial test of its functions." Nothing could inspire more confidence in its efficacy and strengthen the hope for its successful development.[13] The edifice of the League of Nations would rest on shifting ground, if the Peace Congress did not undertake decisive steps for the restoration of order, unity, and liberty in Russia under a strong government.

The London *Times* reported under the date of March 12, 1919 from Ekaterinodar that there was general sentiment in the Army of Volunteers that the first task of the League of Nations should be organizing and regenerating Russia and that this could be done only by occupying one province of Russia after another.[14] In August, Denikin appealed to Wilson: The League of Nations could prove its high mission only if it took a stand against Bolshevism.[15] The protagonists of the idea of a crusade against Russia wanted the

---

10. James L. Garvin, *The Economic Foundations of Peace* (London, 1919), 402.

11. *Literary Digest,* LX (January 18, 1919), 18: "Why we are invading Russia."

12. Hans Delbrück, "Locarno und Russland," *Vor und nach dem Weltkrieg. Politische und historische Aufsätze 1902–1925* (Berlin, 1926), 462.

13. Garvin, 401. Baron A. Heyking, the last London consul general of Czarist Russia, expressed the same opinion: "The League of Nations must be able to command obedience and to force recalcitrant members of the world's society of nations into submission. Russia is a test case, and should be dealt with, if that League is to have any real and practical significance" (*Bolshevism and Pusillanimity* [London, 1919], 14).

14. *Times* (London), April 14, 1919: "The Volunteer Army."

15. United States, Department of State, *Papers Relating to the Foreign Relations of the United States, 1919. Russia,* 772 (Taganrog, August 23, 1919).

peaceful League of Nations changed into a war alliance against Bolshevism "to crush this brutal outrage on modern civilization." [16] An editorial of the London *Times* of April 10, entitled "The Authority of the Conference," pointed out that the prestige of the future League of Nations rested upon its Russian policy: a few more months of a policy which resulted in a weak Poland, a hostile Hungary, an almost helpless Rumania, and, in addition, a "frozen in" army in North Russia and in another retreating in the Russian South would suffice to undermine the authority of the League of Nations, before it really sprang into life.

On the basis of the idea that a "league to enforce peace" should be established, Lloyd George could regard the League of Nations as a weapon against revolution, an organization of the world against Bolshevism. On February 19, 1919 he wrote to Philip Kerr, his private secretary, that Poland, Finland, and the other states carved from Russia should be placed under the protection of the League of Nations and should be given "moral, material, and, if necessary, full military support against Bolshevik aggression." He added that Estonia, Lithuania, and Livonia, if they would come with Poland into the same category, had a right to be supported under the same conditions.[17]

It cannot be doubted that in Paris the League of Nations had been regarded at its beginning as an instrument which could be used for defense against or even to crush the Bolshevist influence, which, originating from Soviet Russia, could be felt everywhere in the world. Wilson's concept was that the League of Nations, as an alternative to Bolshevism, should unite and protect all the forces opposed to Bolshevism; that it should provide "a policy of steady moral, material, political, and diplomatic encouragement to those who are fighting the battle of the Allies in Russia and Asia." This was the way the London *Times* on November 10 characterized a Russian policy that was other than armed intervention.[18]

16. H. S. King, "Russian Trade," *Times* (London), January 21, 1920; *The Financial News* (London), February 22, 1920.

17. David Lloyd George, *Memoirs of the Peace Conference* (New York, 1939), I, 377.

18. *Times* (London), November 10, 1919: "Peace in Russia" (editorial). Apparently the same abstract conception of nonmilitary intervention was the foundation of appeals made by Albert Thomas, a leading French socialist, who pleaded for "intervention in Russia by all moral and economic means on

Chaikovskii, the President of the Provisional Government of North Russia, intimated to Henry White, one of the American Peace Commissioners, that the League of Nations should recruit a large international force, send it to Russia, and force order on the country, if the Allies and the United States did not wish to send their troops against the Bolshevists.[19] In the same vein, Churchill, at a meeting of the War Cabinet on December 31, 1918, had suggested that "collective intervention by a composed force" should establish in Russia a democratic government; general elections under the auspices of the Allies would expose and destroy Bolshevism.[20] Again and again, Churchill, the driving force for intervention in the British Cabinet, reiterated that intervention be made the task of the League of Nations. At the meeting of the Supreme Council on February 15 he declared that Russia was the key to the situation: as long as she was not a living part of Europe, a "living partner" in the League of Nations and a friend of the Allied Powers, there could be neither peace nor victory.[21] He probably thought of a democratic, federated Russia, a Russia which, as the note of May 26 of the Allied Powers to Admiral Kolchak expressed the hope, would share the efforts of the other members of the League of Nations regarding disarmament.[22]

On March 3, Churchill revealed in Parliament more succinctly than before what he believed to be the task of the League of Nations with regard to Russia. England, he mentioned, was fulfilling in the Caucasus only a "duty to the League of Nations or League of Allied Nations."[23] A little later, on March 26, he declared that the course of future military operations in Russia depended on

---

the basis of Wilson's Fourteen Points," and who asked for an intervention which, in contrast to the uncoordinated actions of various Allied governments, "should be directed by the League of Nations in the name of the principles of humanity and international law" (B. W. Schaper, *Albert Thomas. Trente ans de réformisme social* [Assen, 1959], 188).

19. Allan Nevins, *Henry White. Thirty Years of American Diplomacy* (New York [1930]), 370.

20. Lloyd George, *Memoirs of the Peace Conference,* I, 326.

21. David Hunter Miller, *My Diary at the Conference of Paris* (New York, 1924), XIV, 448; United States, Department of State, *Papers Relating to the Foreign Relations of the United States, 1919. Russia,* 62.

22. Ernest Lagarde, *La reconnaissance du gouvernement des Soviets* (Paris, 1924), 57; see below, note 63.

23. *Parliamentary Debates,* Series 5, CXIII, Col. 81.

neither the War Office nor the Cabinet; it was a matter of the League of Nations or the League of Victorious Powers.[24]

During the period of intervention, Churchill repeatedly pointed out that England's Russian policy was not his personal policy or "even a national policy," but "an international, . . . an inter-Allied policy." [25] In his speeches of March quoted above, he built a direct link between intervention and the League of Nations. Only the British White Book about the evacuation of North Russia, published in August 1919, revealed that in April Churchill had made a serious effort to justify an interest of the League of Nations in military intervention in Russia.[26] The *Manchester Guardian,* which had led the opposition to the Archangel expedition, interpreted the information in the White Book as Churchill's confession of culpability: Churchill's unexpected interest in the League of Nations should be taken as proof that in a moment of sudden elucidation the real perpetrators of the "prodigious blunder" recognized that their support by the Cabinet, the House of Commons, and the Supreme Council was not enough; therefore, they hoped that the League of Nations would protect them.[27]

Churchill's speech on July 17 before the British Russia Club, when he declared that saving Russia was a duty of the League of Nations, was an official attack on the liberal "Manifesto of the Fourteen." [28] A few days before, this latter publication had deeply impressed the English public; it must be regarded as a milestone in the anti-interventionist movement. Among the signers of the "Manifesto" were numerous outstanding personalities, such as F. D. Acland, Sidney Arnold, G. Lowes Dickinson, Lord Bray, and Lord Eversley. It said that the Government's Russian policy ran counter to the real interests of England; "a strange new principle" was being practiced in international policy, according to which governments not wholly democratic had to be eliminated by forceful intervention from abroad. Contrary to this opinion, Churchill

---

24. Ibid., CXIV, Col. 485.
25. *Times* (London), July 18, 1919: Churchill's speech before the British Russia Club, held on July 17.
26. [Great Britain, Army], *The Evacuation of North Russia, 1919,* Cmd. 818. 1920, 27.
27. *Manchester Guardian,* August 3, 1920.
28. Ibid., July 5, 1919.

pointed out that Europe was seeking protection behind the weak defense of a chain of new and weak states; to these tottering new states, the League of Nations had promised protection. "The League of Nations was on its trial with regard to Russia, and if the League could not save Russia, Russia in her agony would destroy the League." [29]

Taking issue with the declaration of the fourteen that England had no interest in intervention, Churchill linked England's national interest in the defeat of Bolshevism with an alleged Pan-European interest of the League of Nations in an upheaval in Russia.

Churchill's utterance of March 26 that the intervention was a matter of the "League of Victorious Powers" brings to mind Léon Bourgeois's definition of the League of Nations: "Société pour maintien de la paix," [30] during the preparation of the Versailles treaty. Perhaps it must be considered the foundation for David Jayne Hill's famous utterances about the League of Nations made in 1919 and 1922. Soon after the signing of the peace, the American jurist recognized that statesmen had failed to replace the old "balance of power" policy, which was based on a balance of armament, by a "Community of Power." [31] He wrote:

Because all sovereign states are equal before the law, it cannot

---

29. *Times* (London), July 18, 1919, 12: "Allied Policy in Russia. Mr. Churchill's Defence"; also in *Struggling Russia*, I, No. 25 (August 30, 1919), 397–400. The final sentence (missing in the *Times* report) reads: "I appeal to the League of Nations to take a grand review of the whole position of Russia, and to make one united, concerted effort to deliver the Russian nation from her appalling fate and to restore peace to the tortured world."

30. Miller, *Diary*, VIII, 54: Meeting of Commission for the League of Nations, March 3, 1919.

See also Herbert Hoover's pessimistic utterance about the League of Nations and the "armed alliance" of the Great Powers (April 11, 1919): "As the Central Empires and Russia will not be for some years admitted to the League, and if we continue in what is in effect an armed alliance in Europe dominating these empires, the League will become simply a few neutrals gyrating around this armed alliance. It will tend to drive the Central Powers and Russia into an independent League," in Herbert C. Hoover, *America's First Crusade* (New York, 1922), 45. It is somewhat strange that Hoover at this time used the terms "Central Empires" and "Central Powers."

31. *President Wilson's State Papers and Addresses* (New York, 1917), 351 (January 22, 1917). See also Josef L. Kunz, "Konzert, europäisches," *Wörterbuch des Völkerrechts und der Diplomatie*, Karl Strupp, ed. (Berlin, 1924), I, 701.

long subsist merely as a "League," which is essentially a group of Powers within the general Society of States . . . .[32]

and:

To become a real Association for peace it must transform itself fundamentally. At present it is just a "League," not the "Society of Nations." [33]

Farsighted General Smuts was one of the earliest advocates of admitting Russia to the League of Nations. In his famous memorandum of December 16, 1918, "The League of Nations. A Practical Suggestion," [34] he proposed that "Central Russia" as an important intermediate Power should become a member of the Council of the League with a seat of limited duration.[35] He stressed the right of full independence of Finland and Poland. In second place he did not name the nationalities in northwestern Russia (the Lithuanians, Latvians, and Estonians) but rather Russia's provinces in Transcaucasia and Transcaspia, a significant order for an English assessment of Russian territorial and national problems. Smuts doubted that these territories were ripe for self-government and that they could conduct an independent foreign policy. He went so far as to recommend that, for peoples and territories formerly belonging to Russia, the League of Nations should be regarded as reversionary in the widest sense, entitled to make final decisions applying certain principles. Furthermore, he suggested that

any authority, control, or administration which may be necessary in respect of these territories and peoples other than their own self-determined autonomy, shall be the exclusive function of and shall be vested in the League of Nations and exercised by or on behalf of it.[36]

In Smuts's view, Russia, like Austria and Turkey, was a defeated and fragmented state; therefore, he recommended that the

---

32. David Jayne Hill, *Present Problems in Foreign Policy* (New York, 1919), x.
33. Hill, "The Second Assembly of the League of Nations," *American Journal of International Law*, XVI (1922), 65.
34. Jan Christian Smuts, "The League of Nations. A Program for the Peace Conference," in Miller, *Diary*, III (Doc. 110); and David Hunter Miller, *The Drafting of the Covenant* (New York, 1926), II, 23–64.
35. Smuts, 58 (Miller, *Covenant*).
36. Ibid., 38.

League's system of mandates be applied to certain Russian territories as a permanent solution. David Hunter Miller and James Brown Scott, in their "Summary Observations on the Memorandum of General Smuts," prophesied that the whole world would intervene in Russia, if Smuts's proposals were accepted.[37] Smuts's idea to apply the League's system of mandates to certain Russian territories was unjust toward a former ally. Harold Williams remonstrated in April against the intention of dealing with Russia "in the position of an Empire defeated and broken up by the war," in the same way as with the former enemies, Austria-Hungary and Turkey.

Only someone who started out from the faulty theory that Russia no longer existed [38] could imagine "that the mandatory system of the League of Nations might be made permanently operative in certain areas of Russian territories." [39]

The ideas of General Smuts about mandated territories under a "trusteeship" of the League of Nations, providing for these territories an indispensable "guiding hand of some external authority to steady their administration," [40] slowly gained ground during the Peace Conference. Even for Poland, Smuts stressed the necessity of education for self-government. His ideas culminated in the conviction that nations (like individuals) needed an apprenticeship for attaining political freedom. Therefore, he proposed as a guarantee of peace an occupation of Poland within the frontiers of 1772.[41] Charles Sarolea prophesied that the new Poland from the point of view of foreign policy would become "the most vulnerable of all the European states" and in her internal policy "the most artificial political structure." From this he concluded that this state, endangered from outside and internally artificial, could hope for survival only if guaranteed by the League of Nations. Poland was not able to protect Europe against Germanism or Bolshevism. On the contrary,

---

37. Miller, *Diary*, III, 239 (Document 138).

38. Robert H. Lord, "The Russian [Soviet] Government, whose existence the Peace Conference could not pretend to ignore, but never felt able to recognize," in Edward M. House and Charles Seymour, eds., *What Really Happened at Paris* (New York, 1921), 67.

39. Harold Williams, "Russia and the Peace Conference," *Edinburgh Review*, CCXXIX, Number 463 (April 1919), 281–282.

40. Lloyd George, *Memoirs of the Peace Conference*, II, 624.

41. Tadeusz Wolski, "Le rôle de la Pologne," *La Paix des Peuples*, I, 1 (February 25, 1919), 111.

Europe would have to protect Poland against these two external and internal dangers threatening her existence.[42]

Lt. Colonel E. F. Riggs, the chief of the American Mission to South Russia, went so far as to suggest appropriate foreign guarantees for Russian internal policy in the future. Convinced of the overshadowing importance of the agrarian question, he hoped to win over the Russian peasant by giving him moral support and by promising land. The Council of Ten in a formal proclamation should make an appeal to the Russian people guaranteeing to the peasantry a full and sufficient land reform; then, Admiral Kolchak and General Denikin should initiate the necessary steps.[43]

In this connection, closer examination is needed of the question of extending the League's mandatory system, anchored in the Covenant and originally intended only for colonies, to Russian territories. Perhaps at the urging of General Smuts, Wilson at the sixth meeting of the Commission for the League of Nations, on February 8, 1919, proposed additions to the draft of Article XVII of the Covenant which should be applied only to territories of the former Russian Empire. The proposal was defeated by the opposition of the representatives of Belgium, Portugal, and Rumania.[44] It is possible that Wilson also had been influenced by a report of Pleasant A. Stovall, the American Minister to Switzerland. Haidar Bammat, who paraded as "Minister of Foreign Affairs of the Republic of the United Peoples of the Territory of the Cherkessians and of Daghestan," had expressed to Stovall his hope that the territory which he represented be placed under the protection of the "Society of Nations" and that the League of Nations would make the United States the mandatory Power.[45] This was only one of numerous similar proposals for Caucasian territories.[46]

On April 19, the London *Times* published a letter suggesting that a mandatory Power take over the government of Georgia, Azerbaidzhan, and Armenia as a federated system for about a

---

42. Charles Sarolea, *Europe and the League of Nations* (London, 1919), 162.

43. United States, Department of State, *Papers Relating to the Foreign Relations of the United States, 1919. Russia*, 756 (Odessa, March 28, 1919).

44. Miller, *The Drafting of the Covenant*, I, 186; II, 272–273.

45. United States, Department of State, *Papers Relating to the Foreign Relations of the United States, 1919. Russia*, 44 (Berne, February 5, 1919).

46. Firuz Kazemzadeh, *The Struggle for Transcaucasia, 1917–1921* (New York, 1951), ch. 17: "Transcaucasia and the Versailles Peace Conference."

decade, thus making possible education for self-government. At the end of the educational process, these states should enter the system of the United States of Great Russia. Avetis Aharonian, the president of the Armenian National Council, who headed the Delegation of the Armenian Republic, and Boghos Nubar Pasha, the leader of the Armenian National Delegation, on February 12 had sent a joint memorandum to the Peace Conference. They proposed placing the Armenian states temporarily (i.e., for no longer than twenty years) under the collective guarantee of the Allied Powers and the United States or under a guarantee of the League of Nations.[47] The Delegation of Azerbaidzhan applied to the Peace Conference asking to be recognized as an "absolutely independent State under the name of Democratic Republic of Azerbaidzhan" and to be admitted to the League of Nations "under the high protection of which this Republic wishes to be placed like other States." [48] Wilson informed the delegation that the Peace Conference did not intend to split the world into small national states. It did not oppose in principle a Caucasian federation under a mandate of the League of Nations, but the final decision regarding Azerbaidzhan had to wait, until the whole Russian question had been solved.[49]

Lloyd George, at the meeting of the Big Four on May 21, proposed that, as long as Russia was not yet reorganized, the United States should accept the mandate for the Caucasus. There had been at this time a vivid discussion of the question of an American mandate over Constantinople and Asia Minor, including parts of Russian Armenia.[50] The influence of this discussion on Russo-

47. The Armenian Question before the Peace Conference (delegation propaganda, Hoover Institution files); extracts in William Henry Cook and Edith P. Stickney, eds., *Readings in European International Relations since 1879* (New York, 1931), 665–674.

48. *Claims of the Peace Delegation of the Republic of Caucasian Azerbaijan. Presented to the Peace Conference in Paris* (Paris, 1919), 49.

49. Richard Pipes, *The Formation of the Soviet Union. Communism and Nationalism, 1917–1923* (Cambridge, Mass., 1954), 216; Kazemzadeh, 266.

50. Kazemzadeh, 260–264; Gotthold Jäschke, "Präsident Wilson als Schiedsrichter zwischen der Türkei und Armenien," *Mitteilungen des Seminars für orientalische Sprachen Berlin*, XXXVIII (1935), 2, Abt.: Westasiatische Studien, 75–80; Luigi Aldrovandi Marescotti, "Un ipotetico mandato degli Stati Uniti d'America in Turchia (1919) e la dottrina di Monroe," Centro italiano di studi americani. Comitato storico-politico, *Pubblicazioni* 7 (the two studies are not listed by Kazemzadeh); Robert L. Daniel, "The Armenian Question and American-Turkish Relations, 1914–1927," *Mississippi Valley Historical Review*, XLVI, Number 2 (September 1959), 260–261.

American relations has hardly been touched upon in Western European and American literature.

No more far-reaching official proposal was made than the recommendation in the report of the King-Crane Mission

> that the United States be asked to take this general single mandate (for the whole of Asia Minor, not assigned to Mesopotamia or Syria) together with its inclusive mandates for the Armenian State, the Constantinopolitan State, and the continued Turkish State.[51]

Albert Howe Lybyer, the mission's expert on Armenia, defined the frontiers of the "definite territory" of an Armenian state suggested by him, as follows: [52]

> This area should be taken from both Turkish and Russian territory. The wars of the 19th century divided the proper Armenian land between these two empires.
>
> The proposed large Armenia, to extend from the Black Sea to the Mediterranean, is probably impossible of realization, and therefore should not be planned for.[53]
>
> An Armenia reduced to the Armenian highlands in both Turkey and Russia, with an outlet on the Black Sea, would have a good chance of establishment and continuance. The Turkish area which the Russians held in 1917 may be taken approximately as the Turkish portion of this "Small Armenia," and the present territory of Russian Armenia as the remainder . . . . This land having secure frontiers, as was tried out thoroughly during the Great War, gives promise of self-defensibility.

The report on Armenia of Major-General James G. Harbord did not limit his recommendations to Armenia; he went further, proposing that the Power entrusted with the mandate over Armenia should simultaneously exercise the same rights for Anatolia (Rumelia), Constantinople, and Transcaucasia.[54] Brigadier General

---

51. The King-Crane Report on the Near East (Report of the American Section of the International Commission on Mandates in Turkey): United States, Department of State, *Papers Relating to the Foreign Relations of the United States. Paris Peace Conference 1919*, XII (1947), 842.

52. Ibid., 821–823.

53. Albert Howe Lybyer, "Turkey under the Armistice," *Journal of International Relations*, XII, Number 4 (April 1922), 458.

54. James G. Harbord, "Report of the American Military Mission to Armenia (October 16, 1919)," *International Conciliation*, No. 151 (June 1920). Kazemzadeh mentions only Harbord's report and does not analyze Lybyer's proposals.

Moseley estimated in the fall of 1919 that 59,000 men would be needed for an American mandate in Asia Minor; not less than 200 million dollars would be needed for the maintenance of this force during the first three or four years of the occupation.[55]

Kolchak's reply to the Allies' note had strengthened the Caucasian republics' intention to establish a union of the Caucasian states to be placed under the protection of the League of Nations. From this time on, the efforts of the leaders of the anti-Bolshevik national Caucasian movements—Haidar Bammat, Z. Avalov, and A. Chkhenkeli from Georgia, Mir Vaqub from Azerbaidzhan, and others—increased to mobilize the League of Nations to represent their interests.[56]

In the discussions concerning how to interest the League of Nations in the newly established states, the states set up in the Russian Northwest ranked next to the Caucasian states. As early as November 1918 the governments of the Crimea as well as of Estonia approached British Navy officers suggesting those areas become British protectorates. On May 3, 1919, an American Navy officer reported from Libau that Russia, after having lost Finland, could not renounce the Baltic ports; recognition of an independent Finland seemed doubly dangerous with a view to peace with Russia at a later date. He said that there was a general desire to be independent, and that a League of Nations' protectorate seemed very acceptable. Paets, the Estonian Prime Minister, would not object to a governor general appointed by the Allies; his authority should be similar to that exercised by the British governor general in Egypt. Estonian and Latvian circles which favored full internal autonomy recognized the economic and political necessity of entering in the future into a union with a "sane" Russian state and to accept Russian sovereignty.[57]

In Paris at the end of June 1919, Colonel Warwick Greene, the

---

55. George Van Horn Moseley, "The Military Problem of a Mandatory," *International Conciliation*, No. 151 (June, 1920), 42.

General Sir Hubert Gough, who recommended a British mandate in Transcaucasia, had estimated in the spring that probably only two Divisions of British or Indian forces would be needed for one to two years: Sir Hubert Gough, "British Policy on Caucasus Republics," *Times* (London), April 19, 1919.

56. Pipes, 216–217.

57. United States, Department of State, *Papers Relating to the Foreign Relations of the United States, Paris Peace Conference 1919*, XII (1947), 155–160.

head of the American Mission to Finland and the Baltic States, proposed in vain a United States mandate over Latvia and Lithuania, and that Great Britain, as mandatory Power for Estonia, take responsibility for the Petrograd front.[58] When Jaan Poska, the Estonian delegate at the Peace Conference, protested that his country could not accept less than recognition of its complete independence, Sir Esme Howard assured him that the League of Nations would guarantee an agreement between Estonia and Soviet Russia and that Russian sovereignty over Estonia would be a mere formality.[59] The Supreme Council instruction dated October 28 for General Niessel, the chief of the Inter-Allied Mission for supervising the evacuation of the Baltic provinces by the Germans, indicated that the League of Nations would intervene in the relations of the Baltic states and the future Russian government, if they should be unable to reach a direct agreement.[60]

At the time of the establishment of the League of Nations, recognition of the independence and sovereignty of new states, in the sense of international law, and admission to the league were linked with each other; [61] it seemed uncertain that the vacuum between Germany and Russia would be filled by sovereign states. In the meeting of the Big Four on May 20, Lloyd George pointed out that the various groups fighting against the Bolsheviks should recognize frontiers determined by the League of Nations.[62]

The note sent by the Supreme Council to Admiral Kolchak on May 26 [63] clearly showed the uncertainty concerning the future status of the nationalities, according to state law as well as by international law. Articles 4 and 5 of the note envisaged gradually in-

---

58. Ibid., 211; United States, Department of State, *Papers Relating to the Foreign Relations of the United States, 1919. Russia,* 683.

59. O. Greiffenhagen, "Jaan Poska, ein Baumeister des heutigen Estland," *Jahrbücher für Geschichte Osteuropas,* II (1937), 91–98.

60. Albert Niessel, *L'évacuation des pays baltiques par les Allemands* (Paris, 1935), 32; *Documents on British Foreign Policy, 1919–1939,* Series 1, II, 97.

61. Malbone W. Graham, *In Quest of a Law of Recognition,* Faculty Research Lecture at the University of California at Los Angeles, delivered May 15, 1933, No. 8 (Berkeley, 1933).

62. United States, Department of State, *Papers Relating to the Foreign Relations of the United States, 1919. Russia,* 354.

63. Ibid., 367–370; *Documents on British Foreign Policy,* Series I, III, 332–333, 362–364, 376.

dependent states and various sorts of autonomy and self-government for the nationalities in Russia's northern and western borderlands. It expressed unconcealed sympathy with the separatist tendencies of the Transcaucasian and Transcaspian nationalities. While the note mentioned Finland, Poland, Estonia, Latvia, Lithuania, and Bessarabia, it passed with silence over the Ukraine [64] and White Russia.[65] From the note, the great contours of the political map of the Russia of the future can be outlined as imagined by the leading Entente statesmen at the time of its dispatch. The mentioning of separatist tendencies, which was tantamount to supporting them, since their realization depended on the aid provided by the Entente, depicted British evaluation of the situation rather than French. The communication to Kolchak stressed that questions of the frontiers between Russia, Poland, and Finland should be submitted to the League of Nations for arbitration if no direct agreement could be reached between the litigants. Point 5 of the note, however, went much further and must at least be regarded as "diplomatic intervention" in Russian affairs in a wide sense. It read:

---

64. To a declaration made on May 21, 1919 by the Ukrainian delegate Hryhorij Sydorenko at the meeting of the Supreme Council, Lloyd George remarked that there was one point only on which Bolsheviks and anti-Bolsheviks were in agreement: "Ils veulent que l'Ukraine reste partie intégrante de la Russie" (Paul Mantoux, *Les délibérations du Conseil des Quatres* [24 mars—23 juin 1919] [Paris, 1955], I, 149).

65. Appeals for aid and protests were addressed to the Peace Conference by the powerless bourgeois Government of the White Russian National Republic (Belorusskaia Narodnaia Respublika), which in December 1917 had been proclaimed by resolution of the Minsk White Russian Congress to comprise the White Russian nationality within its geographico-historical confines. On January 8, 1919, it made its first appeal to "The diplomatic representatives of America, England, France, and Italy at Spa," asking that the Great Powers protect it against partition of its territory by its neighbors: the Ukraine, which had taken possession of ten White Russian districts of the governments of Grodno, Minsk, and Chernigov; the Russian Soviet Republic, which had occupied the whole of eastern White Russia; and especially the Poles, who were about to occupy western White Russia (K. Ezovitov, *Belorussy i Poliaki. Dokumenty i fakty iz istorii okkupatsii Belorussii Poliakami v 1918 i 1919 godakh* [Kovno, 1919], 27–29).

On May 8, 1919, a note addressed to the president of the Peace Conference protested against the establishment of a Polish civilian administration and the preparation of a plebiscite under abnormal conditions in the Polish-occupied White Russian territory. It predicted that the Polish action, by increasing national conflicts, would result in "new Balkans" in eastern Europe (Ibid., pp. 66–68). See also Eugen Freiherr von Engelhardt, *Weissruthenien. Volk und Land* (Berlin, 1943), 116–121 (based on J. Voronko [Varonka], *Belorusskii vopros k momentu Versal'skoi konferentsii* [Kaunas, 1919; in White Russian, 1924]).

That if a solution of the relations between Esthonia, Latvia, Lithuania and the Caucasian and Transcaspian territories and Russia is not speedily reached by agreement, the settlement will be made in consultation and co-operation with the League of Nations.

Kolchak, in his reply,[66] pointed out that the delineation of the frontier between Russia and Poland and the final solution of the Finnish question would have to depend on decisions of the future Russian Constituent National Assembly. With regard to Point 5 of the note, he declared that his Government was inclined to make the preparations necessary for solution of the questions concerning policies for the nationalities in Estonia, Latvia, and Lithuania and in the Caucasian and Transcaspian territories. If difficulties should arise in determining the autonomy of the various nationalities, his Government was prepared "to have recourse to the collaboration and good offices of the League of Nations."

Since the notes exchanged between the Peace Conference and the Kolchak Government contain basic declarations concerning nationality policy in the Russian East, it seems appropriate to quote the relevant paragraphs side by side:

Peace Conference note, May 26, 1919 [67]

Kolchak Government note, June 4, 1919 [68]

Fourthly, that the independence of Finland and Poland be recognised, and that in the event of the frontiers and other relations between Russia and these countries not being settled by agreement, they will be referred to the arbitration of the League of Nations.

3. Considering the creation of a unified Polish State to be one of the chief of the normal and just consequences of the world war, the Government thinks itself justified in confirming the independence of Poland, proclaimed by the Provisional Russian Government of 1917, all the pledges and decrees of which we have accepted. The final solution of the question of delimiting the frontiers between Russia and Poland

---

66. United States, Department of State, *Papers Relating to the Foreign Relations of the United States, 1919. Russia,* 375–378; S. P. Mel'gunov, *Tragediia Admirala Kolchaka* (Belgrade, 1931), III, 323–326.

67. United States, Department of State, *Papers Relating to the Foreign Relations of the United States, 1919. Russia,* 369 (May 26, 1919).

68. Ibid., 377 (June 4, 1919).

Fifthly, that if a solution of the relations between Esthonia, Latvia, Lithuania and the Caucasian and Transcaspian territories and Russia is not speedily reached by agreement, the settlement will be made in consultation and co-operation with the League of Nations, and that until such settlement is made the Government of Russia agrees to recognise these territories as autonomous and to confirm the relations which may exist between their de facto Governments and the Allied and Associated Governments.

Sixthly, the right of the Peace Conference to determine the future of the Roumanian part of Bessarabia, be recognized.

must, however, . . . be postponed till the meeting of the Constituent Assembly.

We are disposed at once to recognise the *de facto* Government of Finland, but the final solution of the Finnish Question must belong to the Constituent Assembly.

4. We are fully disposed at once to prepare for the solution of the questions concerning the fate of the national groups in Esthonia, Latvia, Lithuania, and of the Caucasian and Transcaspian countries, and we have every reason to believe that a prompt settlement will be made, seeing that the Government is assuring as from the present time the autonomy of the various nationalities. It goes without saying that the limits and conditions of these autonomous institutions will be settled separately as regards each of the nationalities concerned.

And even in case difficulties should arise in regard to the solution of these various questions, the Government is ready to have recourse to the collaboration and good offices of the League of Nations with a view to arriving at a satisfactory settlement.

5. The above principle, implying the ratification of the agreements by the Constituent Assembly should obviously be applied to the question of Bessarabia.

There must have been grave internal dissensions before the Kolchak Government formulated and dispatched its reply. General Miller, the military governor of Archangel, regarded Points 5 and 6 of the note addressed to Kolchak as a menace to the Russian patrimonium. It seemed to him economically impossible that small units such as Estonia be permanently and completely detached from Russia. The separation of Lithuania from Russia, together with other temporary alienations, would result "in throwing Russia again back to the territorially unsatisfactory situation which Peter the Great had faced when ascending to the throne." [69]

A telegram of the Omsk Government to the Allied Main Powers dated June 24, asking their support in persuading Mannerheim to attack Petrograd, contained the assurance that all open questions between Finland and Russia could be peacefully settled with the help of the League of Nations.[70]

The Supreme Council regarded its letter to Kolchak as the basic document for all future negotiations. In August, it informed Kolchak that the Allied and Associated Powers, in consultation and cooperation with the League of Nations, would settle the issue if the new states and Russia would not soon reach agreement. As long as such an agreement had not yet been attained, these states should be recognized as autonomous and entitled to relations with the Allied and Associated Powers.[71] Advocates of the League of Nations pleaded for recognition of the independence of the Baltic and Caucasian states, of Finland, and eventually of the Ukraine in order to accelerate the establishment of the League of Nations and thus enable the Supreme Council to make the solution of the Russian problem its first great task.[72]

In the consultations of the Big Four about the content of the note to Kolchak, it was important that Wilson opposed the idea of obligatory military service. With regard to Russia, he had tried before to obtain a pledge from the groups fighting against the Bolsheviks to desist from compulsory recruiting of peasants, a completely unrealistic demand. Clemenceau as well as Orlando objected to making abolition of universal compulsory military service a condition for Kolchak. Wilson regretted that abolition of compul-

---

69. Ibid., 370 (May 29, 1919).

70. Ibid., 681. It should be noted that the Omsk Government mentioned the League of Nations only in its telegram to the governments of Great Britain, France, and the United States, but omitted reference to the League in Kolchak's telegram to Mannerheim, dated June 23 (Leonid I. Strakhovsky, *Intervention at Archangel* [Princeton, 1944], 204–205).

71. Hoover Library, American Relief Administration, XVII (1932), 492–493 (August 21, 1919).

72. "We should like to see the League of Nations constituted forthwith, so that the Council of the League might take up the Russian question as its first great task. If that is not possible, the existing Supreme Council of the Allies should assume the responsibility . . ." ("The Russian Problem," *The Spectator* [London], CXXIII, November 22, 1919, 684).

sory service had not been inserted in the Covenant. Lloyd George envisaged that Russia could mobilize six million men if it did not abolish compulsory service. Abolishing compulsory service would result in great dangers, bringing Russia into the German sphere of influence. Wilson finally agreed to a compromise according to which a condition for recognition of the Kolchak Government by the Supreme Council was not abolition of compulsory service but Kolchak's consent that armaments be limited.

[Point 7]: That as soon as a government for Russia has been consti-tuted on a democratic basis, Russia should join the League of Nations and co-operate with the other members in the limitation of armaments and of military organization throughout the world.[73]

The parallel to the juridical situation created by the Vienna "Kongressakte" of 1815 for the German Confederation was made complete by the intention that the autonomy of the newly estab-lished states be guaranteed by the League of Nations.

When the Peace Conference came to its close, Wilson did not hide his apprehension caused by the fact that Germany and Rus-sia, "the most dangerous elements of Europe," remained outside the league.[74] At Lloyd George's request, two military experts of the Peace Conference, Lt. Colonel C. N. Buzzard and Colonel R. H. Beadon, submitted a memorandum on June 19. It concluded with the naive proposition that the League of Nations should com-mission a group of military, diplomatic, and civilian experts to investigate all the questions which separated the various Russian groups from each other.[75] Lt. Colonel Malone, a liberal member of Parliament, in November 1919 proposed an international con-ference on Eastern Europe and asked in this connection for a new orientation of the League of Nations' idea as far as Germany and Russia were concerned.[76]

When the Allies lifted the blockade of Russia in January

---

73. United States, Department of State, *Papers Relating to the Foreign Relations of the United States, 1919. Russia,* 355–358.

74. Luigi Aldorrandi, "Le ultime sedute dei 'Quattro'," *Nuova Anto-logia,* XXXIX (1937), 78 (June 3, 1919); reprinted in his *Nuovi ricordi e frammenti di diario* (Milan, 1938), 19.

75. Roger H. Beadon, *Some Memories of the Peace Conference* (London, 1933), 106.

76. *Parliamentary Debates,* Series 5, CXXI, Col. 739 (November 17, 1919).

1920, it seemed that a propitious moment had arrived to have the situation in Soviet Russia investigated by experts. By its note of February 24, the Supreme Council made known its intention to ask the League of Nations to undertake the task; [77] thus, the council undertook what General Smuts had suggested on January 21, 1919, at a meeting of the British Empire delegation, entrusting the League of Nations, as one of its first tasks, with an examination of the situation in Russia.[78] In order to circumvent the difficulty of "recognizing" the Soviet Government, Smuts had proposed involving the future League of Nations in the conflict between the Western capitalist world and Bolshevism, as a neutral, supranational creation, so to speak, with power to arbitrate. The Bolsheviks should appear before a court! "As soon as the League of Nations was created it might appoint a Commission to summon all *de facto* Governments before it," were Smuts's words. An armistice should be proclaimed for the period of investigation. To this, Balfour replied:

> It would be a most unfortunate precedent if the League of Nations concerned itself with an enquiry between factions within a country, especially a country which was not part of the League.[79]

Smuts's suggestion was a remarkable early attempt not to limit the authority of the League of Nations to relations between states, but to extend it to internal, civil-war situations, a problem which in the era of the United Nations has assumed new proportions with the liberation movements in Asia and Africa.

The resolution of the Supreme Council had no consequences. It only shows to what extent illusions prevailed, not only underestimating the consciousness of sovereignty of the Bolshevik leaders but wholly neglecting to take it into account. Official declarations of the Soviet Government a few months later made its attitude toward the League of Nations crystal clear.

---

77. Wilhelm von Bülow, *Der Versailler Völkerbund* (Berlin, 1923), 375–377; Manley O. Hudson, "Membership in the League of Nations," *American Journal of International Law,* XVIII (1924), 452–453. Soviet declaration of May 13, 1920: Jane Degras, ed., *Soviet Documents on Foreign Policy,* I: *1917–1924* (London, 1951), 186–187.

78. Lloyd George, *Memoirs of the Peace Conference,* I, 230 (January 21, 1919).

79. Ibid., 231.

On July 17, when the Russo-Polish war was raging, Chicherin, in one of his sarcastic notes to the British Government, rejected any intervention by the League of Nations, which for him did not officially exist, for the Soviet Government "never received from the so-called League of Nations any communication as to its creation and existence." Ironically, he continued:

When acquainting itself from unofficial press sources with the Covenant of the so-called League of Nations, the Soviet Government could not leave unnoticed the fact that, according to Article XVII, the non-members in case of a conflict with members of the so-called League of Nations can be invited to submit to its decision as if they were members.

Chicherin contested this paragraph:

The Soviet Government can in no way agree that one group of Powers should assume the role of supreme body over all the states in the world. Watching over the full inviolability of the sovereign rights of the Russian working people, the Soviet Government absolutely rejects the pretensions of any foreign groups of Powers claiming to assume the role of supreme masters of the fate of other nations.[80]

A few months later, the Council of the League of Nations intended to send an international police force to the Vilna district in order to ensure a correct plebiscite. Joffe, the leader of the Russian delegation to the Riga Peace Conference, in a note to the leader of the Polish delegation "emphatically" objected to the dispatching to Vilna of armed contingents of various alien states, "ostensibly

---

80. *The New Russia,* II (1920), 414; Bulletin de l'Institut interméd. internat., III (1920), 241. See also, C. Salvioli, "La jurisprudence de la Cour Permanente de Justice Internationale," 89, 96; "La situation juridique de l'Etat non-membre," *L'Académie de Droit international. Recueil des cours,* XII (1926, Vol. 2), 1927.

Kathryn (Wasserman) Davis, *The Soviets at Geneva. The U.S.S.R. and the League of Nations, 1919–1933* (Geneva, 1935), remains the leading work about the relations between the Soviet Government and the League of Nations.

For Lenin's negative attitude toward the League of Nations, see *Diplomaticheskii Slovar'* (Moscow, 1950), II, col. 25. Chicherin, in his note to Wilson dated October 24, 1918, ironically analyzed the President's program of a League of Nations (Degras, *Documents on Soviet Foreign Policy,* I, 116–118).

on the recommendation of an institution styled the 'League of Nations,' an association of states which is not recognized by the Soviet Republics." He declared that the presence of these armed contingents could encourage the preparation of new hostile actions against the Soviet Republics. When the Swiss Government withdrew its pledge to enter into the intended international force for safeguarding the lines of communication, its spokesman stressed the enmity of the Soviet Government toward the "intervention" of the League of Nations and accused the Soviets of preparing a military offensive in connection with the revolutionary movements in Europe.[81]

In July 1921 the Secretary General of the League of Nations invited the Great Powers and all the Baltic coastal states (with the exception of Soviet Russia and Lithuania) to a conference about the neutrality of the Aland Islands. The Soviet Government protested when the League of Nations assumed an active role in this question.[82] In an official communication of June 1922, Chicherin likewise sharply rejected the claim of the "so-called League of Nations" to deal with the internal situation of Karelia. He declared that the Soviet Government would regard as a hostile act any attempt to apply to Soviet Russia Article XVII of the Covenant in a conflict between a member state and a nonmember.[83]

Malbone W. Graham has dealt in an exemplary and exhaustive manner with all questions arising from the recognition of the Baltic states and their admission to the League of Nations.[84] Therefore, this study can limit itself to a short survey of the handling of applications for admission submitted by successor states of the former "one and indivisible" czarist Russia. At the first assembly of the

81. Paul Mantoux, "A Contribution to the History of the Lost Opportunities of the League of Nations," *The World Crisis*, by the Professors of the Graduate Institute of International Studies (London, 1938), 17, 19, 21–22.

82. Samuel Shepard Jones, *The Scandinavian States and the League of Nations* (Princeton, 1939), 252–254; Norman J. Padelford and Gösta A. Anderson, "The Aland Islands Question," *American Journal of International Law,* XXXIII (1939), 477.

83. Publications of the Permanent Court of International Justice, Series B. Collection of Advisory Opinions, No. 5: Advisory Opinion given by the Court on July 23rd, 1923 (regarding eastern Karelia), 13; Davis, *The Soviets at Geneva,* 97–102: "The Eastern Karelia Case."

84. Malbone W. Graham, *In Quest of a Law of Recognition, The Diplomatic Recognition of the Border States,* Pt. 1: Finland (Berkeley, 1935), Pt. 2: Estonia (1939), Pt. 3: Latvia (1941).

League of Nations at the end of 1920, the applications of Armenia, Azerbaidzhan, Georgia, and the Ukraine were declined.[85] Viviani, the main French representative to the assembly, in December opposed the applications of Lithuania, Latvia, and Estonia because they opened the Russian question, which should be solved as a whole.[86]

This French opposition against the applications of the Baltic states was generally interpreted as a sign that French policy was still adhering to the idea of a unified Russian state. Nevertheless, a few weeks later France recognized *de jure* Latvia, Estonia, and an independent Georgia.[87] On September 22, 1921, Estonia, Latvia, and Lithuania were admitted to the League of Nations.[88]

Instability was the cardinal mistake in the operations of the Supreme Council, especially in the recognition of new states. This uncertainty can be traced back and attributed to the uncertain relationship and to the disparity between the prewar idea of the balance of power and the League of Nations' idea.[89] The reluctance of the Allied Great Powers to admit to the League of Nations certain Russian successor states has been explained as wishing to avoid the functioning of the League of Nations as a supranational state.[90] Reasons of equity with regard to Russia, their wartime ally, had made the Powers hesitant to recognize the new states; by agreeing to the admission of the new states in the East, they reversed their previous stand. An article in *Round Table* (London) explained in June 1920 that in 1919–20 the Supreme Council, as "Executive Agent of the Allies," exercised the function of a *de facto* government over undetermined territories, the future status of which was uncertain. When the League of Nations declined the invitation of the Supreme Council to accept responsibility for the Government of Armenia, it had acted in accordance with Washington's principle that

---

85. Manley A. Hudson, "Membership of the League of Nations," *American Journal of International Law*, XVIII (1924), 445–446.

86. Zurab D. Avalov, *Nezavisimost' Gruzii v mezhdunarodnoi politike 1918–1921 g.g.* (Paris, 1924), 238.

87. Ibid., 309–310.

88. Ants Piip, "Estonia and the League of Nations," Grotius Society (London), *Transactions*, VI: "Problems of Peace and War" (1921), 35–44.

89. "Confusion of Ideas," *Westminster Gazette* (July 20, 1920).

90. C. R. Pusta, "Le Statut international de l'Esthonie et la reconnaissance des nouveaux états," *Académie diplomatique internationale. Séances et travaux*, IV (October–December 1928), 23.

"influence is not government." For the same reason, it was impossible for the League of Nations to accept responsibility for Russia.[91]

On January 10, 1922, in a speech at Bristol, Lord Grey held that there had been "too much Supreme Council and not enough League of Nations" in the relations of the Western Powers to the Soviet Government. The same, and more justly, could be said about the relations of the Western Powers to Germany. It is pathetic that the Peace Conference tried to impose the solution of the most difficult questions which it could not master on an organization which existed merely on paper.

In reading private utterances and official declarations concerning the innumerable hints to the League of Nations (only a selection of those relating to Russia and Eastern Europe are presented here), one almost becomes disturbed by the magic of the word. It seems that mentioning the "League of Nations" created the conception that it was a power which could simultaneously restore order and overcome the chaotic situation in the East at the end of the war. We must leave undecided how much was the desire and wishful thinking of honest idealists, cunning and self-deception by professional politicians, or even conscious deceiving of their followers. Incessantly, self-determination and the League of Nations were hailed as the ultimate goals in realizing democratic ideas.[92] Both ideas had become ideologies which dominated the atmosphere of the Peace Conference. It was possible to juggle with them as terms of political philosophy and political propaganda, but their realization met with unexpected difficulties which often could not be overcome. In the case of the Russian nationalities, it resulted in conflict between the idea of self-determination and the idea of the unified Russian state.

---

91. "Problems of Europe: The Work of the Supreme Council," *Round Table,* Number 39 (June 1920), 599–605.

92. It has been said of Wilson that the idea of "self-determination as such" exercised on him a certain magic; but he always linked it with the creation of democratic institutions. (Sir Llewellyn Woodward, "A British View of Wilson's Foreign Policy," in Edward H. Buehrig, ed., *Wilson's Foreign Policy in Perspective* [Bloomington, Ind., 1957], 65).

VII

Germany's Eastern Policy
in the First World War

IN 1928, ULRICH NOACK, in his book on Bismarck's policy of peace and the problem of the decay of German power,[1] written on the basis of the great publication of German pre-World War I documents,[2] propagated a new image of Bismarck in an effort tantamount to deflating the prevalent hero-worship of the chancellor. He described the policy of the aging statesman as utterly timid; otherwise, between 1878 and 1888 he would not have avoided the "preventive war" in the East aimed at establishing a federative order of the "young nations" in the East under a German protectorate. The opponents of speculative history sharply attacked Noack's scheme.[3]

About the First World War, Noack passed the following judgment: it was the underestimation of Germany's mission in Eastern Europe that must be regarded as the real cause of Germany's collapse in 1918:

Comments on the book by Fritz Fischer, *Griff nach der Weltmacht. Die Kriegszielpolitik des kaiserlichen Deutschland 1914–1918*. (Düsseldorf: Droste Verlag, 1961). 896 pp. This article was originally published in *Jahrbücher für Geschichte Osteuropas*, X, No. 3 (1962), 381–394; reprinted in *Deutsche Kriegsziele 1914–1918*, Ernst W. Graf Lynar, ed., 1966, 158–174 (Ullstein Buch No. 616).

1. Ulrich Noack, *Bismarcks Friedenspolitik und das Problem des deutschen Machtverfalls* (Leipzig, 1928).

2. *Die Grosse Politik der europäischen Kabinette 1871–1914* (Berlin, 1922–27).

3. See especially the review by Hans Rothfels in the *Deutsche Literaturzeitung*, LI, No. 44 (November 1, 1930), col. 2091–2101.

If strategy had been subordinated to political goals, instead of the Verdun bloodletting in the spring of 1916, it would have Russia—already half-defeated in the autumn of 1915—completely finished and thus would have brought Rumania to the German side in the course of the year 1916. During the winter of 1916–17, Germany could have organized the new states in the East, could have saved the Russian monarchy after its internal collapse, and could have concluded a separate peace with it. Furthermore, Persia and Afghanistan could have been won over for the Central European Federation, which might have resulted in expelling the British from Mesopotamia and in keeping them busy at the Indus. Simultaneously, all of Turkey's military power could have been used against the Suez Canal; and, finally, Germany's Eastern army, on its way to the Western front in the fall of 1916, could have mounted on the side-line a victorious campaign in Venetia against Italy. Then, in the spring of 1917 Germany would have stood exactly at the point where—after a year had been lost—she stood in the spring of 1918 before the great offensive . . . . [Noack, p. 493]

Noack thinks that in the spring of 1917 "victory or a peace of mutual concessions (*Verständigungsfrieden*) in the West and *in any case* [italics the reviewer's] recognition of the new order in the East" could have been attained.

It is a strange experience to compare the utopias of 1914–1918 with the utopian expansionist prescription for victory of an historian in 1928, a rebel against the Bismarck myth, and with another, not less utopian, prescription to be found in Erwin Hölzle's book, *Der Osten im Ersten Weltkrieg* (Leipzig, 1944). On the basis of an overwhelmingly large and confusing mass of documents, Fritz Fischer has for the first time laid bare in a comprehensive narrative the utopias which influenced the leaders of Germany during the First World War.[4] Fischer is no less a rebel than Noack. He assumes that the best way to penetrate the immense amount of material would be to elucidate the history of the years preceding

---

4. It seems that Fischer disregarded among relevant documentation the files of the Investigation Committee (and its subcommittee) of the National Assembly and the Reichstag kept in the Political Archives of the German Foreign Ministry at Bonn. They include certain compilations of wartime documents prepared by the Foreign Ministry for the committee, but not for publication. See *Index of Microfilmed Records of the German Foreign Ministry and of the Reich's Chancellery Covering the Weimar Period* (Washington: The National Archives, 1958), 87–95.

the First World War, its outbreak, and its course by starting out from the war aim ("Griff nach der Weltmacht"?) or aims of Germany. This is, no doubt, a daring way of looking at the problem at hand. Fischer has based his novel mode of judging the past on a sensational find among the documents, a program of war aims which Chancellor Bethmann Hollweg prepared in an early stage of the war. He has declared that this document, although its origins (by no means irrelevant for its evaluation) remain in the dark, represents fundamentally, with only tactical changes, the consistent line of the chancellor's war policy. That is, he attributes to the memorandum an importance which does not take sufficiently into account changes of the war situation and their impact.[5]

The following review of Fischer's book will not play down certain doubts and silently pass over the reviewer's reservations, and it must be said that there are many matters on which he disagrees. Nevertheless, he is compelled to confess, as his general impression, that this book is one of the few German historical works of our days in which the author has achieved a breakthrough that is more than a timely "revision" of judgments that have long been generally tolerated and firmly accepted. It *is* a breakthrough; otherwise the acerbity in refuting the book could not be understood and justified. The book is revolutionizing in many respects; it upsets accustomed standards in judging the policy of imperial Germany in the First World War. No longer can the view be upheld that this policy largely lacked direction, plans, and aims.

For a long time the opinion had been held that the victories in the East were a major embarrassment to the civilian government in assessing what could be considered a just equivalent for the sacrifices. It seemed that the caution and discretion of the responsible political leaders who abstained from proclaiming Eastern war aims

---

5. In spite of Fischer's attempt to depict Bethmann Hollweg (usually regarded as a weak chancellor) as a strong-willed man, it seems that the development which under his chancellorship led from the Supreme Command's right to be heard to the right of participating in decisions has rightly been stressed in the section "Aussenpolitik" (pp. 43–47) of "Die Generalstäbe in Deutschland 1871–1945" (Beiträge zur Militär- und Kriegsgeschichte, III, Freiburg, Militärgeschichtliches Forschungsamt, ed. [Stuttgart, 1962]). Stress is laid (p. 45) on the fact that Bethmann Hollweg's effort at self-justification (*Betrachtungen zum Weltkriege*), although perceptive in conceiving the psychological causes which brought about the overwhelming military influence, does not sufficiently recognize his own mistakes and omissions.

could hardly be reconciled with the great military successes in the East; it helped to evoke unbridled annexationist war aims advocated by irresponsible orators and writers.

Before the German diplomatic archives became accessible for research, Hans W. Gatzke, an American historian, had examined Germany's Western and colonial war aims under the provocative title, *Germany's Drive to the West* (Baltimore, 1950). The documents which have since become available have not only complemented the author's findings but have also completely confirmed them in their basic outlines. Now Germany's Eastern war aims also have their historian, Fritz Fischer. Readers of the book will certainly wonder how firmly the lines drawn by Fischer on the basis of the German war documents will stand, because Fischer's conviction that Germany's war aims since the beginning of the war remained basically unchanged has put the war in a wholly new perspective.

There will be people who, even after having read Fischer's book, will continue to maintain the thesis that Germany fought a war which was purely defensive. However, under the weight of authentic utterances adduced by Fischer, they will at least have to concede that military, political, and economic claims were made in the course of the war which went far beyond Germany's needs for defense. What is new and what is of decisive importance for evaluating Fischer's book is the following: claims of irresponsible people which could not be taken seriously and sometimes bordered on the grotesque have been known for a long time. But Fischer reveals the details of hitherto secret, unrealistic hopes and plans of responsible political and military leaders. By far the greater part are claims which came up during the war. It cannot be denied that these claims were detrimental to all peace efforts, but in this connection Fischer should have discussed whether or not the war aims in both camps contributed to lengthening the war, and to what extent Germany's war aims might be regarded as a reaction to those proclaimed by her enemies.[6]

---

6. Erwin Hölzle's article, "Das Experiment des Friedens im Ersten Weltkrieg 1914 bis 1917," *Geschichte in Wissenschaft und Unterricht*, XIII 1962, 465–522, supplements Fischer's book, which centers upon German war aims, insofar as it makes clear that the extreme annexationist aims on both sides made it practically impossible to negotiate a peace of mutual moderation. It should

The suggestive title of the book, which may have been the publisher's contribution in order to heighten the book's appeal, is misleading. It creates the impression that in the First World War Germany tried to subjugate the world. This distorts the meaning of the book. Fischer wanted to show that in the First World War Germany tried to change her status from that of a Great Power to that of a World Power by becoming equal to the existing three World Powers—the British Empire, Russia, and the United States. This goal might have been achieved by realizing the idea of a broadened Mitteleuropa or by ruling an economic area (p. 460) extending from Antwerp to Brest-Litovsk (or Rostov) and from Riga (or Reval) to Salonica and Constanza (if not Baghdad and Suez). Also, colonies and bases overseas as a consequence of and supplementary to the extension of power in Europe popped up in discussions over war aims.

It cannot be concealed that the composition of the work as a whole, its chronological division into three main parts, "1914–1916," "1917," and "1918," is not entirely satisfactory. The content of the book defies such a chronological scheme. One could think of periodizations within the course of the war derived from certain topics, but thematic synchronizations of events within different regions are divided according to years. The book would have been more compact, penetrating, and impressive if the author had followed the development of the main themes throughout the entire duration of the war, without chronological breaks. In this connection, the lack of a topical index is regrettable. It is, for instance, very difficult to find a very informative survey of the cost of German propaganda and special expeditions during the war (hidden on p. 176 in note 27). Often, cross-references are missing (for instance, in dealing with the great conferences on war aims at Spa early in July 1918, pp. 836–838, there is a suggestion to see pp. 703–704 but not vice versa). The chronological scheme of the work makes it rather difficult (in spite of the detailed table of contents) to obtain quick information on certain topics (for instance, on Germany's Flemish policy, pp. 120, 335–339, and 577–

---

be realized, however, that the German aims were often more "realistic" in the sense that they were based on the reality of German occupation of coveted territories, while realization of the war aims of the enemies seemed a long way off until the last months of the war.

586, or on the development of the war policy of the German navy, pp. 410–411, 464–466, and 789–791).[7]

It is impossible in a short resume to give an adequate idea of the variety of documents used by the author. But it also seems unnecessary, for in the future whoever writes or speaks on Germany's war aims in the First World War will have to pay careful attention to the book. The relations between Germany and her allies are touched upon only so far as it is of immediate significance for an understanding of Germany's war aims, for instance, by dealing with German-Austrian negotiations about the future of Poland. Not a word is said about Austrian colonial propaganda during the war. Fischer is convincing in pointing out that the best Austria-Hungary could do in the late summer of 1917 was to fight for the *status quo;* taking this into account, Germany had to develop a formula which made the former German war aims no longer appear directly annexationist, but envisaged indirect rule over spheres of influence based on economic and military agreements, without, however, sacrificing substantial gains (p. 537). From Fischer's narrative, it becomes clear that Germany's aim to keep Valona and Constanza and her plans regarding the Crimea and the Caucasus made deep inroads into her allies' spheres of interest and made it questionable whether the war alliance would survive in peacetime. It could almost be said that Germany pursued aims

---

7. Persons are sometimes mentioned at random with no explanation of their role for the nonspecialist; this is true, for instance, for the "Haniel-McCormick" peace move in August 1918 (p. 839). There is no hint concerning the position of the American negotiator (his name is omitted in the index of names) from which the significance of the diplomatic step could be judged. (This peace move is discussed by Klaus Schwabe in his article, "Die amerikanische und die deutsche Geheimdiplomatie und das Problem eines Verständigungsfriedens im Jahre 1918," *Vierteljahrshefte für Zeitgeschichte,* XIX, No. 1 [January 1971], 6–9.)

On the basis of a German diplomatic report from Stockholm, Fischer did not question the strange news of a proclamation allegedly directed by the Czar at the beginning of the war "To my beloved Jews." This proclamation must be classed as an invention: the origin of the rumor which circulated widely in August and September 1914 (see, for instance, *Jüdische Rundschau,* August 14, 1914; and J. Kreppel, *Juden und Judentum von heute* [Zürich, 1925], 169–170) is not clear. It might be assumed that it was the work of Entente circles in order to gain the sympathies of American Jewry, which was critical of the cooperation between the Western democracies and autocratic Czarism. (See also Egmont Zechlin, *Die deutsche Politik und die Juden im Ersten Weltkrieg* [Göttingen, 1969], 114, note 58.)

directed equally against her foes and her friends.[8]

According to Fischer's second chapter, "Germany and the Outbreak of the World War," Germany has to bear a greater share of responsibility for the outbreak of the war than usually admitted in German historical literature. Unjustifiably limited use of available sources has exposed this chapter especially to violent criticism. While Bethmann Hollweg was usually reproached for diplomatic failure in the July crisis due to illusions and lack of perspicacity, Fischer accused him of a *dolus*. But it must be stressed that Fischer did not make use of the customary arguments and alleged "proofs" of earlier advocates of Germany's "war guilt": writings of Heinrich Kanner, the Eisner documents, Prince Lichnowsky's memorandum, "My London Mission, 1912–1914," or a frequently cited letter of W. Muehlon, a member of the Krupp directorate before 1914. Fischer's dealing with the July crisis and the end of his second chapter were disappointing to all those who believed that discussion of the war-guilt question in the 1920s and Ludwig Dehio's analysis of the foreign policy of Wilhelminian Germany (which he repeated in his exemplary review of Fischer's book in *Der Monat,* February 1962, pp. 65–69) [9] had produced a deeper understanding of the causes of the First World War and had relegated to the background a criminalistic approach to the last weeks before the outbreak of the war. Although Fischer spoke out against isolating the events of July 1914 from the general framework of German foreign policy since the turn of the century, his narrative of the last week of July 1914 made audible again the strokes of the clock before the outbreak of the war. His critics have to meet his challenge in trying to refute his contention that Bethmann Hollweg, in complete self-deception over British policy, had decided to run the risk of war by humiliating Russia, a conviction which is an affront to the conception that all the Powers had slid or stumbled simultaneously into the war.[10]

---

8. Wilhelm van Kampen in his review of Fischer's book in *Das Parlament,* No. 29, July 18, 1962, intimates that Fischer's treatment of Turkey as a German "war aim" cannot be upheld.

9. See also Ludwig Dehio, "Kriegsziele im Ersten Weltkrieg," *Der Monat* (July 1962), 96.

10. Fischer's second chapter, on the outbreak of the war, became the target of Ritter's article, "Eine neue Kriegsschuldthese?" *Historische Zeitschrift,*

If German historians had taken more seriously certain un-orthodox findings of F. I. Notovich,[11] instead of disregarding the polemical and offensive argumentation of the Soviet author, they might have been more tolerant and more understanding toward Fischer's effort to produce conclusions of his own which were at variance with those of other scholars who had gone over the same documentation.[12]

Efforts have been made to declare the often carelessly straight-forward, temperamental marginal notes of the German Emperor as essentially unimportant for the conduct of affairs and hence-forth for the course and for an understanding of the foreign policy of imperial Germany. Histories of the war period show the stereo-type of a weak emperor who completely failed in his task to mediate between the civil government and the Supreme Command. This picture must be amended, since Fischer has clearly shown that the differences between the civil government and the Supreme Com-mand were often merely quantitative, and in method rather than in substance, as far as war aims were concerned. Before the publication of Fischer's book it was not known to what extent the thoughts and actions of those who took part in discussions on war aims, the

---

CXCIII (1962), 648–668. This article is moderate compared with his harsh con-demnation of Fischer's book in a newspaper article (see below, note 29).

In this connection, attention might be called to Siegfried A. Kähler's refu-tation of modern historical legends, such as Germany's sole responsibility for the outbreak of the First World War, in his *Studien zur deutschen Geschichte des 19. und 20. Jahrhunderts. Aufsätze und Vorträge* (Göttingen, 1961), 309–314.

11. In his contribution, "Fashistskaia istoriografiia o 'vinovnikakh mirovoi voiny'," in the symposium *Protiv fashistskoi fal'sifikatsii istorii* (Moscow, 1939).

12. By applying the methods of content analysis, three staff members of the Stanford University Project on International Conflict and Integration (Dina A. Zinner, Robert C. North, and Howard E. Koch), have recently come up with a new explanation of the outbreak of the First World War, which differs from the traditional yardsticks in forming historical judgments, and which has been disregarded in Germany, at least in historical literature. In 13 pages, "Capability, Threat, and the Outbreak of War," in *International Politics and Foreign Policy. A Reader in Research and Theory*, James N. Rosenau, ed. (The Free Press of Glencoe, 1961), 469–482, the result of a study of about 3,000 documents from the weeks between the plot of Sarajevo and the outbreak of the war is described. Like Fischer (p. 92), the scholars make use in their research of the Emperor's marginal notes to a telegram from St. Petersburg from Count Pourtalès, dated July 30, 1914, illustrating that at the end of July Germany distinctly reacted to ideas of enmity and to threats and did not act with cool rationalization. The method used by the team leaves little room for the individual responsibility of the historical personality.

Emperor, the Supreme Command, the Navy, the civil government (especially the Foreign Ministry and ministries of the Reich and Prussia), the several rulers of federal states, influential industrialists, and the parties of the Right were on the same level. Fischer is right in citing numerous utterances of the Emperor which in their spontaneity often offer a refreshing comment on simultaneous complicated diplomatic formulas and which remove the curtain from concealments.

Although for the prewar period Fischer often does not make sufficiently clear distinctions among advocates of German world power, and he reduces the wartime literature promoting German annexations in the East almost to a catalog of names (pp. 346–347), one feature clearly emerges: during an initial period, patriotic excitement engulfed the German people like a wave, and spokesmen of German public opinion made claims which they later disavowed under the sobering effect of the war situation and eventual possibilities of peace.[13] With the progress of time and often competing with each other, considerations and concrete proposals of representatives of agriculture (settlement plans), industrialists, and bankers came to the fore. We must recognize as a lasting and irrefutable result of Fischer's research (which only scratches the surface) that the role of the German economy and the influences which it tried to exercise or actually exercised on German policy during the First World War have been elevated to a research topic of first rank dealing with claims in the West and East and with demands for German colonies. Fischer's concise survey (pp. 711–725) of the conflict between state economic and private interests in the Ukrainian economic sphere [14] and of considerations of German big industry and of big banking houses indicates that monographs on German economic interests in the European East in peacetime and on preparations of postwar economic penetration and rule are a

---

13. See the letter from Friedrich Meinecke to Erwin Hölzle of January 13, 1947: "The idea of power [*Machtgedanke*], the hypertrophy of which we have experienced with horror, did once pervade all of us—though in a different degree—excessively. I myself have slowly, but since the First World War resolutely and consciously, overcome it as far as historical insight demanded it" (Meinecke, *Ausgewählter Briefwechsel* in *Werke*, VI, 267).

14. See Peter Borowsky, *Deutsche Ukrainepolitik 1918 mit besonderer Berücksichtigung der Wirtschaftsfragen* (Lübeck, 1970).

great necessity. It would be a pity if such themes, which are ready-made for publicistic exploitation, became a monopoly of the foes of the "bourgeois" order of society.

Fischer made clear the extent to which interests of the German economy determined German war aims, a topic already ably illuminated by the work of G. Gratz and R. Schüller, *Die äussere Wirtschaftspolitik Österreich-Ungarns. Mitteleuropäische Pläne* (Vienna, 1925).[15] In view of the fact that in the main body of his work Fischer stresses the intention to penetrate and exploit economically the territories in the German sphere of power, it is strange and surprising that the initial chapter of the book dealing with German economic interests in these areas before the war provides a colorless, vague, and unsubstantiated picture. In a cursory view (p. 35), Fischer mentions that by substantial investments Upper-Silesian industry had gained control of Polish mines and Polish iron "up to Radom," that German heavy industry won a foothold in the Ukrainian deposits of raw materials of Krivo Rog and Ciatury (Thyssen interests in the metals of the Don territory and the manganese of the Caucasus), and that German banks envisaging armament deals developed links to Russian banks; and he also mentions strong German economic interests in Rumania. But figures and indications of sources are missing, in spite of the fact that there are available excellent Russian works by N. Vanag, I. F. Gindin, A. L. Sidorov, and others, especially for foreign capital in Russia in the prewar period.[16]

The scattered information about the interests and wishes of the German iron industry in the East (pp. 117, 321, 633–635, 713, 720, 736) is no substitute for the missing chapter conveying basic information. Likewise, in spite of information in the section "Longwy-Briey: Hauptziel der deutschen Schwerindustrie," pp. 316–319, the book lacks a substantial chapter on German investments and industrial interests in France and Belgium as a German counterpart to the admirable description given in the chapter "The Western Industrialists and Their War Aims," in Hans Gatzke's

---

15. Not used by Fischer.
16. Recent literature is listed in the article by K. N. Tarnovskii, "K itogam izucheniia monopolisticheskogo kapitalizma v Rossii," *Sovetskaia istoricheskaia nauka ot XX k XXII s'ezdu KPSS* (Moscow, 1962), 294–330.

Germany's Drive to the West, written without access to the German documents.

From Fischer's work, several conclusions can be drawn which illuminate the difficulties involved in the study of contemporary diplomatic history.

1. Even for the limited period of the four years of the First World War, the mass of German diplomatic documents is overwhelming. The amount of work done by Fischer in coping with the material, in addition to his regular duties as a university teacher, must be admired and respected. The fact that Fischer expresses thanks to two assistants, not only for work in the archives but also (and this is significant) "in exploiting the large masses of material," shows that he had undertaken a task which no single researcher could fulfill. Since delineations in the cooperation are not made clear, Fischer must also take responsibility for any shortcomings of his assistants; one of them, Imanuel Geiss, whose monograph about the Polish border strife, 1914–1918, was no less an original contribution than Fischer's book, has exposed himself to justified criticism about his manner of evaluating documents. It cannot be doubted that the few competent reviewers of Fischer's work include quite a number who have a better knowledge than the author of special issues, and likewise special studies can bring about changes of emphasis. The bibliography shows that the number of new German studies, especially published ones on questions of German internal and foreign policy during the First World War, is disappointingly small, notwithstanding the availability of large masses of documentary material for many years. It is strange that so far these sources have attracted only a few scholars. Nobody guessed their explosive force with regard to prevailing traditional views and honest convictions. Fischer's courage is the more praiseworthy, since he did not refrain from undertaking a comprehensive work, although previous work based on the documents was lacking for large parts of his narrative.

The large extracts from original papers are gratifying for professional historians, since even the best paraphrase can never be a full substitute for the original wording and because the documentation kept in German Democratic Republic archives is at present practically inaccessible to Western scholars. The question must be asked whether or not Fischer's picture is not too close to the files, reflecting in too one-sided and uniform a manner the viewpoints of certain offices and relegating too much to the background the variety of historical forces and the diversity of the motivations of the persons involved. To this must be added that Fischer's deliberate exclusion of the war aims of Germany's enemies and his cursory treatment of German internal developments during the war, which cannot be ignored in dealing with foreign policy, are undeniable weaknesses of the book and lay it open to criticism. Up to now, German scholarship has not produced an equal counterpart to Z. K. Eggert's well-documented, but one-sided, treatment of German domestic politics between August 1914 and October 1917.[17]

2. Fischer's work proves that a single scholar can no longer maintain complete command and a firm grasp of secondary literature on the First World War and deal with it, if desirable or necessary, critically. More than half of Fischer's book is devoted to questions of Eastern and Southeastern Europe and of the Near East. The historian specializing in East European history must voice regret that Fischer abstained from systematic use of relevant literature in the Slavic languages, although it must be admitted that it is often difficult to track it down bibliographically and to find it in German libraries. The chapter on German policy in the Caucasus would have profited from quoting Z. Avalov's monograph.[18] There is no allusion to the only monograph about the peace of Bucharest (1918).[19] Completely isolated are two Finnish titles (p. 674). A sentence where "conversations with Miljukov" in the summer of 1918 are mentioned (p. 769) lacks any precision; it is not noted that Miljukov's conversations with a representative of the German High Command in the Ukraine constituted one of the few anti-Bolshevik soundings concerning a total revision of the Brest-Litovsk Treaty, soundings about which we knew until now only from Russian sources.[20] In the section about the treaties of August 1918,

---

17. *Bor'ba klassov i partii v Germanii v gody mirovoi voiny* (Moscow, 1957).

18. *Nezavisimost' Gruzii v mezhdunarodnoi politike 1918–1921 g.g.* (Paris, 1924).

19. F. I. Notovich, *Bukharestskii mir 1918 g.* (Moscow, 1959).

20. Winfried Baumgardt, *Deutsche Ostpolitik 1918. Von Brest-Litowsk bis zum Ende des Ersten Weltkrieges* (Vienna and Munich, 1966), 136–139, deals with the Miljukov episode on the basis of Russian and German sources,

additional to the Brest-Litovsk Treaty (pp. 766–778), the publication of the simultaneously exchanged secret notes between Hintze and Joffe (*Europäische Gespräche,* IV [1926], pp. 148–153) is not mentioned. And it is surprising that the bibliography omits a spirited discussion in the columns of the *Historische Zeitschrift* which preceded the publication of Fischer's book and which all scholars on this subject must know.[21]

3. The author may have purposely risked the weaknesses of his book sketched above because his intention to present for the first time a comprehensive picture of Germany's war aims based on German documents was his overriding consideration. One of the reasons to salute the publication of the book is the fortunate fact that for a considerable time to come it will represent the last massive work in the field of recent German history for which the holdings of archives in both parts of divided Germany were used. Denying users from the West access to the German Democratic Republic archives means not only that checking Fischer's extracts from Potsdam and Merseburg materials will be very difficult but that there might also be very undesirable effects for future work on themes dealt with or intimated by Fischer.

To a certain degree, the book must serve as a substitute for comprehensive German documentation on the history of the First World War, which, though a desideratum of first order, cannot be hoped for within the foreseeable future. But just as the imminent publication of documents from the Political Archives of the German Foreign Ministry concerning peace efforts between August 1914 and the end of January 1917 [22] will illustrate a much-debated, very problematic complex of questions, Fischer should provide a volume of documents supplementing his work. It should include, for instance, the complete text of a memorandum on the Russian question written by Secretary of State Admiral von Hintze in August 1918, in

---

21. Fritz Fischer, "Deutsche Kriegsziele, Revolutionierung und Separatfrieden im Osten 1914–1918," *Historische Zeitschrift,* CLXXXVIII (1959), 259–310; Hans Herzfeld. "Zur deutschen Politik im Ersten Weltkriege. Kontinuität oder permanente Krise?" ibid., CXCI (1960), 67–82; Fritz Fischer, "Kontinuität des Irrtums. Zum Problem der deutschen Kriegszielpolitik im Ersten Weltkrieg," ibid., 83–100.

22. *L'Allemagne et les problèmes de la paix pendant la première guerre mondiale,* André Scherer and Jacques Grunewald, eds., I: August 1914 to January 31, 1917 (Paris, 1962) [II: February 1 to November 7, 1917 (Paris, 1966)].

rebuttal to Ludendorff and Helfferich (analyzed by Fischer on pp. 762–765). This memorandum, hitherto unknown, has been put by Fischer on a par with Bethmann Hollweg's memorandum of September 1914, on which, as has been mentioned before, Fischer's judgment of Bethmann Hollweg's wartime policy is too rigorous. Fischer characterizes Hintze's memorandum as "the summit and crowning of the policy of the German Reich as far as realization of its expansionist aims in the East was concerned."

Against the repeated warnings of a reviewer that no more works should be written about the First World War based exclusively on sources of one side in the struggle,[23] it must be stressed that Fischer deserves great merit for his far-reaching use of German archival deposits. The hope must be expressed that the war aims of Germany's enemies be likewise elucidated by comparable works making similar broad use of the relevant wealth of "one-sided" documentation. Thus, conditions for dealing with First World War policy under "universal" historical aspects will be decidedly improved.[24] Thus, what has rightly been said about the Second World War applies also to the First: only a research institute could provide the opportunity for a comprehensive study of all extant documents and of interviews conducted with all those still alive who took part in formulating the war aims of their respective states.[25] The term "research institute" should not be pressed. What is envisaged are rather common tasks for research on the period of the First World War, comparable to the writing of the social and economic history of the First World War which was sponsored by the Carnegie Foundation. Today a coordinated program for the publication of important documents of the First World War, arranged according to themes, can be envisaged. On the German side, compilations of documents prepared by the Foreign Ministry for the Investigation Committee of the National Assembly, of which

---

23. Erwin Hölzle, *Das historisch-politische Buch* (March 1962) and *Die Welt,* July 7, 1962; the opposite view in *The Times Literary Supplement,* May 4, 1962, 323.

24. In this respect, the reviewer disagrees with Fritz Ernst, who wrote in his review of Fischer's book: "At a time when loud claims can be heard to write history in a supranational sense, the strictest national isolation has been applied to a theme which can be dealt with only supranationally" (*Stuttgarter Zeitung,* August 15, 1962).

25. Anne Armstrong, *Unconditional Surrender* (New Brunswick, 1961), x.

numbered copies were made accessible to the experts, could serve as starting points.

It will be up to Fritz Fischer to come to grips with his critics; he started with a letter to the editor of the Hamburg weekly, *Die Zeit* ("Die Schuld am Ersten Weltkrieg," November 17, 1961), and with an article, "Drang zum 'Platz an der Sonne'," in the daily *Die Welt* of July 7, 1962.

The interest of the public, an initially positive reaction of the press, and the utterly critical, often negative, and sometimes even hostile attitude of professional historians, who went so far as to declare the book pernicious or superfluous, explain why a detailed review seemed appropriate and necessary in a journal devoted to the history of Eastern Europe read by specialists, since Germany's war aims in the East are the book's main concern. With respect to the criticism leveled by colleagues of the author, this reviewer wishes to state the following:

From the outset, the author can hardly have doubted that his disregard of national biases, not to say taboos, especially in judging nationalism in Wilhelminian Germany, would result in misinterpretations and sharp condemnation.[26] But the rigidity of reactions to the book, negative as well as positive, and especially the vehemence in uttering displeasure, was surprising and indicated that Fischer had touched an overly sensitive nerve in passing judgments about vital questions of the nation. Noteworthy objections regarding the composition as a whole as well as details have been brought forward. But even those who remain unconvinced by Fischer's thesis of a continuity of German foreign policy from William II to Hitler, especially of his evaluation of the Bethmann Hollweg era, must recognize that the book has put historical knowledge about German wartime policy on a new basis. This achievement must neither be obscured nor underestimated, for there is no period

---

26. The range of interpretation in reviewing Fischer's book can be seen in the utterance of Erwin Hölzle, who speaks of the "beloved self-accusation" ("beliebte Selbstbeschuldigung") in *Das historisch-politische Buch,* (March 1962), No. 3, 69, while Fritz Ernst considered the trend of the book rather predetermined by the author's generally negative prejudice toward nationalism (see note 24, above).

of modern German history for which elucidation was more needed. Compared to the preceding period and in part to the postwar period as well, sufficient documentation has been lacking. Fischer has thrown merciless light on the period between 1914 and 1918, but some of his critics seemed almost to prefer the hitherto prevailing twilight, with its illusions, to embarrassing national self-criticism. There were those among Fischer's critics who disagreed with his basic attitude and with his method in dealing with innumerable themes and who were fearful of the influence the book might have on uncritical readers. Why, it must be asked, did they never attempt to present their views with the same penetration and profundity? The manner in which Egmont Zechlin [27] has taken up certain questions which Fischer dealt with in his book shows that Fischer's narrative is not to be considered the last word on many details and indicates that deeper insights can be gained.[28]

The reviewer very much regrets having to disagree with Professor Gerhard Ritter (Freiburg), a distinguished colleague, for whom he has the highest regard. A pitiless critic of Fischer's book,[29] he has written: "Whoever would correct all the misinterpretations would have to write an even larger and surely very tedious book." Nevertheless, this book should be written, since Ritter's indignation went so far as to include the worst reproach imaginable to a colleague in the free world. He charged that "there was no true effort made for historical understanding, for an interpretation of the sources without prejudice," but that "a preconceived basic thesis was to be cemented by quotations from sources." In the opinion of this reviewer, Fischer's interpretation of the sources cannot be set aside by a sovereign wave of the hand and the assertion that "someone who is sufficiently familiar with the documentary material used by Fischer does not need to examine every detail." The

---

27. "Friedensbestrebungen und Revolutionierungsversuche im Ersten Weltkrieg," *Aus Politik und Zeitgeschichte,* Beilage zum "Parlament," B 20/61; B 24/61; B 25/61; B 20/63; B 22/63.

28. Zechlin's article, "Die 'Zentralorganisation für einen dauernden Frieden' und die Mittelmächte," *Jahrbuch für internationales Recht,* XI (1962), 448–511 (Festschrift in honor of Rudolf Laun) also shows that bourgeois critical voices against annexationist tendencies must be taken more seriously, instead of summarily dismissing them (as Fischer does, p. 211) as "the opposition of a few bourgeois groups with pacifist inclination."

29. "Griff nach der Weltmacht?" *Lübecker Nachrichten,* May 20, 1962.

present reviewer holds the view that every detail needs reexamination in the laboratory of historical science. If this contention is denied, the impression could be created that a premise which does not allow minimal doubt is being made the starting point and that all opinions which differ from the prevailing one must *a limine* be regarded as wrong. It would be an offense against the conscience and the conscientiousness of the historian, who is bound and expected to reexamine the sources seriously, simply to accept as valid the premises of traditional views.

Ritter regards German imperialism before the war as a desire for recognition as an "equal partner" (*Gleichberechtigung*). Fischer takes more seriously certain outward appearances, actions, and utterances which were felt abroad as German imperialism. For the intent of Fischer's book, it is basically irrelevant whether or not an "aggressive and bellicose imperialism" of other nations also existed, but it cannot be denied that Fischer's exclusive concern with German imperialism has created the impression that he regards German imperialism as more damnable than any other. Some of Fischer's critics seemed especially angered by the fact that Fischer did not present German imperialism as a reaction to the imperialism of other nations in peace and war directed against Germany and imperiling her; this merely replaced Fischer's one-sidedness by another.

A notable and justifiable objection has been made by Golo Mann, who has pointed out that Fischer underestimated "events, decision-making, sentiments, pressures" which have left no record in documents and which were present on both sides and against each other.[30] He also thought that comparison, dialectics, and drama were missing in Fischer's book; these are features which belong to the art of the historian who is eager to go beyond establishing and linking facts. It must be assumed that Fischer obviously does not aspire to the laurels of a philosophically minded historian, but such self-limitation and self-moderation do not in any way diminish the significance of the work as a compendium of Germany's world war policy, even if the author's viewpoints for selecting and organizing the materials as yardsticks remain controversial.

---

30. *Neue Züricher Zeitung*, April 28, 1962.

It is an unintended result (or merit) of the book that it reveals the limits set for a single historian in analytical penetration of the material on the First World War and likewise makes clear the limitations inherent in the quantity and the dispersion of the material. The book has opened up new avenues in the discussion of the First World War; in particular, "Brest-Litovsk" is no longer a "forgotten peace." [31] The problems posed by this peace, which Theodor Schieder pointed out at the twentieth anniversary of its conclusion,[32] have only now, almost a quarter of a century later, been taken up again by Werner Hahlweg [33] and Fritz Fischer.

---

31. J. Wheeler-Bennett, *Brest-Litovsk. The Forgotten Peace* (London, 1938) (1956, 1963).

32. *Osteuropa*, XIII, No. 5 (February 1938), 375–377.

33. *Der Diktatfrieden von Brest-Litowsk 1918 und die bolschewistische Weltrevolution* (Münster, 1960).

VIII

The Accessibility of Source Materials Illuminating the History of German Foreign Policy.

THE PUBLICATION OF DOCUMENTS OF THE GERMAN FOREIGN MINISTRY AFTER BOTH WORLD WARS: A COMPARISON OF METHODS

IN 1915, THE FIRST YEAR of the First World War, Justus Hashagen published a pamphlet, *Das Studium der Zeitgeschichte,* in Bonn. Hashagen had a long and distinguished career as Professor of Modern History at the University of Hamburg; he died in November 1961 at the age of 84. In this work, he took German historians (who were otherwise wont to edit anything they touched) to task for their indifference toward editing contemporary materials. He addressed himself particularly to the sloppy manner in which diplomatic papers of the recent past, i.e., on the negotiations which preceded the outbreak of war in 1914, had been published. From a scholar's point of view, the gross sin of omission, the failure of the editors of these collections to explain the drafting of the papers and to indicate exactly the times at which they were sent and received, made it practically impossible to arrange in

---

This paper consists of part of an address on the "Source Materials on the Foreign Policy of the Hitler period" ("Die Quellen zur Aussenpolitik der Hitlerzeit"), given on the Dies Academicus (December 6, 1961) at the University of Bonn. It was originally published in *Die Welt als Geschichte,* XXII (1962), 204–219.

chronological order the papers published on the outbreak of war. Yet, correct chronological arrangement was an indispensable prerequisite for determining causal relationships, equally important from the historical and the political point of view.

The historians of 1914 will have to be defended against Hashagen's reproach, for the "color books" (*Farbbücher*)—epitomized by an enterprising publisher in a collection called "rainbow books" —were not the work of historians, but rather of ministerial officials, for whom political purposes, not historical precision, were the leading concerns. The aim and object, then, of these publications was to vindicate one's own actions and to put the enemy in the wrong. They were weapons in the political struggle, raw material for publicists to exploit; and, insofar as historians used them, not a few essays give more evidence of the patriotism and blind faith of their authors than of a critical attitude toward the *Farbbücher*, from which one could indeed only expect a colored presentation of the events treated.

In his work, Hashagen defined contemporary history (*Zeitgeschichte*) as history insofar as it sheds light on the current situation. Many of the things that he designated as desiderata almost fifty years ago have since been realized in teaching and research at German universities. Hashagen belongs among the godfathers of the teaching of recent history at the German university, along with Theodor Schiemann and Otto Hoetzsch.

Historians were, so to say, first discovered by the German Foreign Ministry during the First World War, when historical and political support were needed for the policies of the Reich Government: in the period of the Armistice, prior to the Peace Conference, experts were commissioned to prepare reports—Friedrich Meinecke on the question of the western border and Dietrich Schäfer on the nationalities problem in the German East; Hans Delbrück was called to Versailles to refute the note of the Allies on the war guilt; and when the peace was concluded, preparation of the monumental publication of documents for the period 1871 to 1914 was placed in the hands of historians.

Today, historians have long since obtained citizenship in the German Foreign Ministry as well as in the foreign offices of other nations, and the custodians of political archives are generally on the best of terms with the institution's historical experts (if these functions are not some kind of "personal union" exercised by the same persons, as in the German Foreign Ministry). The great publications of documents between the World Wars and after the Second World War have created an entirely new type of modern historian: the editor of modern documentation, who, because of the mass of source material to be sifted, is a member of a work team rather than the lone editor, who typically has edited medieval sources. He, of course, ordinarily has close connections on administrative and organizational matters with the agency in whose archives he is working and, as supreme proof of the agency's confidence in him, he has even been guaranteed unqualified independence and freedom from any kind of official interference in exploring the archives and in publishing documents.

The scholarly independence of the editors in selecting documents was underscored by appointing nationally known historians of international reputation as the heads of these projects, men, who, in signing as responsible editors, assumed personal responsibility before their contemporaries and posterity. One can gauge the importance which the governments attached to the objective and workmanlike execution of the publication of documents after the First World War from the fact that in Germany Johannes Lepsius, Albrecht Mendelssohn Bartholdy, and Friedrich Thimme were chosen, in Austria Konrad Bittner and Hans Übersberger, and in England George Peabody Gooch and Harold Temperley. This meant also recognition of the scholarly achievement, the objectivity, and the integrity of the scholars chosen for the task.

Anyone who is familiar with the great publications of documents on the history of the modern period is staggered by the enormous amount of painstaking editorial work evidenced by each volume. Yet it is of decisive importance that the publication of every single document be preceded by a thorough examination of both its significance in a larger context and its own relative weight.

The post-World War I publication of Foreign Ministry documents represented a "novum" [1] in the history of international rela-

---

1. Veit Valentin, "Bismarck und Österreich," *Neues Wiener Tageblatt,* June 2, 1922.

tions, for the great lines as well as the details of the policies of one of the Great Powers were revealed for the first time. The series *Die grosse Politik der europäischen Kabinette 1871–1914,* the so-called *Grosse Politik,* was conceived under an unlucky star, in that a primarily political motive, the politically necessary opposition to the war-guilt paragraph (Article 231 of the Treaty of Versailles), gave impetus to its publication and determined its character as an instrument for the rehabilitation of the German people by removing from them the burden of guilt for the war.[2] Thus, the editor-in-chief, Friedrich Thimme, who considered the publication of the documents a German national undertaking of the noblest order, strove unremittingly to adhere to the fundamental principles of unconditional truthfulness, openness, and impartiality, to which the editors had been bound upon conferral of the commission, without losing sight of the interests of German foreign policy in the 1920s.

Thimme, an ardent patriot, stated in a memorandum in May 1925 [3] that it was more and more his earnest aspiration to serve with the publication of the documents not only historical truth but also, as much as possible, the interests of his country's foreign policy. Indeed, he admitted that he subscribed to the view that it would not be in the interest of Germany's foreign policy if her own statesmen were unnecessarily compromised by publication of the documents.

---

2. Because of the propagandistic intent of the series, even naming it raised considerable problems. In lengthy deliberations, its editors sought an alluring title, one capable of exercising an inducement to buy it both at home and abroad. Such a title was thought to have been found in *Die europäische Geheimpolitik 1871 bis 1914 nach den deutschen Archiven,* because one could hear in it an echo of Wilson's condemnation of secret diplomacy and because it contained a challenge to the enemy nations to follow Germany's example and open their secret archives. A memorandum of Department IX D, dated May 7, 1921, stated: "The great document publication is not being prepared so that its volumes, which cost one and a half million marks, might only gather dust in archives or be studied by isolated historians with effects which will be apparent only after years" (Politisches Archiv des Auswärtigen Amtes, *Akten betr. Herausgabe der amtlichen Dokumente zur Vorgeschichte des Krieges,* I: "Vom Januar 1921 bis 30. Juni 1922").

3. Memorandum of Dr. Thimme on the contents of the series being published on May 10 (Fourth Series, Second Half, Volumes 22–25), submitted by Herr Stieve on May 4, 1925 (Auswärtiges Amt, *Nachlass Stresemann,* Volume 350): "Aus dem Nachlass Stresemann von Konsul Bernhard dem Auswärtigen Amt übergebene Schriftstücke, 1924–1930" (7414 H 175, 484–487).

The editors of the documents, Thimme explained, clung tenaciously to the principle that nothing was to be published which might give offense to neutral nations or statesmen. In the selection of documentary material and in the footnoting they were as circumspect as possible with regard to those foreign statesmen who, although on the enemy side, were not outspoken Germanophobes and who might still be of importance for shaping relations between their countries and Germany in the future.

As shown in the foregoing, the work has many aspects which its users do not exactly have to consider departures from the publicly proclaimed supreme principle of unqualified openness, but which nevertheless constitute a substantial self-restriction in the presentation of documents. We should, however, be wary of drawing hasty conclusions. It is only through a fortunate accident, the discovery of Thimme's memorandum among Stresemann's secret papers, that we are in a position to see and judge the dilemma of the editor of *one* of a number of national document publications. That the editors of the French documentary work, *Les Documents diplomatiques français,* similarly saw themselves confronted with arguments demanding restrictions in publishing certain documents, due to the alleged national interest invoked by former participants in negotiations, emerges from 1930 correspondence cited in the *Revue Historique* between Ambassador Maurice Paléologue and former President Poincaré.[4] Yet Thimme's acknowledgement of the compromises due to political considerations, with regard to the political aim of publication, cannot remain without future effect on the world's confidence in the unconditional reliability of the published material, especially since it has become clear that the firm denial of requests to use certain files was related to the fear that serious criticism might be leveled at the selection of documents for the *Grosse Politik* and that the publication's effectiveness might thus be diminished.[5] We cannot suppress our feeling that certain features of international politics which might have been obscured would have

4. Pierre Renouvin, "Les Documents diplomatiques français 1871–1914," *Revue Historique,* CCXXVI (1961), 148–152.
5. See Norman Rich and M. H. Fisher, eds., *The Holstein Papers* (Cambridge, England, 1955), I, 8, note 1, concerning the German selection of documents on the acquisition of Kiaochow.

emerged rather clearly had there been less solicitude for the reputations of German and foreign statesmen. Here, hitherto unasked questions arise of a critical comparison of the published documents with the original files. In 1924, Thimme wrote that as a politician he could not accept the view that the publication of the documents existed for the study of contemporary history as an end in itself: "The political end, to which the documents also owe their existence, stands higher. And whenever contemporary documents are being published . . . , one does well to suspect political ends." [6]

In 1926, Thimme's coeditor, Professor Mendelssohn Bartholdy, countered certain objections as "minor misunderstandings concerning a major publication." He wrote at the time: "We knew that we had to turn this work out in an unmanageable form. . . . For our document collection is indeed intended to serve the future, not the past." [7] Therein lies as well an acknowledgment of the primarily political character of the publication. It must be stressed, however, that the publication's deficiencies are minor in comparison with its great merit.

The document publication, by shedding light on German foreign policy since the foundation of the Reich, transformed the question of war guilt into one on the causes of the war and thus effected a revolution in the study of recent history. Above all, it determined the direction American research took in the 1920s, and it is due primarily to American historians that the psychological, emotional argument, on which Gemany's defamation was based, has been relegated to the background in favor of efforts to arrive at a more objective causal determination in the discussion of the war's origins.

The editors of the *Grosse Politik* and Germany's champions in the war-guilt question were justified in seeing a major moral and political victory in the fact that Germany's monumental effort to vindicate with her own documents German policy from 1871 to 1914 led the governments of Germany's major war enemies to further the knowledge of the origins of the World War through simi-

---

6. Friedrich Thimme, "Die Aktenpublikation des Auswärtigen Amts und ihre Gegner," *Archiv für Politik und Geschichte,* II (1924), 475.

7. "Kleine Missverständnisse über eine grosse Publikation," *Europäische Gespräche,* IV, No. 7 (July 1926), 387.

lar publications of documents. If Germany's former enemies were not to yield to an interpretation of the events in recent diplomatic history decisively influenced by the German document publication (whereby its arrangement of the documents according to topics promoted the impression of a tendentious compilation),[8] then they had to set against the German publication something of similar character and value. The two series, *British Documents on the Origin of the War, 1898–1914* and *Documents diplomatiques français, 1871–1914,* owe their existence to a certain "pressure to publish" ("Publikationszwang") [9] in order to keep Germany's head start in the publication of documents from giving her a monopoly throughout the world in shaping opinion on the origins of the war. In this context, Bernhard Schwertfeger has written of an intellectual "World War of documents" after the World War itself.[10]

The foreign document publications were important for the critical evaluation of the "Grosse Politik," for the reflection of the actions and motivations of German foreign policy in foreign diplomatic reports provided a certain amount of control material against which the completeness and objectivity of the German picture could be measured. Moreover, it must be remembered that in recent decades major portions of the archives of the foreign ministries of Belgium, Czechoslovakia, Poland, Yugoslavia, and France have been temporarily in German possession as captured documents. Under certain circumstances, elucidation of international relations by foreign diplomatic observers could prove more effective than efforts at self-defense, especially when the observer allowed one to presuppose an anti-German bias. We must view in this propagandistic light, then, German publications in both World Wars from Belgian, Czech, and Polish diplomatic archives, as well as the publication of the correspondence of Russian statesmen, such as Izvol'skii and Benckendorff, which was delivered to the Germans by the Russian emigration.[11]

---

8. Bernhard Schwertfeger, "Das grosse Aktenwerk des Auswärtigen Amtes und die Geschichtsforschung," *Kriegsgeschichte und Wehrpolitik. Vorträge und Aufsätze* (Potsdam, 1938), 292.

9. Ibid., 284, 293.

10. Ibid., 310.

11. That Bismarck did not scorn to use documents captured in the Franco-Prussian War had been totally forgotten in Germany until Article 245 of the

Because it had been linked with the question of reparations, in the 1920s the question of war guilt was eminently a political question.[12] As the scholarly examination of the causes of the war advanced, the German parties on the Right urged steadily that the question of war guilt be taken up with Germany's former enemies on an official level. Indeed, as early as 1919, the German Government had asked for the establishment of a neutral court to examine the charge of Germany's war guilt.[13]

It was in keeping with the political aim of the document publication that in 1924 the German Government contemplated a diplomatic action in which the question of revising the Treaty of Versailles would be raised by a call for reconsideration of the question of war guilt from the point of view of the document publication. In August 1924 Chancellor Marx confidentially apprised the British prime minister, Ramsay Macdonald, that once the document publication was completed Germany intended to challenge the Allies to convene an international court of arbitration to inquire into the causes of the war and to hand down an impartial decision.[14] The English statesman advised strongly against such a step, for which public opinion in the lands of Germany's former enemies was not yet ripe. He wrote Marx:

> I should strongly advise you, not to raise this question at present.
> It has now become a matter for the historian. The life of nations
> goes on in defiance of these hasty verdicts and, in the end, the truth
> is discovered and everybody agrees to forget falsehoods and errors.
> Were I in your position, I should content myself and wait for the
> verdict.

Treaty of Versailles called for the return of diplomatic correspondence discovered in November 1870 at Cerçay Castle and taken from there.

12. See Hajo Holborn, *Kriegsschuld und Reparationen auf der Pariser Friedenskonferenz von 1919* [Grundfragen der internationalen Politik, No. 3] (Leipzig, 1932) (Lectures of the Carnegie Chair of Foreign Policy and History at the Deutsche Hochschule für Politik).

13. Private organizations such as Norway's Neutral Commission for the Investigation of War Guilt and the Dutch Committee to Study the Causes of the War could be considered preliminary stages in the establishment of an international investigating committee. The whole "guilt-question" complex warrants an exhaustive presentation from the documents of the Foreign Ministry.

14. Politisches Archiv des Auswärtigen Amtes, Büro Staatssekretär. *Akten betr. Kriegsschuldfrage,* I: "August 1924 bis Oktober 1926," 4519 H/E 134 073 (letter of August 16, 1924) and E 134 077 (Macdonald's reply of August 22).

Macdonald's reply made clear the limits of the direct use of a document publication like the "Grosse Politik" for political aims.

It must have come as a shock to the editors of the German documents at the beginning of 1925 when their work met with very sharp criticism from the Italians, apparently due to distorted announcements in the press. On February 16, 1925, the ambassador at the Quirinal, von Neurath, sent a telegram to Stresemann personally, in which he commented as follows on the publication of documents pertaining to Italy:

> I must point out with all due emphasis that our document publication in its present form is likely not only to spoil the improving mood in Italy but also to provide our enemies with an instrument for assailing us. If we persist in insulting and compromising foreign sovereigns and statesmen still alive by tactless and indiscreet publication of past reports, directives, and comments, then we ought not to be surprised if we fail to regain the sympathies of the world.
>
> Mussolini spoke to me last evening . . . and expressed his amazement that such publications, whose damaging effect on current and future German politics was obvious, should have been allowed by responsible organs of the Reich . . . .

Then followed the lapidary sentence:

> The events of the period presently being published (the first decade of this century) are still of too recent vintage to allow the publication of the pertinent documents according to the criteria of historical research alone. . . .[15]

In 1924 the prime minister said: "It has now become a matter for the historian." The German diplomat in 1925 was of a different opinion: the prewar period was too actual, too near to the present for documents to be published according to the criteria of historical research alone.

Stresemann instructed the ambassador to explain, when the opportunity arose, that the publication of prewar documents was an act of self-defense on the part of the German people against the

---

15. Ibid., 4519 H/E 134 136–7.

unheard-of charge of sole responsibility for the World War, an attempt to lay Germany's case before the public because the Entente Powers had disregarded her repeated requests for an inquiry by an impartial tribunal into the causes of the war. As far as the Italian complaint in particular was concerned, the foreign minister pointed out that all volumes of the document publication were examined by a former diplomat before they were printed in order to avoid any unnecessary offense to a statesman still alive, and said that he would ensure in the future that the parts pertaining to Italy would be given special attention.[16]

When one considers the many political precautions taken from the beginning to safeguard the German document publication of the 1920s, von Neurath's statement must have been alarming, if not to a certain extent disheartening.

Since the end of the 1920s, the Soviet Union has also contributed to the foundations of our knowledge of history. The Russian document publication on the origins and history of the First World War, entitled *Die internationalen Beziehungen im Zeitalter des Imperialismus, 1878–1917,* of which only the volumes covering the period immediately prior to the war and the first two years of the war have appeared, does not differ fundamentally from the general kind of politico-diplomatic documentation.[17] Economic reports receive somewhat greater attention than in the publications of the bourgeois countries. Upon seizing power, the Bolsheviks used the publication of documents with consummate skill to denounce the war as imperialistic. By revealing secret war-aims agreements, they made bitter enemies of the Entente governments. Understandably, the Soviet document publication was also conceived, as is evident in its title, as an indictment of the imperialist Powers.

From the beginning of the Second World War, both sides systematically confiscated documentary material for use in intelligence and propaganda. Both sides organized operational detachments whose primary function was to obtain the enemy's foreign policy documentation. The German Foreign Ministry and military

---

16. Ibid., 4519 H/E 134 140 (Stresemann to von Neurath, February 18, 1925).

17. Otto Hoetzsch, "Die russische Aktenpublikation zur Vorgeschichte des Weltkriegs," *Zeitschrift für osteuropäische Geschichte,* V (1931), 348–376.

agencies conducted methodical searches for documents in occupied territories; great quantities of documents were assembled at various collection points: "East" in Danzig-Oliva, "Central" in Berlin-Wannsee, "Southeast" in Vienna, and "South" in Munich (the first three were captured by the Russians). In order to exploit the captured diplomatic documents, the Foreign Ministry created an archive commission. Yet German historical scholarship drew only minimal profit from the masses of documents temporarily in German possession.[18] What did not go up in flames in bomb attacks or were not otherwise destroyed, were returned to the original owners at the end of the war.

But despite efforts to safeguard, hide, or destroy them, unimaginable quantities of *German* documents, far in excess of the number Germany had confiscated, found their way into the hands of Germany's enemies in the East and West. Among the most valuable and historically important of these were the files of the Political Archive of the Foreign Ministry. In the spring of 1945, the major part of the papers of the Foreign Ministry, weighing more than 300 tons, was discovered by the Americans and the British virtually unharmed at various evaluation centers in central Germany. Gaps in the Foreign Ministry papers captured in the West were due in part to accidents, in part to last-minute attempts to destroy papers to keep them from enemy hands, and in part to the fact that large files remained in areas occupied by the Russians.[19]

One of the most important discoveries of American and British search details was a crate containing notes by Minister Paul Otto Schmidt, the Chief Interpreter of the Foreign Ministry during the Hitler period, and a number of German microfilms, the substance of which proved on close examination to consist of nearly 10,000 pages from the war papers of the Reich's Foreign Minister. Since the summer of 1943 Ribbentrop had had filmed papers of the

18. Gerhard L. Weinberg, "Information on Documents Captured by the Germans before and during World War II," in *Guide to Captured German Documents* (War Documentation Project Study No. 1, 1952), 69–70; Erwin Hölzle, *Der Osten im Weltkrieg* (Leipzig, 1944).

19. See *Akten zur deutschen auswärtigen Politik 1918–1945*, Series D, I (1950), General Introduction, x. The files of the Paris embassy and the papers of the legations in Athens, Budapest, and Helsinki and of the general consulates in Milan and Toulouse are among the known war losses, but copies of numerous items have appeared in other recovered files.

Office of the Foreign Minister of the Reich (*Büro Reichsaussenminister*). He kept them with him in his special train for reference in case the files at the Foreign Ministry were destroyed. We can consider these microfilmed documents, the originals of which have disappeared, the most important part of Ribbentrop's working papers of the war period to 1943. Nowhere else can one find as many key documents on National Socialist foreign policy of the first war years compressed into such a small space; enlargements are now on file in the Political Archive of the Foreign Ministry. In all his vanity Ribbentrop would never have permitted himself to dream that his sole enduring merit would lie in his preserving a portion of the materials of his term of office for historical scholarship.

The most important discoveries of German documents from the period of the Second World War thus include: 1. Hitler's correspondence with foreign heads of state and statesmen, including the major part of his correspondence with Mussolini; 2. the notes of the chief interpreter, Minister Schmidt, on Hitler's and Ribbentrop's conversations with foreign heads of state and statesmen; 3. the most important correspondence with German missions abroad.[20]

After an odyssey which, between 1946 and 1948, led them from the collection point at Marburg Castle to Berlin-Tempelhof, then to Berlin-Lichterfelde, and then, in 1948, to the country seat Whaddon Hall in the county of Buckinghamshire, the documents of the Foreign Ministry since 1867 returned to Bonn three years ago [1958] to form the nucleus of the Political Archive of the German Foreign Ministry then being rebuilt.[21] The restitution of papers taken from Germany to England and America at the end of the war has been under way for many years and is approaching completion. The Soviet Zone, unfortunately, has shown itself superior to the Federal Republic in making propaganda on the restitution of documents: each time the Soviet Union, which carted off

20. See Paul Otto Schmidt, *Statist auf diplomatischer Bühne, 1923–1945* (Bonn, 1949); and *Staatsmänner und Diplomaten bei Hitler. Vertrauliche Aufzeichnungen über die Unterredungen mit Vertretern des Auslandes,* A. Hillgruber, ed. (Munich, 1967–1969), two volumes.

21. See Hans Philippi, "Das Politische Archiv des Auswärtigen Amtes. Rückführung und Übersicht über die Bestände," *Der Archivar,* XIII, No. 2–3 (July 1960), 199–218; Thomas E. Skidmore, "Survey of Unpublished Sources on the Central Government and Politics of the German Empire, 1871–1918," *American Historical Review,* LXV, No. 4 (July 1960), 851–852.

archives, libraries, and art treasures to an unknown extent, restores papers, the action is used to show "German-Soviet friendship." [22] On the other hand, the West German public hardly takes notice of the much more extensive restitutions from the United States and England. To be sure, the victorious enemy did not confiscate the source materials in recent German history with the intention of "saving" them.[23] Yet, only one who loses sight of the chaotic situation in Germany at the end of the war will find it difficult to acknowledge that without measures taken by the Allies to protect the documents, we should have to regret a still greater loss than actually occurred.

No one knows better, and no one regrets more, than the Director of the Political Archive of the Foreign Ministry that the files in his keeping constitute only a fraction of those in the former center for foreign policy documents. In 1957, even before the Soviets restored great numbers of papers, the *Übersicht der Bestände des Deutschen Zentralarchivs Potsdam* had listed holdings of nearly 61,500 volumes of papers of the Foreign Ministry from the years 1821–1945.[24]

The foregoing general orientation can give only a very approximate picture of the document situation which confronted, and still confronts, historians, particularly the international editorial commission of the series *Documents on German Foreign Policy, 1918–1945* and *Akten zur deutschen auswärtigen Politik 1918–1945*. From the examples cited, one can see the great difficulties with which scholarly editorial work and historiography from the documents have to contend in a divided Germany.

The Western Powers first examined and evaluated the captured documents from an intelligence standpoint in preparation for

---

22. Skidmore, 852 n.; Helmut Lötzke, "Bericht über die von der UdSSR an die DDR seit 1957 übergebenen Archivbestände," *Archivmitteilungen,* X, No. 1 (1960), 12–15; "Archivalische Quellen zur deutschen Aussenpolitik bis zum Ende des zweiten Weltkrieges," *Deutsche Aussenpolitik,* II, No. 10 (1957), 873–879.

23. Hans Rothfels, preface to *Hitlers zweites Buch,* edited by Gerhard L. Weinberg (*Quellen und Darstellungen zur Zeitgeschichte,* VII) (Stuttgart, 1961), 8.

24. It cited around 6,000 volumes for the Nachrichten- und Presse-Abteilung of 1914–1945 (Department of Intelligence and Publicity) and around 4,400 volumes for the legation (later embassy) in Peking, 1862–1945.

the Nürnberg Trials. Through these trials, the public in Germany and in the rest of the world first became aware of the extent and the political and historical importance of the documents. Between 1945 and 1948, 62,000 documents were registered in Nürnberg, including a great many items from the Political Archive of the Foreign Office. Robert M. W. Kempner said of the documentation assembled at Nürnberg: "The growing source book of history has been the backbone of the Nürnberg story"; [25] but, despite oft-encountered notions, the benefit which research into contemporary history has derived from the war trials has been slight. The reasons for this are various: only an infinitesimal fraction of the Nürnberg documentation has been published (unpublished trial documents, transcripts of hearings, and protocols are estimated to total some 2½ million pages); the documents were assembled with the juridical view of incriminating or exonerating defendants; the registers of official publications on the trials are, except for a few, thoroughly unsatisfactory, and the card indexing of the materials by German research institutes has only just now reached completion.

An editorial preface to Rudolf Holzhausen's first provisional survey of the sources available for research on the history of the Third Reich [26] pointed out that diplomatic and scholarly circles of the Western Powers were, after the war, aware of the responsibility which the confiscation of the Reich's archives brought with it. At an early stage, voices could be heard in America advocating that the Foreign Ministry documents be subjected to systematic scrutiny by historians. It was through the influence of historians working in Washington wartime agencies that the Department of State discussed with the Foreign Office in 1945–1946 the possibility that German diplomatic papers be examined by scholars with a view to preparing a publication from them. The champions of a publication of the diplomatic files of the Hitler period answered with an unqualified "yes" the question of whether or not these documents should be made accessible without restriction to historical research. Two considerations were decisive in this connection. First, the historians wanted to elucidate the diplomatic background of the

25. Fritz T. Epstein, "Zur Quellenkunde der neuesten Geschichte," *Vierteljahrshefte für Zeitgeschichte,* II (1954), 325.
26. "Die Quellen zur Geschichte des 'Dritten Reiches' von 1938 bis 1945," *Europa-Archiv,* IV, No. 21 (1949), 2585–2590.

prewar period, i.e., to gain secure documentary foundation for analysis of the years just preceding the outbreak of the Second World War. The second aim was didactic: they desired that the truth concerning Hitler's policies be brought to the attention of the German people, who had affirmed his foreign policy and had entrusted themselves to his leadership right up to the bitter end, and who had approved policies that, from the very beginning, not only took into account the eventual necessity of war for achieving their aims but resolutely steered a course toward war because they could not consider realizing their aims without threat of war or war itself.

We can consider the deliberations thus entered into as part of the spirited and controversial debate during and after the war on the so-called political reeducation of the German people. But just as the American reeducation program was transformed into an information program, so any didactic aims in the publication by American, English, and French scholars of the documents of the Hitler period (begun in 1948 and not yet completed) have become totally unimportant. What has remained, and what is being produced by experts, is a document publication for specialists, men who recognize that sources are never historical truth, but a means of finding the truth,[27] that, to use an expression of Hermann Oncken's,[28] the triumph of historical truth is at all times due to the exploitation of source materials. It will probably be imperative one day to consider making the most important papers in the document publication for the years 1918–1945 accessible to a larger public than the professional historians by presenting them in a more suitable form, as the abridged or popular edition of the *Grosse Politik,* which, under the title *Die auswärtige Politik des Deutschen Reiches 1871–1914,* presents in four volumes an extract of the fifty-four volumes of the original.

The history and achievement of the Inter-Allied Commission for the Publication of German Diplomatic Papers (1946–1958) have hitherto received little attention in Germany, and there are many mistaken notions concerning the commission. The project, which terminated officially at the end of 1958 (although the finish-

---

27. Michael Freund, *Die politische Meinung,* VI, No. 66 (November 1961), 92.
28. Hermann Oncken, *Die Rheinpolitik Napoleons III von 1863–1870 und der Ursprung des Krieges von 1870/71* (Stuttgart, 1926), I, x.

ing touches are still being put on five volumes of papers from the Hitler period), is without parallel in the history of large-scale document publication, as a successful experiment in international cooperation in the field of history, and as the first international publication project in the field of recent history.[29]

On December 13, 1946, a conference of the Foreign Office-State Department "German War Documents Project" in Berlin set down certain "observations" after four days of meetings. In various respects these observations modified the recommendations for the publication of German foreign policy papers of the period between the World Wars and of the Second World War which had been approved by historians and government representatives at an Anglo-American conference in London in June 1946. Together with the June recommendations, the "observations" served as the basis for the publication of the series *Documents on German Foreign Policy, 1918–1945—Akten zur deutschen auswärtigen Politik 1918–1945*. The December conference recommended the following arrangement for the proposed document publication:

VOLUMES

Series A:	1937–1941	4
B:	1942–1945	2
C:	1933–1937	4
D:	1924–1933	4
E:	1918–1924	4
F:	1914–1918	4
G:	1890–1914	2
H:	1871–1890	2
I:	1866–1871	2

The editors thus hoped to cover the period from 1918 to 1945 with a total of eighteen volumes. They proposed four further series

29. See Maurice Baumont, "The Publication of Documents of the German Ministry of Foreign Affairs" (lithographed), summary of a talk given at the conference "World War II in the West," held by the Netherlands State Institute for War Documentation, September 5–9, 1950, in Amsterdam; Margaret Lambert, "Source Materials Made Available to Historical Research as a Result of World War II," *International Affairs* (London), XXXV, No. 2 (April 1959), 188–196; Raymond J. Sontag, "The German Diplomatic Papers: Publication after Two World Wars," a paper presented at the annual meeting of the American Historical Association in Washington, D.C., on December 28, 1961: *American Historical Review*, LXVIII, No. 1 (October 1962), 57–68.

with a total of ten volumes: four volumes supplementing the *Grosse Politik,* two volumes covering the decisive years in Germany's unification, and four volumes covering the First World War. In support of this plan, the editors maintained that knowledge of the aims and methods of German diplomacy during the First World War and of Bismarck's policies in the years between the wars of 1866 and 1870/71 had hitherto been fragmentary and that German foreign policy of the years 1871–1914 had been seen only through the eyes of the German editors of the *Grosse Politik.*

The aim of the publication has remained unaltered: "to give a substantially complete and correct account on the highest possible level of scientific objectivity" (June 1946 program); or, to repeat Professor Baumont's formulation at the Amsterdam Conference on the Second World War in the West (1950): to provide "a complete survey of German diplomatic activity on a basis of the highest scientific objectivity." Professor Baumont was justified in stressing the unique, truly international character of this project, in which Germany's former war enemies had mutually agreed that historians of independent judgment undertake a publication of German documents strictly according to scientific principles, an unbiased publication, entirely free from propagandistic considerations.

The original editorial plans of 1946 subsequently underwent drastic revision. By 1950, the editors planned sixteen volumes for the years 1937–1945, when only eighteen volumes had been envisioned for the period 1918–1945. Between 1949 and 1961 the project, expanded to a Tripartite (Anglo-American-French) Project by the addition of France in April 1947 and remodelled in 1960/61 as a Quadripartite (Anglo-American-French-German) Project, published seventeen volumes dealing exclusively with the foreign policy of the Hitler period: five volumes of a Series C (1933–1937), thirteen volumes of a Series D (1937–1941), and one volume of a Series E (1941–1945). Series A and B (originally proposed as Series E and D), covering the period of the Weimar Republic, were postponed for the time being, while publication of papers from the period between 1866 and 1918 was abandoned entirely.[30]

---

30. In addition to the governments participating in the document publication, various other governments as well as American and English scholarly institutions carried out rather extensive microfilming operations on particular themes from the period between 1867 and 1914. As a by-product of the work of

The particular interest of both scholarly circles and the general public in the direct antecedents and history of the Second World War dictated that the Tripartite Project concentrate its energies on the Hitler period and publish first the series originally envisioned as A, B, and C as C and D. The editors of Series C and D were cognizant that the history of the interwar period formed a unit in the history of international relations, being the history of the new system of states resulting from the First World War and of its problems, and that, for a deeper understanding of Hitler's policy, a document collection covering the period from the end of the First World War to the National Socialist revolution also had to be considered.

Upon invitation of the German Federal Republic, an editorial conference convened in Bonn in December 1960 to establish an international editorial commission [31] and to establish the guidelines for a quadripartite (Anglo-American-French-German) publication of documents on the history of the foreign policy of the Weimar Republic. This conference had an importance equal to the Berlin editorial conference of 1946, and had to consider in part the same questions. However, it also had the benefit of the combined experiences of the Tripartite Project.

The official German designation *Gemeinschaftspublikation* (cooperative publication) aptly expresses the fact that the four participating governments regard and recognize the cooperative selection of documents to be published as the guiding principle of the new project. The Foreign Ministry has taken the initiative for the continuation of the document publication, with considerable per-

---

the first project, in 1959 Oxford University Press published a complete list of the papers of the Foreign Ministry and all existing microfilms for the period 1867–1920: The American Historical Association, Committee for the Study of War Documents, *A Catalogue of Files and Microfilms of the German Foreign Ministry Archives, 1867–1920*, foreword by Howard M. Ehrmann, 1920 cols. (detailed review by I. Schmid in *Archivmitteilungen*, XI, Number 4 [1961], 124–126). This reference work is indispensable for research in modern history. See also *A Catalogue of Files and Microfilms of the German Foreign Ministry Archives 1920–1945*, compiled and edited by George O. Kent, published by the Hoover Institution, Stanford University, I, 1920–1936 (1962); II, 1920–1936 (1964); III, 1936–1945 (1966).

31. The Editors-in-Chief of the series are: for Germany, Hans Rothfels; for France, Maurice Baumont of the Sorbonne; for the United Kingdom, Alan L. C. Bullock (since December 1960, United Kingdom Historical Adviser) [Ronald Wheatley, Editor-in-Chief since January 1963]; for the United States, Howard M. Smyth, Editor-in-Chief, December 1960 to February 1964 [Hajo Holborn, February 1964 to June 1969, and Hans W. Gatzke, since October 1969].

sonal engagement of the Foreign Minister, Herr von Brentano. With decisive cooperation of the Political Archive, the Foreign Ministry has taken up a suggestion made years ago by the Allies for a cooperative document publication and has paved the way for its realization. The collaboration of German, American, English, and French historians on the cooperative project rests on the conviction, confirmed by the experiences of the preceding Tripartite Project, all of whose spadework is at the new project's disposal, that it is possible for Western historians to define jointly, in the spirit of scientific objectivity, the criteria to govern the selection of documents and to apply these criteria accordingly.[32] German participation in the selection of each document to be published is assured by establishing, in each instance, a German-American, Anglo-German, and Franco-German work group. This procedure at the same time precludes the emergence of any tendency towards apologetics.[33]

The editors supplemented the guidelines for the editorial task in both projects—greatest possible scientific objectivity and the editors' complete independence in the selection and publication of documents—with an extremely important stipulation, as a result of which they exposed themselves to public criticism in a manner hitherto unprecedented in document publications. That stipulation was possible only in this technological age: microfilms of all documents, of both those which, because of their immediate importance for an understanding of German foreign policy, were being published, and those which could not be published for lack of space, are being made accessible to the public without limitation. It would be most unwise of the editors to publish a selection from the documents which could be accused of being tendentious in any sense and which could not survive the very rigorous criteria of historical criticism. The selection made and the objectivity of the editors can at any time be checked for reliability against the originals in Bonn or the microfilms in Washington, London, and Paris.

It has been necessary to pursue in greater detail some ques-

---

32. See Hans Rothfels and Fritz T. Epstein, "Die Akten der Weimarer Zeit," letter to *Christ und Welt*, XIV, No. 1 (January 5, 1961), 20.

33. See Alain Clément, "Le couronnement d'une Odyssée: la publication quadripartie des archives diplomatiques de Weimar," *Le Monde*, December 24, 1960, 4.

tions connected with the Allies' publication of documents from the Hitler period, since the preparatory work of the Tripartite Project and the combined experiences of the Allied historians during the project provided an important basis for the preparation of the new cooperative publication. The new project first addressed itself to Series B, covering the period from the Treaty of Locarno to the seizure of power by the National Socialists, because for this period considerable spadework had already been done through microfilming. Series A, covering the period from the Armistice of November 1918 to Locarno, and Series E (1941–1945) were to follow later.

As an immediate reaction to the plan of the Western Powers (and before any actual publication), a late reflex of the war-guilt discussion which dominated the Weimar period in Germany produced the demand for a counter-publication upon restitution of the documents, a work demonstrating the guilt of Germany's enemies for the outbreak of the Second World War. To be sure, today no one seriously entertains the notion of confronting the volumes hitherto published by the Allies with an opposing series. Those responsible for this publication were aware from the very first that if they proceeded unencumbered by the need to be solicitous for national biases and sensibilities, they would find much in the German papers of the prewar and war periods which would place events and personalities in the Allied camp as well in an unaccustomed and unusual, and perhaps even unfavorable, light. And this has doubtless been the case over and over again. There is no need to enumerate the events which the editors of the volumes already published have laid bare without regard for persons still alive or national sensibilities and protestations.

The papers hitherto published on the history of the foreign policy of Hitler's Germany shed light primarily on the diplomatic history of the years 1933 to 1941, i.e., a period during which Ribbentrop's office (*Büro Ribbentrop*), the *Auslands-Organisation,* Alfred Rosenberg's *Aussenpolitisches Amt,* and special emissaries of Hitler, Ribbentrop, and Göring competed with the officially accredited German representatives abroad. German diplomats abroad were often intentionally left in the dark about policy aims (even the ambassador in Moscow prior to the invasion of the Soviet Union), and they were often reduced to runners or postmen. Hitler never concealed his low opinion for German diplomats of the old school.

It is often necessary to consult in addition papers of other agencies in order to illuminate economic, financial, and military negotiations or to determine the influence of propaganda abroad.

The key to Hitler's inmost thoughts and to the genesis of his decisions is not to be found in the papers of the Foreign Ministry. Their value lies in the incomparable view they afford of the everyday diplomatic routine of the Ministry in a period when the author of Germany's destiny in foreign affairs, as he himself said on March 14, 1936, was carrying out with the certainty of a sleepwalker the mission set before him by Providence (a metaphor which disregarded the fatal fall of many a somnambulist). The personal style of Hitler's diplomacy is probably best illustrated in his correspondence with Mussolini and in the notes on his conversations with foreign statesmen such as Chamberlain and Darlan, Horthy and Franco, and Matsuoka and Molotov, but also with men such as Sven Hedin and Colin Ross.

A document publication is justified when its usefulness as a sound, secure foundation for objective historical research is recognized. The reception given the volumes of the Hitler series by international criticism leaves no doubt that the volumes which have appeared thus far meet our needs and satisfy our expectations and thus constitute cogent evidence for the harmonious cooperation of historians of various nations. The guidelines for the continuation of the project for the Weimar period were thus implicitly affirmed by this positive reception. Where reviewers voiced reservations, these were as a rule concerned with the fact that too little, rather than too much had been published on a particular topic,[34] or with the language of the English translation, which perhaps struck the English as too "American."

---

34. See, particularly, Manfred Merkes's appreciation of the series in the preface to his work, *Die deutsche Politik gegenüber dem spanischen Bürgerkrieg 1936–1939* ("Bonner Historische Forschungen"), XVII (1961). Ludwig Denne's criticism, *Das Danzig-Problem in der deutschen Aussenpolitik 1934–1939* (Bonn, 1959), that the editors of the German papers had not sufficiently penetrated the situation of the authors of the papers published is untenable, for it misses the point of the publication. The task of the editors has been confused with that of the historians who will consult and interpret the documents.

The records of the National Archives in Washington and the Political Archive of the Bonn Foreign Ministry show a sharp increase in the use of the microfilms of German documents deposited with the former [35] and of the pertinent originals held by the latter. We can be sure that the number of investigations based on the German documents will increase by leaps and bounds. The student of contemporary history will see himself confronted with an avalanche of primary source materials once the document publication for the Hitler period currently under way in America, Great Britain, Italy, and the Soviet Union and the French new series, *Documents relatifs aux origines de la guerre 1939–1945*,[36] are available in completed form. As far as the history of German-Japanese relations is concerned, we can note that the Library of Congress has microfilms of over two million pages from the Archives of the Japanese Ministry of Foreign Affairs, covering the period 1868–1945; these the Library had filmed in Tokyo between 1949 and 1951. The Library of Congress also possesses microfilms of some 400,000 pages from the Japanese Army and Navy archives, filmed in Washington before the archives were restored to Japan in 1958.[37]

When the series for the period 1918–1945 being prepared by the two international editorial commissions are completed, and if it is possible to publish, according to topics, the sorely needed documentation of German policies in the First World War, one will be able to survey German foreign policy continuously from the founding of the Reich in 1871 to the end of the unified Reich in 1945. Thus, the precondition will be met for the historiography not only of the "rise and fall of the Third Reich," at which William Shirer tried his hand, but of the rise and fall of the modern Reich.

---

35. See (in addition to the Oxford catalogs cited in footnote 30) Skidmore (cited in footnote 21), 851, n. 11.

36. Décret no. 61–444, May 2, 1961 (Ministère des affaires étrangères), *Journal Officiel de la République Française*, May 7, 1961, 4216.

37. *Checklist of Archives in the Japanese Ministry of Foreign Affairs, Tokyo, Japan, 1868–1945*, microfilmed for the Library of Congress, 1949–1951, compiled by Cecil H. Uyehara (Washington; Library of Congress [Photoduplication Service], 1954); *Checklist of Microfilm Reproductions of Selected Archives of the Japanese Army, Navy, and Other Government Agencies, 1868–1945*, compiled by John Young (Washington, D.C.; Georgetown University Press, 1959).

IX

New Literature on the History
of German Eastern Policy
in the First World War

IA. Fritz Fischer, *Griff nach der Weltmacht. Die Kriegszielpolitik des kaiserlichen Deutschland 1914–1918* (Düsseldorf: Droste, third revised edition, 1964), 902 pp., 4 maps. DM 34.80.

IB. Gerhard Ritter, *Staatskunst und Kriegshandwerk. Das Problem des "Militarismus" in Deutschland*, III: *Die Tragödie der Staatskunst. Bethmann Hollweg als Kriegskanzler (1914–1917)* (Munich: Oldenbourg, 1964), 707 pp. DM 48.00.

II. Hellmuth Röszler, ed., *Weltwende 1917. Monarchie. Weltrevolution* (Göttingen: Musterschmidt, 1965; published for the Ranke Society), 214 pp. DM 19.80.

III. Eberhard von Vietsch, ed., *Gegen die Unvernunft. Der Briefwechsel zwischen Paul Graf Wolff Metternich und Wilhelm Solf 1915–1918 mit zwei Briefen Albert Ballins. Zeugen ihrer Zeit. Erlebnisse. Berichte. Dokumente* (Bremen: Schuenemann, 1964), 145 pp. DM 9.80.

This article was originally published in *Jahrbücher für Geschichte Osteuropas*, XIV, No. 1 (1966), 64–93. The reviews of the following three books have been omitted in the translation: Wolfgang Steglich, *Die Friedenspolitik der Mittelmächte 1917/1918*, I (Wiesbaden, 1964); Gerd Linde, *Die deutsche Politik in Litauen im Ersten Weltkrieg* (Wiesbaden, 1965); Bernhard Mann, *Die baltischen Länder in der deutschen Kriegszielpublizistik 1914–1918* (Tübingen, 1965).

As an informative new book on Britain's policy in the First World War points out, we are living "at a time of revival in First World War studies on both sides of the Atlantic." [1] Germany, in particular, has seen in recent years the publication of noteworthy studies on the period of the First World War. Of these, Fritz Fischer's provocative and highly controversial book, *Griff nach der Weltmacht,* has the merit of being the first to illuminate long stretches of the secret political history of the war which had hitherto lain in the dark, such as Germany's revolutionary activities in Russia, and of having given impetus to renewed examination of the problems of the First World War.

I A

Fischer's book has now appeared in a third, only slightly altered edition. Owing to the topicality of its theme, it has received an unusual amount of attention and has had astonishing impact far beyond the borders of Germany, as have only a few German historical works of the nineteenth and twentieth centuries. On the whole, agreement balances disagreement. It is indisputable that Fischer's book has introduced a new phase in the discussion of the political history of the First World War. Since the start of the sixties, it has functioned as a catalyst for analyses of the war: it has met with opposition; it has given impetus to a critical elucidation of sources; it has occasioned renewed scrutiny of notions accepted unquestioningly for too long.[2]

The heated discussion is anything but a mere professors' quarrel. The deep personal involvement of the participants and the unusual animosity and bitterness with which the discussion was (and

---

1. Paul Guinn, *British Strategy and Politics, 1914 to 1918* (Oxford, 1965), vii.

2. For reviews of Fischer's book, see the list of reviews (pp. 195–198) in the collection *Deutsche Kriegsziele 1914–1918. Eine Diskussion,* edited by Ernst W. Graf Lynar (Berlin, 1964). This volume contains reprints of essays and reviews by Fritz Fischer, Gerhard Ritter, Hans Herzfeld, Michael Freund, Golo Mann, Rudolf Neck, and the present reviewer. See also Egmont Zechlin's criticism of the selection of articles in his essay "Deutschland zwischen Kabinettskrieg und Wirtschaftskrieg," *Historische Zeitschrift,* CIC (1964), 433. In the introduction (265–276) and the epilogue (p. 346) to his essay "Weltpolitik, Weltmachtstreben und deutsche Kriegsziele," 265–346, Fischer comes to grips with his critics. *Historische Zeitschrift,* CC (1965), 783–787, contains a reply by Gerhard Ritter, "Zur Fischer-Kontroverse."

is still being) pursued bring to mind similar clashes, the conflicts between Max Lehmann and Albert Naudé, between Georg von Below and Veit Valentin, between Johannes Haller and Otto Hoetzsch, which have entered the annals of German scholarship as paradigms for how such discussions should not be conducted. Numerous reviews in the daily press and magazines give evidence of the breadth of the book's effect; they included outbursts of disfavor over Fischer's treatment of the beginning of the war (the *Deutsche Soldatenzeitung* drew up its heaviest artillery: "a thorough job of German self-defilement"). But the book also had an effect in depth. No work on the history of the First World War can neglect Fischer's book or avoid taking a position on it.

If in 1962 Gerhard Ritter thought that Fischer's book represented a high point in the "self-beclouding of Germany's historical consciousness," today he might perhaps agree that the discussion it has occasioned has contributed more than Fischer's critics would ever have thought possible to the elucidation of German history of the period of the First World War. Erwin Hölzle, who first bluntly rejected Fischer's book,[3] now confines himself in his brief review of the third edition to the observation that the book is "for the most part a wearisome account of documentation." [4]

It seems, however, that the book, both in its thesis and in its argument, has had anything but a wearisome effect on Fischer's opponents; rather it has worked like a red flag. Numerous respected historians have given Fischer's work critical attention; the weaknesses have been given detailed treatment, particularly in essays by Ritter and by Hölzle.[5]

The thematic parallelism between Hölzle's essay and Fischer's work can be seen in Hölzle's section headings: "L'écrasement, 1914–1916," "The German and American Offers, 1916," " 'World Democracy,' 'Papal Mediation,' and the Soviets, 1917," "Revolution and Separate Peace in the East," "Motives of German Policy," "Eastern Colossus and Western Civilization," "Peace through

---

3. *Das historisch-politische Buch*, X, No. 3, (1962), 65–69.
4. Ibid., No. 9 (1965), 277–278.
5. Erwin Hölzle, "Das Experiment des Friedens im Ersten Weltkrieg 1914–1917," *Geschichte in Wissenschaft und Unterricht*, XIII (1962), 465–522; for Ritter, see note 2, above.

Victory and Negotiated Peace," "Germany as a 'World Power'."

The essays of both Ritter and Hölzle derive from extensive preliminary studies; it was not the publication of Fischer's book that first occasioned treatment of the same range of themes. Both Ritter and Hölzle pointed out gaps in German research of the World War, such as the need for a documented history of the Hindenburg Program,[6] of the ignominious Belgian deportations, and of Russophobia in Germany.

In my review of Fischer's book,[7] I wrote:

> The question that will pose itself to each reader of the book is whether the description Fischer has drawn on the basis of German war documents will prove enduring, especially since the continuity of aims from the very beginning of the war that he has outlined has put the war in a wholly new perspective.

Although after careful consideration of the book's strengths and weaknesses, I assessed it positively, I made plain that Fischer's reasoning, based as it was on Bethmann Hollweg's war aims program of September 1914, did not seem conclusive. I stated that Fischer attributed to that memorandum a universality "which does not sufficiently take into account or do justice to changes in the war situation and their impact." I considered the intentional exclusion of the war aims of Germany's adversaries and the all too brief treatment of domestic political developments during the war, from which foreign policy cannot be isolated, "undeniable weaknesses of the book, which therefore provided much opportunity for attack."

The original impression I received upon studying Fischer's book, that differences between the Reich leadership and the Supreme Command in questions of war aims were primarily differences in degree and means and not differences in substance, cannot be allowed to stand after Ritter's analysis. It is valid in a limited way for Bethmann's relation to Falkenhayn, that is, to the

---

6. Now in part filled by Robert B. Armeson's monograph *Total Warfare and Compulsory Warfare* (The Hague, 1964). See the review by Hans W. Gatzke, *American Historical Review*, LXXI (1965), 228–229. See also Gerald D. Feldman, *Army, Industry, and Labor in Germany, 1914–1918* (Princeton, 1966).

7. *Jahrbücher für Geschichte Osteuropas*, X., No. 3 (October 1962), 381–394.

second Oberste Heeresleitung,[8] but not for his relation to Hindenburg and Ludendorff (to Ober-Ost 1914–1916 and the third Supreme Command) and to the "demigods" of the coterie of Colonels Bauer, Bartenwerffer, and von Oldershausen.

Today there are two distinct schools of thought in assessing Fischer's book. One accepts the continuity of aims set forth by Fischer, that is, agrees that the leaders of the Reich pursued expansionist aims that could only have been realized through German victory and that these leaders were in perpetual error over Germany's strength and the enemies' will to wage a victorious war. The other school, chiefly represented by Gerhard Ritter, Egmont Zechlin, and Wolfgang Steglich, maintains the view that German war policy was fundamentally a peace policy; the guarantees which it sought were not conceived as immutably fixed war aims on which it would let a peace founder if efforts for peace endangered those aims. In the course of the war, as the general military situation of the Central Powers deteriorated and German leaders found themselves in increasingly strained circumstances, above all economically, and before America's intervention tipped the military scales in favor of the Entente, the idea of safeguards and guarantees was supplanted by the idea of self-determination, realization of which could still have been considered a victory. The historian will have to come to terms with these opposing views, and the controversy over Fritz Fischer will doubtless find historians for or against Fischer or neutrally disposed.[9]

Fischer states [10] that by July 7 and 8 Tisza had not yet been

---

8. See the detailed study of Karl-Heinz Janssen, *Der Kanzler und der General. Die Führungskrise um Bethmann Hollweg und Falkenhayn (1914–1916)* (Göttingen, 1967).

9. In *Weltmacht oder Niedergang. Deutschland im Ersten Weltkrieg* (Hamburg, 1965) Fischer addressed his main critics, Ritter and Zechlin, and defended his method. Against Hans Herzfeld (see above, note 2) and Karl D. Erdmann ("Zur Beurteilung Bethmann Hollwegs," *Geschichte in Wissenschaft und Unterricht,* XV [1964], 525–540), he defended the factual content of his book, which he summarized in eight theses. Ritter's *Der Erste Weltkrieg. Studien zum deutschen Geschichtsbild* (Bonn, 1964) similarly recapitulates *in nuce* the main lines of Fischer's book.

A comparison of the positions of the two historians is made difficult by the fact that Ritter based his pronouncements against Fischer on the first edition of Fischer's work, rather than on the somewhat altered later editions, of which the third (1964) has different pagination from the first two.

10. Fischer, *Weltmacht oder Niedergang,* 66.

won over to a vigorous campaign on the part of the Monarchy against Serbia, but that he finally gave in on July 14. Josef Galántai has traced the reasons for Tisza's change of mind between July 10 and July 14.[11] In his biography of Berchtold, Hugo Hantsch has simply recorded the total agreement of the two prime ministers on July 14.[12]

Despite his overestimation of the significance of the September directives, it remains clear that Fischer did not go so far as to characterize Bethmann as an obdurate annexationist. He himself pointed up the difference between the eras of Bethmann Hollweg and Ludendorff when he wrote: "Not Kühlmann and Bethmann Hollweg, *with their ideas of possible negotiation* [reviewer's italics], but rather those forces which compelled them to proceed, represented the will of the German nation." [13] The expression "will of the nation" may seem infelicitous, since there is sufficient evidence for the dissolution of the national united front at the beginning of the war, but Fischer himself qualifies it in the same paragraph, intending it to mean the will of "the overwhelming majority of the German people." He would have done better to speak of the bourgeoisie or middle class, almost all of whom stood behind the Supreme Command; he avoided this in order not to use Marxist terminology.

It is unfortunate that Fischer has not yet published a volume of documents, which is the much desired and indeed absolutely necessary complement to his work. In the face of concentrated opposition to his conception of the outbreak of the war, he has been content to rely upon the support fire provided by Imanuel Geiss in his impressive document collection, *Julikrise und Kriegsausbruch* (Hannover, 1964).[14]

Had Fischer limited his book to the theme sharply defined in his subtitle, that is, elucidation of German war aims policy for the years 1914–1918, instead of including in his treatment in a provocative way the question concerning responsibility for the outbreak

---

11. Josef Galántai, "Stefan Tisza und der Erste Weltkrieg," *Österreich in Geschichte und Literatur,* VIII (1964), 474–476.
12. Hugo Hantsch, *Leopold, Graf Berchtold* (Graz, 1963), II, 598.
13. Fischer, *Griff nach der Weltmacht,* p. 838 in the first edition, p. 844 in the second.
14. See also the introduction by I. Geiss to *Juli 1914. Die europäische Krise und der Ausbruch des Ersten Weltkriegs* (Munich, 1965).

of the war, irrelevant to such an elucidation, the discussion would never have become so heated and so complicated. The barrage directed at Fischer's view on the outbreak of the war thus precluded a coherent discussion of the main elements and tendencies of his work, until Ritter's book appeared.

The following fundamental insights have crystallized from the discussion of Fischer's book:

1. The description provided by Fischer of German discussions on war aims can be made fruitful for scholarship "not by [providing] the substance of an alleged continuity in German foreign policy, of a design never abandoned, but by [providing] access to problems of domestic and foreign policy created in Germany by the reality of the world war." [15]

2. From the discussion of Fischer's book there has emerged a more differentiated picture of ideas on politics and war aims during the course of the war in German and Austrian government circles, among the military leadership (army and navy), and in the educated classes, particularly as this related to Russia, eastern Europe in general, and southeastern Europe.

3. "German policy in the First World War [recognized], particularly in its peace aims, neither the realities of, and developments in, power politics nor the ideological tendencies of the world." [16]

I B

In my earlier assessment of Fischer's work, I cited a statement by Gerhard Ritter,[17] one of Fischer's sharpest critics: "Whoever would correct all the misinterpretations would have to write an even larger and surely very tedious book." Ritter's description of German policy up to the downfall of Bethmann Hollweg in July 1917, covering nearly 600 pages, stands not opposed to, but alongside of, the nearly 900 pages of the third edition of Fischer's book. Ritter's

---

15. Egmont Zechlin, "Probleme des Kriegskalküls und der Kriegsbeendigung im Ersten Weltkrieg," *Geschichte in Wissenschaft und Unterricht*, XVI, No. 2 (1965), 82.
16. Hölzle, "Das Experiment des Friedens im Ersten Weltkrieg" (see above, note 5), 521.
17. See above, p. 166.

book is anything but tedious; the author himself found the job of
working through and presenting an immense quantity of primary
and secondary sources "extremely absorbing, indeed, exciting."
Ritter's talent is such that he causes the reader to feel his own excitement. He writes diplomatic history without taking shelter in
overlong excerpts from documents and in such fashion that it never
seems tedious.

It must be emphasized that Ritter's book did not receive its
impetus from Fischer's study. It is the third volume of *Staatskunst
und Kriegshandwerk,* Ritter's treatment in depth of the problem of
militarism in Germany. The wealth of material forced Ritter, who
had undertaken to carry his survey to the Hitler period and the
Second World War, to envisage a fourth volume, in addition to the
three originally planned. The question must remain open whether
Fischer's prior treatment of the First World War caused Ritter to
present and substantiate his divergent view in far greater detail
than would otherwise have been the case. What was said of Fischer's
book applies equally to Ritter's work: only he who has familiarized
himself thoroughly with the book's contents can enter into discussion of aims in the First World War.

One can concur with Ritter's placing the division between his
third and fourth volumes in the World War, since, for his particular
theme, "statecraft and warcraft," the year 1917 marked for Germany the end of diplomatic efforts toward a negotiated peace associated with Bethmann Hollweg's name. The continuation of Bethmann Hollweg's policy by Kühlmann was doomed, in the face of the
all-too-powerful Supreme Command, which brought about Kühlmann's downfall in the summer of 1918. Hertling's struggle against
the Supreme Command at the time of the Brest negotiations
achieved no enduring success. More and more headway has been
made by the notion, supported understandably by Soviet historians
and by German historians as well (see below), that it is not 1914,
the year the war broke out, or 1918, the year the war ended, but
rather 1917 that marks a watershed, because that was the year in
which the October Revolution occurred in Russia and the Supreme
Command gained an ascendancy in Germany which in 1917–1918
was tantamount to military dictatorship. One has only to add to
this the entry of the United States into the war, which raised the

question of the legitimacy after 1917 of a perspective on world affairs that was Europe-centered. It also brought with it more declarations of war against Germany in the last years of the war than had been made in preceding years, so that Germany saw herself literally opposed by a world full of enemies.

Ritter's book, as has been stated, was not conceived as a refutation of Fischer, but in the long run it has become one. Ritter thought it better to keep his text free of the dead weight of a polemic against Fischer, and in this he largely succeeded. His criticism of Fischer is concentrated in the notes. That he presents his own view continuously, without digressing, has been of extraordinary benefit for the readability of his book, and his method causes no difficulty whatsoever in checking the sources he cites.

As in my review of Fischer's book, I shall comment here only on the contribution of Ritter's work to East European research and to the assessment of Germany's aims in the East, in other words, on only one aspect of Bethmann Hollweg's war policy.

On the question of the outbreak of the war, I should like to confine myself to the following remarks. The pessimistic conviction of the Chief of the General Staff, von Moltke, that Germany's political and military position was deteriorating steadily, and Bethmann Hollweg's fatalism, which considered military confrontation with the Slavic nations inevitable, certainly did not have the effect upon the leaders of the Reich and its chief military advisers of preventing war in 1914, but still one cannot charge the latter for that reason with warmongering. Ritter's characterization of Austria's war with Serbia (p. 17) as "purely defensive, a defense against mortal dangers, not an offensive action to conquer Slavic territory" applies equally well to Germany's war with Russia. Germany did not seek war, but neither did it do everything to avoid it, because according to the view of those in power—which had become an idée fixe—war could not be avoided in the long run. Thinking it necessary to take advantage of the last opportunity for victory (which would have meant as well the preservation of her ally), Germany exposed herself to the reproach of war lust from the contemporary world and to the burden of opprobrium for a preventive war in the judgment of posterity. In the summer of 1914, no difference existed between the military and political authorities in their assessments of the political situation, so far as the threat to Germany from the East was concerned, so that at that point the unequal distribution of weight between military and political authorities (the predominance of the former a "structural error of the Bismarck Reich," Ritter, p. 19) was less in evidence than during the course of the war. The first conflicts between the political and military leadership at the beginning of the war were merely quiet preludes to the opposition which developed during the war into an unbridgeable gap between Bethmann Hollweg and the General Staff. After the struggle for declarations of war, a second clash occurred in the middle of August, when the plans of the General Staff for an insurrection in Poland resulted in an appeal to the Poles promising them national independence. Bethmann Hollweg recognized at once that such an appeal would inevitably cause difficulties in domestic policy over the status of the Poles in Prussia (p. 33). It is characteristic that the military dispelled the chancellor's misgivings by appealing to the authority of Bismarck, who, in 1866, did not oppose the idea of supporting insurrections of Czechs and Hungarians against the Hapsburg monarchy.

In his introductory chapter, Ritter points out that the idea of necessary "guarantees," a notion which admitted the extension of power for purposes of security, had its origin in the conviction that a defensive war was being waged. A prime instance in this connection is afforded by a memorandum by Erzberger at the beginning of September 1914, which, apart from designating aims in western Europe and Africa, also called for German military supremacy over and economic incorporation of eastern Europe (p. 37). Ritter stresses the fact that at an early date (the end of October 1914) the Prussian Minister of Internal Affairs, von Loebell, like the historian Otto Hoetzsch, already wanted to avoid anything that could perpetuate the split with Russia, and that von Loebell in a carefully worded note would not go beyond calling for improved protection of East Prussia's Niemen and Narev borders. Ritter considers von Loebell among the opponents of annexation in the East (an objection that Fischer acknowledges in *Weltmacht oder Niedergang*, p. 32) and derives the minister's position from his fundamentally conservative attitude, while Fischer (p. 132) summarily brands von Loebell a confirmed annexationist. It is difficult to reconcile this interpretation with von Loebell's statement: "We will naturally have to demand much more from Russia in the beginning to obtain what we actually desire in a way that makes it relatively easy for Russia to console herself privately and before the world for the loss of border territory." [18]

"Security through extension of power" was the leading thought in Bethmann Hollweg's early directive of September 9, 1914, on drawing up conditions for peace. Moreover, a new economic organization for Europe under German leadership was to be sought. For the East he envisaged Russia's being driven back as far as possible from the German border and an end to Russian dominion over the non-Russian vassal nations. In a further directive to the Foreign Ministry of October 22, war aims in the East also included arrangement with Russia of a long-term trade agreement which would be especially favorable to Germany and would include a reduction in Russian industrial tariffs (p. 44). This demand could be made only in ignorance of the fierce opposition among Russian landowners and industrialists to a revival of the Russo-German trade agreement of 1904, even in a weakened form.[19]

It is not necessary to follow Ritter's discussion of Bethmann Hollweg's Eastern policy step by step and comment on the role this policy played in the framework of his total policy, especially since Ritter's main differences from Fischer do not concern the East. Let us call attention to only a few points. Ritter's second chapter, on Bethmann's relations with Falkenhayn up to the end of the Polish campaign, has as its subject Falkenhayn's pressure for a separate peace with Russia. Falkenhayn sought at least an attempt to break Russia away from the enemy coalition by German renunciation of territorial acquisitions. A separate peace with Russia, even if it entailed loss of Austrian territory, seemed desirable as well to General Conrad, Chief of the Austrian General Staff, when Italy's entry into the war was imminent; Germany's eastern border, how-

---

18. Erich Volkmann, "Die Annexionsfragen des Weltkriegs," *Die Ursachen des deutschen Zusammenbruchs im Jahre 1918*, XII, No. 1 (1929), 191 (Appendix 11: "Denkschrift des preussischen Innenministers von Loebell vom 29. Oktober 1914 über die Kriegsziele").

19. Not discussed by Ritter. On this, see George W. F. Hallgarten, *Imperialismus vor 1914* (Munich, 1963), II, Part 2, 456–458.

ever, was to remain unchanged (p. 81). Ritter gives relatively brief mention to the abortive German feelers for a separate peace with Russia, referring the reader to the literature on the subject.[20]

Even the major successes of the German offensive against Russia in the summer of 1915 did not mislead Bethmann Hollweg into viewing acquisition of the Baltic provinces as a war aim. This time it was he who played Bismarck's authority against the military; Bismarck, he held, treated the question of the Baltic provinces as a *noli me tangere,* divorced from national sentiments (p. 89). It was not until the spring of 1916 that Bethmann Hollweg, under pressure from public opinion and from military quarters, as Ritter surmises (p. 142), changed his views and called for annexation of a border strip containing two to three million inhabitants (p. 143).

In the discussions the Central Powers held on the questions of Central Europe and Poland in the winter of 1915–1916 (Ritter's fourth chapter), the two questions showed themselves closely connected and fundamentally insoluble: the Germans had no use for Poland, they did not wish the Austrians to have it, and they could not return it to Russia.

In Ritter's treatment of the war years 1915–1917, the part played by the United States occupies the central position: American peace mediation and the submarine war. Germany's situation gradually deteriorated (foundering of the Verdun offensive; failure of the manifesto on Poland; failure of the peace action of December 1916; victory of the Supreme Command in the submarine question, which led to the break with America; and finally, Emperor Karl's Bourbon peace move). The February revolution in Russia awakened in Germany and Austria peace hopes which were disappointed, while the Supreme Command became more and more active in for-

---

20. Ritter gives perhaps too much credence to a single Russian source. He writes: "according to Russian sources," in the summer of 1915 Germany offered Russia among other things the loan of several billion marks (p. 88). This he repeated in his contribution to the *Festschrift Percy Ernst Schramm zu seinem 70. Geburtstag,* edited by Peter Classen and Peter Scheibert: "Bethmann Hollweg und die Machtträume deutscher Patrioten im ersten Jahr des Weltkriegs," II, 212. To my knowledge, the only source for this is the telegram of July 15/28, 1915, from the ambassador in Stockholm, A. V. Nekliudov, to the foreign minister, S. D. Sazonov, in which the sum of 5 to 10 billion marks is mentioned. This telegram is reproduced in E. A. Adamov, *Konstantinopol' i prolivy po sekretnym dokumentam b. Ministerstva inostrannykh del'* (Moscow, 1926), II, 377.

eign policy, prosecuting its war aims in the capitals of Germany's allies ("One almost has the impression that the Supreme Command had created its own foreign ministry," p. 527). It was at the same time so bold in internal affairs as to veto the domestic reforms Bethmann Hollweg considered imperative.

Ritter's analysis of the elements of foreign and domestic policy in Bethmann's struggle against "the powers of political reaction and militarism" (p. 558) that brought about his downfall might have presented as evidence that the fallen chancellor saw Prussian *Staatsräson* as the reason for his failure as a German statesman. Bethmann asserted that he fell victim to the overwhelming strength of Prussian conservatism, which had become the bane of German history.[21]

In reading Ritter's work, it is impossible to overlook or treat lightly the fact that Ritter is compelled by the question he asks to view Bethmann Hollweg as a resolute but moderate statesman and to discount as tactical necessities (as a rule on good grounds) statements that are inconsistent with this view. Similarly, Fischer believed that the memorandum of September 1914 was the key to Bethmann Hollweg's war aims policy, which rejected the *status quo ante bellum* for Germany with a view toward particular goals. While Fischer doubtless goes too far in attributing continuity to the chancellor's war aims, Ritter sometimes does not go far enough toward illuminating the tragic disharmony which arose between Bethmann Hollweg's early acknowledgment of the military situation and the need to tolerate the high expectations fostered by the Supreme Command in the German public and to show a confidence in victory which was in contradiction to his pessimism. He opposed annexationist trends even when he seemed to give in to them, and he did not speak out openly against them in order not to dampen popular confidence in victory. From Ritter's study, and from Erdmann's assessment of the chancellor,[22] Bethmann Hollweg emerges as a much more complex personality than he appears in Fischer's work. Where it seemed advisable, particularly in talks

---

21. Hans Herzfeld, "Oberbefehl und Regierung in der neueren Geschichte," *Faktoren der politischen Entscheidung. Festgabe für Ernst Fränkel zum 65. Geburtstag,* edited by Gerhard A. Ritter and Gilbert Ziebura (Berlin 1963), 177.
22. Erdmann, "Zur Beurteilung Bethmann Hollwegs" (see above, note 9).

with proponents of a "peace through victory," he employed a mastery developed during the war of concealing from his interlocutors without deceit his judgment of the total situation and his ultimate ambitions as he pursued moderate goals. In the words of Egmont Zechlin, Bethmann Hollweg "carried the 'art of the dilatory formal compromise' . . . to the extreme, in order to eliminate the danger of his losing his place to a visionary, and in order to conceal from those abroad his own view of the situation." [23]

I should like to comment on a few points in Ritter's presentation. Ritter writes (p. 105) that in January 1916 the Ministerial Council for Joint Affairs of the Dual Monarchy had declared as a war aim the total partition of Serbia between Austria and Bulgaria, only to meet with the opposition of Tisza, who would have no major annexation of Serbian territory to the Danubian empire. However, one must add that in the Ministerial Council of January 7, 1916, Tisza thought it a foregone conclusion that the northwestern part of Serbia should fall to Hungary. A compromise resulted between the view of the head of the Austrian Government, Count Stürgkh, and that of Tisza, according to which all territories in the northern theater would fall to the Austrian half of the empire and all territorial acquisitions in Serbia to the Hungarian.[24]

In his account of the Petrograd crisis of July 1918 (p. 488), Ritter mentions the publication of "certain documents" on the payment of German subsidies to the Bolsheviks, which "caused the greatest commotion in all barracks." No source is named; the definitive source work on these events (particularly for the claim that Germany financed the Bolshevik party), which shows nothing of such "commotion in all barracks," should have been mentioned: *The Russian Provisional Government, 1917. Documents.* Selected and edited by Paul Browder and Alexander F. Kerensky (Stanford, 1961), III, 1364–1382: "The Charges against the Bolsheviks."

It is now necessary to compare Harold I. Nelson's descrip-

---

23. Zechlin, "Deutschland zwischen Kabinettskrieg und Wirtschaftskrieg. Politik und Kriegführung in den ersten Monaten des Weltkriegs 1914," *Historische Zeitschrift,* CIC (1964), 450.

24. Alexander Fussek, "Graf Stürgkh und Graf Tisza," *Österreich in Geschichte und Literatur,* VIII (1954), 427–431, especially 430.

tion [25] of England's war aims, as called for by the War Committee of the cabinet, with Ritter's discussion (pp. 306–310). The "two outstanding officials" of the Foreign Office (Ritter, p. 307) who drafted a memorandum with Balfour and the General Staff are identified in Nelson's work as Sir Ralph Paget and Sir William Tyrrell. Nelson's conclusion on page 14 reads:

> The authors of these projects had assumed that Russia would remain a Great Power and that the United States' role in world politics would not appreciably alter. Both assumptions had to be seriously modified as a result of the Russian Revolution and of the American entry into the war.

Ritter more than once demonstrates successfully that Fischer cut himself off from a deeper insight into the diplomatic achievement of Bethmann Hollweg because he overestimated the war aims program of September 1914. One is compelled to agree with Ritter's assessment of the conference between the chancellor and Stresemann and Rötger, who represented the War Committee of German industry (p. 50). The chancellor's conciliatory attitude on one point (the Central European Tariff Union) should not have blinded Fischer to the fact that Bethmann Hollweg was otherwise not at all in agreement with the two Pan-Germans and repudiated the form of hegemony they advanced.[26]

Ritter's criticism is particularly severe (*ira cum studio*) when an ill-considered, imprecise expression on Fischer's part flatly invites criticism. For instance, in his account of Bethmann Hollweg's negotiations with Colonel House at the end of January 1916 (not in February, as Fischer writes), Fischer characterized Colonel House's report on his conversations in London as containing, first, "English conditions for peace" (instead of "preconditions"), later, however, an "English offer" and "British recommendations," which Bethmann Hollweg rejected in keeping with his war-aims program.

---

25. Harold I. Nelson, *Land and Power. British and Allied Policy on Germany's Frontiers, 1916–1919* (London and Toronto, 1963), 8–14 and 24–26.

26. Willibald Gutsche also demonstrates this, using documents in the State Archives of Saxony in his review of Werner Basler, *Deutschlands Annexionspolitik in Polen und im Baltikum 1914–1918* (Berlin, 1962), in *Zeitschrift für Geschichtswissenschaft,* XII (1964), 840.

One is compelled to agree with Ritter that Colonel House brought with him no English offer.

Ritter's book makes eminently clear from the documents the discrepancy between the moderate war aims which the leaders of the Reich thought desirable and attainable, once the euphoria of victory had worn off, and the notions on German imperialism prevalent abroad before, during, and after the war (and, indeed, today still). These notions were founded on statements by German publicists, to whose utterances Communist anti-imperialist literature has also clung tenaciously.[27]

Summing up, one can say the following. The picture of Bethmann Hollweg drawn by Fischer [28] does only partial justice to the chancellor, for it fails to acknowledge the "unerringly clear, sober insight into Germany's real situation" (Ritter, p. 586) according to which he acted. In the reviewer's opinion, Ritter has demonstrated that Bethmann Hollweg was not prepared to allow either a general or a separate peace to founder, even if it meant minimum German demands far below those of the original program, if Germany could emerge honorably from the war. However, Fischer makes it appear that Bethmann Hollweg clung to the maximum demands put forth at the beginning of the war. In assessing the extent to which the assurances and guarantees that Bethmann Hollweg hoped to obtain in peace negotiations are annexationist demands, the views diverge hopelessly, and agreement can probably never be achieved. Ritter has carried his study to the threshold of the victory of "militarism" in Germany and believes that the tragedy of German diplomacy was consummated with the downfall of Bethmann Hollweg, in that it brought to the helm a professional soldier with the "fantasies of a cadet's brain" (as Ritter characterizes Ludendorff's plans for the changeover from a war to a peace

---

27. It is a sign of hopeless, self-contradictory obduracy that in 1964 Willibald Gutsche would still write: "The Bethmann Government was . . . prepared to end the war only when all essential war objectives were (in one form or another) in the hands of German imperialism. At no time would it think of foregoing even one objective in order to take advantage of an opportunity for an imperialistic negotiated peace [?]" (Gutsche, "Erst Europa—und dann die Welt. Probleme der Kriegszielpolitik des deutschen Imperialismus im ersten Weltkrieg," *Zeitschrift für Geschichtswissenschaft,* XII [1964], 763).

28. Fischer, *Griff nach der Weltmacht,* 223–224 in the first edition, 229–230 in the third.

economy, p. 549). In describing the struggle of the statesman Bethmann Hollweg with the determined representative of unbridled militarism, Ritter sought to raise the usurpation of the political leadership by the military leadership, the antagonism and clash between Bethmann and Ludendorff, into the sphere of an ideological conflict between statecraft and warcraft. Yet the question arises whether it is really permissible to speak here of a "tragedy of diplomacy." Ritter's book describes the tragedy of Bethmann Hollweg, the personal tragedy of a man who managed his department intelligently and with great conscience and yielded more and more, against his better judgment, to the pressures of the military men, of a man who was unable to overcome opposing forces which he recognized clearly.

The winner in the controversy is neither Fischer nor Ritter: the winner is Bethmann Hollweg, winner in the sense that Fischer has replaced the picture of a weak and irresolute statesman with the boldly negative portrait of a chancellor resolutely intent on annexation, which the opposition counters with the portrait of a resolutely prudent, moderate statesman. Fischer's portrayal of the war chancellor, which identifies Bethmann Hollweg with far-reaching annexationist ideas (official and private), found acceptance in wide circles both at home and abroad all the more readily because it seemed to confirm existing notions about German imperialism in the prewar and war periods. Ritter has corrected this view, but it will be a long time before his revised picture of Bethmann will prevail. This should not, however, obscure the achievement of Fischer, who has the indisputable merit of illuminating, as no one else had, for both the older and the younger generation the intellectual disposition and political judgment—or, more exactly, the lack of geopolitical judgment and political moderation—of the German leading classes as manifested in official and private programs for annexation. However, his critics have been able to show that he went much too far in his interpretation and assessment of the influence actually exerted by these programs on Bethmann Hollweg's policy, and that the source of his error lies in his considering the chancellor's well-known directive of September 9 to the Foreign Ministry an essentially static war-aims program.

Although it is impossible to reduce Bethmann Hollweg's position on the known peace moves between 1914 and 1916 to a common denominator for either east or west, it has been established that in the summer of 1917 he arrived after a long inner struggle at recognition of the status quo in the Belgian question and did not even dismiss entirely concessions on Alsace-Lorraine.[29] Owing to the collapse of the czarist empire, an entirely new situation arose in the east at the time, one in which a settlement on demands for territorial security and national self-determination made a peace free from extreme demands and acceptable to the Central Powers seem possible. After Bethmann Hollweg's departure, Kühlmann sought to make headway in the period of the Brest negotiations for the idea of a general peace based on a general status quo, notwithstanding the demands of the Entente and Germany's promises to her allies. The impossibility of bringing the Entente to the negotiating table; the dilatory tactics of the Bolsheviks, who hoped to be able to transplant the revolution into the camp of the Central Powers; the irreconcilable split which had opened up on conceptions of the right to self-determination of populations in German-occupied territories; and above all, the military necessity of making the strength gained in the east useful for victory in the west brought about the dictated peace, which reflected the distribution of power in the German governmental apparatus. One can agree with Fischer that after Brest-Litovsk the annexationist demands advanced by the Supreme Command were no longer rejected by the Reich leadership with a shrug of the shoulders, as Bethmann Hollweg had done as late as December 1916 in the case of its "Catalog of War Aims" (Ritter, p. 354).

It may seem surprising that the conclusions Ritter has drawn after careful examination of an immense amount of source material agree to a great extent with those of Erich Volkmann in his report "Die Annexionsfragen des Weltkriegs," submitted exactly forty years ago, in 1924, to the fourth subcommittee of the Reichstag's Committee to Investigate Responsibility for the World War.

---

29. The Bethmann Hollweg enigma, which Fischer believed he solved by portraying the chancellor as an annexationist, appears, contrary to Fischer, to turn on the question whether the chancellor believed (or could believe) that it was possible for him to reveal his opposition to annexation to the military leadership and public opinion, both clamoring for annexation, without precipitating his own downfall.

The question of war aims was for him [Bethmann Hollweg] a purely practical question; long-term occupation of extensive non-German-speaking territories in Europe seemed to him neither attainable nor desirable. On the other hand, he would gladly have brought about military improvements along the border and economic benefits . . . . These were, however, not questions over which he would allow an opportunity for peace to fail. It can be safely assumed that at any point in the war he would have agreed to a peace based on the status quo ante.[30]

and

As much as one may criticize German war-aims policy, as much as one may charge particular political and military personalities with leaning in one direction or another, the fact remains that German war-aims policy has not been proved of decisive importance for the course and outcome of the war.[31]

A review of Ritter's book in the *Times Literary Supplement* [32] stressed the personal element in his study, the interweaving of reminiscences and the frank admission of biases which a contemporary witness necessarily shares. The manner in which Ritter has criticized his much younger colleague reveals not only that he writes as a political historian but also that he considers himself a national preceptor. Thus, he could not fail to consider as pamphleteering a study of recent history which made assertions which ran directly counter to his own view of history, his consciousness of national history, and his lifelong convictions. He, therefore, reacted with understandable harshness and acrimony. In *Weltmacht oder Niedergang,* Fischer's rejoinder to his critics, one has to penetrate the smokescreen to realize that in many cases the exchange of shots concerns subtle problems in interpreting documents and relating them to various contexts. The same evidence is brought forth in order to capture and defend opposing positions.

From what has been said, it is possible to question equally both basic positions in the discussion of Germany's aims in the First World War, that which sees a continuity in immoderation

30. Volkmann (see above, note 18), 53.
31. Ibid., 164.
32. September 30, 1965, 876.

(Fischer), as well as that which sees a continuity in moderation (Ritter); and it can perhaps be claimed that the task of future German historiography of the First World War consists in taking up anew the main themes and examining them *sine ira et studio,* now that both sides have drawn lines whose rectilinearity greatly oversimplifies the problem.

II

Under the title *Weltwende 1917,* the Ranke Society has published papers presented and the discussions that ensued at a conference in Arnoldshain in 1963. The papers buttressed the thesis long advanced, principally by Erwin Hölzle, that 1917, the year of America's entry into the war and of the revolution in Russia, marked a caesura in modern history as viewed from the perspective of universal history. Hölzle was able to represent his own viewpoint in two of the eight papers.[33] For years he has concentrated his research on Russo-American relations, and in his studies of war policy he has made identification of the Russian components of Wilson's foreign policy his special concern. He calls Wilson's struggle for a democratic world peace the American democratic world revolution, as opposed to the communist world revolution. Both world revolutions, set in motion by the First World War, considered the autocracies their adversary and were united in their demands for world peace and the right to self-determination. This is certainly correctly observed. But it seems doubtful that Hölzle will succeed with his theory and terminology of "two world revolutions." There was at the time in question only *one* world revolutionist, Lenin. Even if one places a high estimate on the intellectual and political influence Wilson exercised in the West, as Hölzle does, it would not occur to one to consider the top-hatted university president and head of state a "world revolutionist." For Wilson did not effect, or think of effecting, a social-revolutionary upheaval which could be compared to or measured against Lenin's achievement in his own country or in the world. The idea that Wilson and

---

33. "Kriegsziele und Friedensversuche in der sich wandelnden Welt 1917–1918" (138–148), and "Die amerikanische und die bolschewistische Weltrevolution" (169–184).

Lenin embodied ideologies which, after the war, would present claims to world leadership was in no way hidden from their contemporaries. For a man like Clemenceau, who had made the ideals of the 1789 revolution his life ideals, it was unbelievably presumptuous that Lenin should appear in Paris in order to discuss world views with Wilson, with an invitation given to the Bolsheviks at the urging of the Americans and British. (The debates at the peace conference in Brest-Litovsk had given a foretaste of such a discussion.) Moreover, it was intolerable that the pressing problems of the Peace Conference should recede into the background in favor of intellectual questions. One can, however, say this of Hölzle: the picture of Wilson that he presented to his listeners and now asks his readers to accept constitutes more than a revision for a German: it constitutes a revolution, inasmuch as it rehabilitates a statesman misunderstood and maligned for half a century. And Hölzle gives his conviction force and credibility by confronting Wilson with Lenin.

Contrary to Hölzle, who holds that the politics of the First World War should be treated in the context of universal history (p. 138), I should like to see priority given to the presentation and elucidation of the policies of the individual states, and of the Vatican as well, on the basis of their chief documents. The request voiced by the International Congress of Historians in Vienna in 1965 that Britain and France open their archives tends in this direction. Only when such inaccessible documentation has been given scholarly consideration will a "source basis comprising as many major countries as possible" become a reality.[34] The difficulty involved in analysis in terms of universal history can be judged from the fact that Fischer's bold attempt at a "unilateral" presentation has thus far had no counterpart in any of the other states involved in the First World War.[35]

According to Hölzle (p. 135), Fischer has not succeeded in demonstrating that Germany's war aims should have threatened the

---

34. Hölzle, "Das Experiment des Friedens" (see above, note 5).

35. A book appeared in England in 1965 which took military affairs as its point of departure, presenting British strategy in the light of national politics and tactical developments and showing the mutual influence of war policy and domestic politics: Guinn, *British Strategy and Politics, 1914 to 1918* (see above, note 1).

status of Germany's chief enemies as world powers, to say nothing of their allowing Germany herself to become a world power. But if one explains German war aims (even in their confinement to a "lesser-European vista" and to a German Central Africa) as a figment of an overactive fantasy, and if one sees in them immediate war aims (as distinct from the unattainable distant goal, status as a world power), does Fischer not still deserve credit for having pointed up the discrepancy between the war aims called for in Germany and the actual military situation, and for having cast light on the self-deception to which the public as well as the government fell victim, especially after Bethmann Hollweg's downfall? From such a perspective, it is of secondary importance whether one explains, as Hölzle does, German war aims as directed toward a concentration of power in inner Europe, or as a consolidation of power in central Europe, or whether, like Fischer, one considers "utopian" economic, if not political, hegemony sought by Germany in Europe, and its extension into eastern Europe as well as Russia and the Near East, to say nothing of demands for colonies and naval bases.

The papers presented by the other scholars provide supporting evidence for the viewpoint advanced by Hölzle—in the instances of Russia (Georg von Rauch, with an unusually positive accent on phenomena of the prewar period in political, economic, and cultural spheres in "czarist Russia between evolution and revolution," as he expressed it on another occasion), of Austria-Hungary (Ludwig Jedlicka), and of Germany (Karl Heinz Janszen, with provocative statements such as, "The Republic [was] a product of the Bolshevik revolution."). The papers represented noteworthy independent achievements, and the frank discussions, which were kept at a consistently high level, deserve the same consideration as the papers themselves. The freedom of the discussion from any *Gleichschaltung* was remarkable. Thus, during the discussion of the paper on Germany, the following question by Janszen went unopposed:

Will we allow ourselves to be bound in the study of history as well by the anti-Bolshevik disposition in our country at this time? We must have the option of discussing seriously the goals of a Karl Liebknecht, a Rosa Luxemburg. [p. 118]

III

That sense and nonsense can be found in close proximity on the shelves of the same archive becomes evident when the sometimes frivolous statements of Professor Friedrich Lezius of Königsberg University are compared with the letters of Ambassador Wolff Metternich to Wilhelm Solf among the Solf papers deposited in the Federal Archive. Wolff Metternich's harsh judgment of Wilson, which is understandable given the circumstances of the time and which corresponds in great measure with the German view of Wilson after Versailles, seems in retrospect more applicable to Lezius: "Nothing is as dangerous as a fanaticized professor . . ." (p. 106). Eberhard von Vietsch, Solf's biographer,[36] has edited and written a perceptive introduction to letters exchanged during and shortly after the war by the former ambassador in London (1901–1912), Paul Count Metternich, and Wilhelm Solf, the secretary of state of the Reich Colonial Office (from 1911) and secretary of state of the Foreign Ministry from the beginning of October to December 3, 1918.[37]

Both correspondents could be characterized as pronounced "Westerners," to borrow an Anglo-Saxon expression. They were by virtue of their intellectual development more at home with the problems of England and America, with the Anglo-Saxon mentality and the war potentials of the two countries, than with questions concerning Germany's Continental enemies, France and Russia. The book has been called "a psychological contribution to history, nothing more" by one well-wishing critic.[38]

Nonetheless, the historian will not be able to ignore this correspondence, for the correspondents were members of the ruling class, who at times had access to unusual sources of information, and who had the opportunity of presenting their views at the highest levels of government. Metternich's war aims were moderate: integ-

---

36. *Wilhelm Solf. Botschafter zwischen den Zeiten* (Tübingen, 1961).
37. Appended are a letter from Metternich to Albert Ballin, Director General of the Hamburg-America Line and two letters from Ballin to Metternich.
38. Erich Dombrowski, in the *Frankfurter Allgemeine Zeitung*, September 24, 1964.

rity of Germany's borders and restitution or acquisition of colonial possessions, in exchange for cession of occupied regions in the West (letter to Ballin, August 20, 1917, 66). In the East, he still saw many possibilities. As to the "Polish adventure" (p. 66), he was of the opinion that in terms of the proclamation on Poland Germany could be content with a peace treaty in which she succeeded in keeping Poland from being carved up. When peace talks with the Soviets began, talks whose political import could hardly have been overestimated, Solf bemoaned the fact that in preparatory discussions on the peace treaty one of the highest officials in the Foreign Ministry seemed to attach paramount importance to what were basically economic agreements ("stipulations on lubricating oil and barley tariffs," p. 101). Solf and Metternich were in agreement that the right to self-determination was the crucial issue in the Brest negotiations and that the Soviets succeeded in exhausting the diplomats of the Central Powers on this question: the longer the Bolsheviks drew out the negotiations the more aware the world at large would become of the irreconcilable contradiction in the fact that the Germans conceded in theory the right of the Baltic nationalities to self-determination, but that they were not prepared to allow them to exercise this right in practice because that would have meant voluntary surrender of Germany's position of strength in the occupied regions. One should add that Germany employed the "inoffensive designation 'border adjustments for strategic purposes' " (Solf to Metternich, January 11, 1918) for the annexations she sought, a practice that Solf, even before talks were concluded, judged would have a catastrophic effect on German prestige and future peace efforts. "The dishonesty of our policy is a mortgage weighing heavily on our Government and on the entire German people as well" (p. 111). Metternich addressed himself to this on February 5 and wrote: "We need a Czernin who speaks clearly and truthfully and leaves no door open for concealed annexations" (p. 112). To say nothing of the fact that in the fourth year of the war a positive assessment of an Austrian statesman was tantamount to heresy from the German point of view, this statement reveals that competent observers recognized clearly the division in the delegations of the Central Powers at the Brest talks, although everything was done to keep this from the public's eyes.

What Solf meant by the pursuit of "aims of ethical and cultural imperialism" by Germany in Russia in a revision of the Brest-Litovsk treaty (letter of July 31, 1918, p. 124) is unclear. The direction taken by his thoughts is indicated by a talk that he gave before the Deutsche Gesellschaft on August 20, 1918, an address which received a good deal of notice. Prepared to accept the Brest peace only as a skeleton agreement, he explained that the repressed foreign nationalities in Russia were to enjoy German protection, which would constitute a transitional stage on the way to complete self-determination. This protection was never to be made a pretense for German annexations.

In Solf's short two-month term of office, as secretary of state of the Foreign Ministry from the beginning of October to December 3 (the "last Foreign Minister of the Monarchy and the first of the Republic"),[39] the armistice in the West and the effects of the revolution on foreign policy were his most pressing concerns. He was not at all aware that the British and Americans had very strong reservations about him after his opposition to a precipitate evacuation of the Ukraine had become known in the last two weeks of October and had been wrongly interpreted,[40] but that incident probably made him *persona non grata* in London and Washington and militated against his being sent as ambassador of the Weimar Republic to either capital.[41]

Since the correspondence extends only to the end of the war and the revolution, and since thus far there has been no presentation of German Eastern policy between the armistice of Compiègne and the Treaty of Versailles, it is impossible to say anything final concerning Solf's role in the decisions of November 1918 affecting Eastern policy except that the fact that the minister responsible for Joffe's expulsion from Germany was a member of the first revolutionary cabinet was taken by the Soviets as symbolic of how far the revolution was from a real revolution. From a paraphrase of documents originally published in 1957 in the first volume (November

---

39. Eberhard von Vietsch, ed., *Gegen die Unvernunft* (Bremen: Schünemann, 1964), 141.
40. Vietsch, *Wilhelm Solf*, 203–204.
41. Ibid., 238.

7 to December 31) of *Dokumenty vneshnei politiki SSSR*,[42] it emerges that in the November weeks the People's Commissariat for External Affairs considered Hugo Haase, Karl Liebknecht, and the Executive Committee of the Berlin Council of Workers and Soldiers members of a kind of collateral government beside the official cabinet, and that it would have liked to see them elevated to principal government. That Solf saw in Haase his chief adversary and that he resigned because he believed that Ebert had left him in the lurch after a sharp clash with Haase comes out in a memorandum of 1926 published in Solf's biography;[43] to Solf's mind, Ebert was too late in breaking with the independents.[44]

---

42. Günter Rosenfeld, *Sowjetrussland und Deutschland 1917–1922* (Berlin, 1960), 146–152.

43. Vietsch, *Wilhelm Soft,* 381–382.

44. Ibid., 383: Letter to Wolf Metternich, November 11, 1919.

The Works of
Fritz T. Epstein

This list excludes short articles, brief book reviews, and most encyclopedia articles. Those essays published in translation in this volume are marked with an asterisk.

I. MONOGRAPHS

1. The Present Situation of East European Studies in Germany, Especially in the Western Zones. A survey, prepared for the Education and Cultural Relations Division of HICOG. 1950. 80 pp. (Mimeographed.)

2. German Source Materials in American Libraries. An address delivered at the Institute of German Affairs, Marquette University, November 14, 1957. Milwaukee: Marquette University Press, 1958. 14 pp.

3. Die Entwicklung der Auslandsforschung an amerikanischen Universitäten seit dem Zweiten Weltkrieg, mit besonderer Hervorhebung der Tätigkeit auf osteuropäischem und russischem Gebiet. Vortrag gehalten im Forschungsinstitut der Deutschen Gesellschaft für auswärtige Politik am 10. November 1969 in Bonn. 35 pp. (Lithographed.)

4. Hajo Holborn (28.5.1902–20.6.1969) zum Gedenken. Nachruf gehalten im Osteuropäischen Hauptseminar, Sommer-Semester 1969, der Universität Hamburg am 25.Juni 1969. 6 pp. (Mimeographed.)

II. ARTICLES

A. General

*5. "Politische Bildung und Hochschulpolitik in der Sowjetunion," *Neue Blätter für den Sozialismus,* III, No. 11 (1932), 594–604.

6. "Die Hochschulfrage in der Sowjetunion," *Student und Hochschule,* Fifth year, No. 1/2 (February 15, 1932), 6–11.

7. "National Socialism and French Colonialism," *Journal of Central European Affairs*, III, No. 1 (April, 1943), 52–64.

*8. "Friedrich Meinecke in seinem Verhältnis zum europäischen Osten," *Jahrbuch für die Geschichte Mittel- und Ostdeutschlands*, III (1954), 119–144.

*9. "Ost-Mitteleuropa als Spannungsfeld zwischen Ost und West um die Jahrhundertwende bis zum Ende des Ersten Weltkrieges," *Die Welt als Geschichte*, XVI, No. 1 (1956), 64–75.

*10. "Zur Interpretation des Versailler Vertrages. Der von Polen 1919–1922 erhobene Reparationsanspruch," *Jahrbücher für Geschichte Osteuropas*, V, No. 3 (October 1957), 315–335.

11. "Studien zur Geschichte der 'Russischen Frage' auf der Pariser Friedenskonferenz von 1919," *Jahrbücher für Geschichte Osteuropas*, VII, No. 4 (December 1959), 431–478.
(1. Die Russische Politische Delegation, 433–445; 2. Die Nationalitäten Russlands auf der Friedenskonferenz, 445–450; 3. Die Stellungnahme der Vereinigten Staaten zu den Selbständigkeitsbestrebungen der Nationalitäten Russlands, 450–460; 4. *Russland und der Völkerbund, 460–478.)

*12. "Die Erschliessung von Quellen zur Geschichte der deutschen Aussenpolitik. Die Publikation von Akten des Auswärtigen Amtes nach den beiden Weltkriegen. Ein Vergleich der Methoden," *Die Welt als Geschichte*, XXII, No. 3–4 (1962), 204–219.

*13. "Die deutsche Ostpolitik im Ersten Weltkrieg. (Bemerkungen zu Fritz Fischers Buch 'Griff nach der Weltmacht. Die Kriegszielpolitik des kaiserlichen Deutschland 1914–1918.' Düsseldorf, 1961), *Jahrbücher für Geschichte Osteuropas*, X, No. 3 (October 1962), 381–394. Reprinted in *Deutsche Kriegsziele, 1914–1918. Eine Diskussion*, Ernst Wilhelm Graf Lynar, ed. (Berlin, 1964), 158–174.

B. *Published in* Festschriften *and Collective Works*

14. "Argentinien und das deutsche Heer. Ein Beitrag zur Geschichte europäischer militärischer Einflüsse auf Südamerika," *Geschichtliche Kräfte und Entscheidungen. Festschrift zum 65. Geburtstag von Otto Becker.* Martin Goehring and Alexander Scharff, eds. (Wiesbaden, 1954), 286–294. See also No. 179: "European Military Influence in Latin America."

*15. "Otto Hoetzsch als aussenpolitischer Kommentator während des Ersten Weltkrieges," *Russland-Studien. Gedenkschrift für Otto Hoetzsch. Schriftenreihe Osteuropa, No. 3* (Stuttgart, 1957), 9–28.

16. "Germany and the United States: Basic Patterns of Conflict and Understanding," *Issues and Conflicts. Studies in Twentieth Century American Diplomacy*, George L. Anderson, ed. (Lawrence, Kansas, 1959), 284–314.

17. "War-time Activities of the SS-Ahnenerbe," *On the Track of Tyranny. Essays Presented by the Wiener Library to Leonard G. Montefiore, O.B.E.,*

on the Occasion of his 70th Birthday, Max Beloff, ed. (London, 1960), 77–95.

18. "America's Changing View of Europe," *Western Integration and the Future of Eastern Europe,* David S. Collier and Kurt Glaser, eds. (Chicago, 1964), 175–201.
German version: "Der Wandel im Europabild Amerikas," *Westintegration und Osteuropa,* Alfred Domes, ed. (Cologne, 1965), 201–223. [An address given at the Second German-American Congress at Wiesbaden, September 1963.]

19. "Deutschland und die USA—Germany and the USA, 1918–1933," *Schriftenreihe des Internationalen Schulbuchinstituts, Braunschweig,* XIII (1968), 7–12.

C. *Survey of Literature and Periodicals*

a. LITERATURE

20. "Erste Orientierung über Russland und den Bolschewismus," *Neue Blätter für den Sozialismus,* First year (1930), 320–325.

21. "Aus der historischen Arbeit in Russisch-Mittelasien," *Jahrbücher für Kultur und Geschichte der Slaven,* IX, No. 3 (1934), 438–447.

22. "Recent Literature on Minorities," *New Europe* (Monthly Review of International Affairs), IV, No. 6 (July–August 1944), 27–29.

23. "Neue Literatur zur Geschichte der Ostpolitik im Ersten Weltkrieg (I)," *Jahrbücher für Geschichte Osteuropas,* XIV, No. 1 (March 1966), 63–94; (II) ibid., XIX (1971), 110–118, 265–286, 401–418, 557–564; XX (1972), 247–274.

b. PERIODICALS

24. "Übersicht über die historischen Aufsätze und Notizen in der Zeitschrift *Severnaia Aziia,* Nos. 1–13, 1923–1927," *Jahrbücher für Kultur und Geschichte der Slaven,* III, No. 4 (1927), 495–504.

25. *Istorik-Marksist* (Zhurnal Obshchestva istorikov-marksistov pri Kommunisticheskoi Akademii), Nos. 1 and 2 (1926), 3 and 4 (1927), *Jahrbücher für Kultur und Geschichte der Slaven,* IV, No. 2 (1928), 277–294.

26. "Die marxistische Geschichtswissenschaft in der Sovetunion seit 1927," [*Istorik-Marksist,* Nos. 5 and 6 (1927), 7 to 10 (1928), and 11 (1929)], *Jahrbücher für Kultur und Geschichte der Slaven,* VI, No. 1 (1930), 78–203.

27. Short notes, *Jahrbücher für Kultur und Geschichte der Slaven,* III–VI (1927–1930).

28. Short notes, *Historische Zeitschrift,* CXXXV, CXXXVI, CXXXIX, CXL, CXLI, CXLIII, CXLVI, CXLVIII, and CIL (1927–1934).

D. *Contributions to Library Science and Bibliography*

29. "Die 'Bücherkatakombe' Iwans des Schrecklichen," *Frankfurter Zeitung,* No. 590, 1. Morning edition, August 10, 1930.

30. "Aus der historischen Wissenschaft der Sovet-Union (Königsberg, 1929) (Osteuropäische Forschungen, VII)," *Zeitschrift für Politik,* XXI, No. 5 (August 1931), 363–364.

31. "Die Sovet-Union 1917–1932. Systematische Bibliographie," Klaus Mehnert, ed. (Königsberg, 1933), *Zeitschrift für Politik,* XXIII, No. 5 (August 1933), 342–346.

32. Wegerer, Alfred von, *Bibliographie zur Vorgeschichte des Weltkrieges* (1934), and Coulter, Edith M., and Melanie Gerstenfeld, *Historical Bibliographies* (Berkeley, 1935), *Bulletin of the Institute of Historical Research,* XIII, No. 39 (February 1936), 166–167.

33. Yakobson, Sergei, and Fritz Epstein (compilers), "A List of Books in English on Russia Published in 1935," *Slavonic and East European Review,* XV, No. 44 (January 1937), 482–490.

34. Postnikov, S. P., ed., *Bibliografiia russkoi revoliutsii* (Paris, 1938), *American Historical Review,* XLIV, No. 2 (January 1939), 449–450.

35. "A Short Working Bibliography on the Slavs," *Slavonic and East European Review,* XXII, No. 60 (October 1944), 110–119.

36. "Die Hoover Library der Stanford-Universität," *Nachrichten für wissenschaftliche Bibliotheken,* Third year, No. 7–8 (July–August 1950), 103–104.

37. Current Bibliographies on Russian History, 1957–1958, and on the History of Germany, Austria, and Switzerland, 1958–1960, as Contributing Editor to the *American Historical Review,* LXV–LXVII.

38. *East Germany: A Selected Bibliography* (Washington, D.C., 1959). 55 pp.

39. "The Growth of the German-language Collections," *The Library of Congress Quarterly Journal of Current Acquisitions,* XVI, No. 3 (May 1959), 123–130.

40. "Russia and the Soviet Union (including the Russian Empire in Asia)," Section X, *Guide to Historical Literature,* published by the American Historical Association (New York, 1961), 621–645.

41. Claus, Helmut (compiler), *Slavica-Katalog der Landesbibliothek Gotha* (Leipzig, 1962), *Slavic Review,* XXII, No. 3 (1963), 614–615.

42. Bruhn, Peter (compiler), *Gesamtverzeichnis russischer und sowjetischer Periodika und Serienwerke in Bibliotheken der Bundesrepublik Deutschland und Westberlins* (Berlin, 1963) (Bibliographische Mitteilungen des Osteuropa-Instituts an der Freien Universität Berlin), *Slavic and East European Journal,* VII, No. 3 (Fall 1963), 133.

43. Hammond, Thomas T., ed., *Soviet Foreign Relations and World Communism* (Princeton, 1965), *Jahrbücher für die Geschichte Osteuropas,* XIII, No. 4 (December 1965), 531–538 ("Eine neue amerikanische Bibliographie über die Sowjetaussenpolitik und den Kommunismus"). See also review in *Slavic Review,* XXV, No. 1 (March 1966), 173–174.

44. Kehr, Helen (compiler), *After Hitler. Germany 1945–1963. The Wiener Library, Catalogue Series No. 4* (London, 1963), *Jahrbücher für Geschichte Osteuropas,* XIII, No. 1 (April 1965), 148.

45. Maichel, Karol, *Guide to Russian Reference Books.* Vol. I: *General Bibliographies and Reference Books* (Stanford, 1962); Vol. II: *History, Auxiliary Historical Sciences, Ethnography, and Geography* (Stanford, 1964). Edited by J. S. G. Simmons (Hoover Institution Bibliographical Series, Nos. 10 and 18), *Slavic and East European Journal,* IX, No. 4 (1965), 469–470, and *Slavic Review,* XXV, No. 2 (June 1966), 370–372.

46. Horecky, Paul L., ed., *Basic Russian Publications. An Annotated Bibliography on Russia and the Soviet Union* (Chicago, 1962); Horecky, Paul L., ed., *Russia and the Soviet Union. A Bibliographic Guide to Western-Language Publications* (Chicago, 1965); Shapiro, David (compiler), *A Select Bibliography of Works in English on Russian History, 1801–1917* (Oxford, 1962), *Slavic Review,* XXV, No. 2 (June 1966), 370–372.

47. *Bibliothek für Zeitgeschichte. Weltkriegsbücherei* (Stuttgart, Jahresbibliographien, Vols. XXXII–XXXVII, 1960–1965) (Frankfurt a.M., 1961–67), *Erasmus,* XIX, No. 23/24 (December 25, 1967), Col. 752–758.

48. Harvard University Library (Widener Library), *Widener Library Shelflist No. 4: Russian History since 1917* (Cambridge, Mass., 1966), *Slavic and East European Journal,* XII, No. 2 (Summer 1968), 264.

49. Kuehl, Warren S., ed., *Dissertations in History . . . 1873–1960* (Lexington, Kentucky, 1965), *Jahrbücher für Geschichte Osteuropas* XVI, No. 4 (December 1968), 559–561; "The History of Austria in United States and Canadian Dissertations," *Austrian History Yearbook,* VI–VII (1970–1971), 221–238.

50. Goy, Peter A., and Laurence H. Miller, eds., *A Biographical Directory of Librarians in the Field of Slavic and East European Studies* (Chicago, 1967), *Jahrbücher für Geschichte Osteuropas,* XVII, No. 1 (March 1969), 135.

51. Scherer, Anton (compiler), *Südosteuropa-Dissertationen 1918–1960. Eine Bibliographie deutscher, österreichischer und schweizerischer Hochschulschriften* (Cologne, Vienna, 1968), *Austrian History Yearbook,* VI–VII (1970–1971), 359–366.

52. *Dokumentationsarchiv der österreichischen Widerstandes.* Catalogs 1–6 (1963–1969); see below, Nos. 66–68.

E. *Analyses of Publications of Sources*

a. PUBLICATIONS OF DOCUMENTS

53. "Documents diplomatiques français (1871–1914)," *Erasmus*, XVI, No. 15/16 (August 25, 1964), Col. 486–490.

54. Nishikawa, Masao, *Survey of Source Materials on Modern History* (in Japanese), *Historische Zeitschrift*, CLXXXXVIII, No. 3 (1964), 784.

55. Deuerlein, Ernst (and others), eds., *Dokumente zur Deutschlandpolitik.* III. *Reihe*, Vols. I and III (for 1955 and 1957) (Frankfurt a.M., Berlin, 1961–1967), *Erasmus*, XIX, No. 23/24 (December 25, 1967), Col. 752–758.

56. *Allianz Hitler-Horthy-Mussolini. Dokumente zur ungarischen Aussenpolitik*, Lajos Kerekes, ed. (Budapest, 1966), *Journal of Modern History*, XLI, No. 2 (July 1969), 269–271.

57. *Protokolle des Gemeinsamen Ministerrates der Österreichisch-ungarischen Monarchie 1914–1918*, Miklós Komjáthy, ed. (Budapest, 1966) (Publikationen des Ungarischen Staatsarchivs. II. Quellenpublikationen, X), *Jahrbücher für Geschichte Osteuropas*, XIX, No. 1 (March 1971), 111–115.

58. Scherer, André, and Jacques Grunewald, eds., *L'Allemagne et les problèmes de la paix pendant la première guerre mondiale (août 1914— Novembre 7, 1917)*. I (Paris, 1962), II (1966), *Jahrbücher für Geschichte Osteuropas*, XIX, No. 1 (March 1971), 115–118.

b. ARCHIVAL SCIENCE

59. "Das sovetrussische Archivwesen (Literaturbericht)," *Archivalische Zeitschrift*, XXXIX (1930), 282–308.

60. "Aus dem Archivwesen der Sovetunion. I. Wissenschaftliche Verbindung zum Ausland. II. Die neuere Archivliteratur des Westens im russischen Urteil," *Zeitschrift für osteuropäische Geschichte*, V (1931), 314–319.

61. "Washington Research Opportunities in the Period of World War II," *American Archivist*, XVII, No. 3 (July 1954), 225–236. The same: "Zur Quellenkunde der neuesten Geschichte. Ausländische Materialien in den Archiven und Bibliotheken der Hauptstadt der Vereinigten Staaten," *Vierteljahrshefte für Zeitgeschichte*, III, No. 2 (July 1954), 313–325.

62. "Archive Administration in the Soviet Union," *American Archivist*, XX, No. 2 (April 1957), 131–143.

63. "Übersicht der Bestände des Deutschen Zentralarchivs Potsdam," Helmut Lötzke and Hans-Stephan Brather, eds. (East Berlin, 1957), and Forstreuter, Kurt, *Das preussische Staatsarchiv Königsberg* (Göttingen, 1955) (Veröffentlichungen der Niedersächsischen Archivverwaltung, 3), *American Archivist*, XXI, No. 2 (April 1958), 212–214.

64. DDR. Ministerium des Innern, Staatliche Archivverwaltung, *Fünf Jahre Archivarbeit, 1952–1957* (East Berlin, 1957), *American Archivist*, XXII, No. 3 (July 1959), 342–343.

65. Heinz, Grete, and Agnes F. Peterson (compilers), *NSDAP Hauptarchiv. Guide to the Hoover Institution Microfilm Collection* (Stanford, 1964) (Hoover Institution Bibliographical Series, 17), *Jahrbücher für Geschichte Osteuropas*, XIII, No. 2 (June 1965), 248–250.

66. *Dokumentationsarchiv des österreichischen Widerstandes. Katalog, Nos. 1 and 2* (Vienna, 1963), *Austrian History Yearbook*, II (Vienna, 1966), 321–324.

67. The same. *Katalog, Nos. 3 and 4* (Vienna, 1966), *Austrian History Yearbook*, IV–V (1968–69), 503–507.

68. The same. *Katalog, Nos. 5 and 6* (Vienna, 1969), *Austrian History Yearbook*, VI–VII (1970–1971), 447–451.

F. *Biographical*

69. "Heinrich von Staden," *Westfälische Lebensbilder*, II, Part 1 (1931), 51–70.

70. "Bogoslovskii, M. M." (obituary), *Historische Vierteljahrsschrift* (1931), 695.

71. "Michail Nikolajewitsch Pokrovskij. Ein Kollektiv-Historiker in U.S.S.R.," (obituary), *Frankfurter Zeitung*, No. 407/08 (Evening edition, 1st morning edition), June 3, 1932.

72. "M. N. Pokrovsky," *Encyclopaedia of the Social Sciences*, XII (1933), 181–182.

73. "Tirpitz," *Encyclopedia Britannica*, XXII (1957), 19–20.

74. "Michael Karpovich" (obituary), *Jahrbücher für Geschichte Osteuropas*, VII, No. 4 (December 1959), 515–516.

75. "William E. Lingelbach und Guy Stanton Ford" (obituaries), *Historische Zeitschrift*, CLXXXXVII, No. 2 (1963), 514–516.

76. "Hamburg und Osteuropa. Zum Gedächtnis von Professor Richard Salomon (1884–1966)." Gedenkrede gehalten als Vortragsveranstaltung der Deutschen Gesellschaft für Osteuropakunde und der Philosophischen Fakultät der Universität Hamburg am Dienstag, dem 17. Mai 1966. 35 pp. (Mimeographed.) The same, with bibliography (compiled in cooperation with Norbert Angermann), *Jahrbücher für Geschichte Osteuropas*, XV, No. 1 (April 1967), 59–98.

77. "The [Boris Ivanovich] Nikolaevskii Collection at Indiana," *Indiana University Library News Letter*, I, No. 4 (April 1966), 1–2.

III. BOOK REVIEWS

1928

78. Korostowetz, Wladimir Konstantinowitsch, *Von Cinggis Khan zur Sowjetrepublik* (Berlin, 1926), *Zeitschrift für Politik*, XVIII, No. 11–12 (1928–29), 816–820).

79. Böttger, Eugen (E. K. Betger), *Novyi avtograf Ulrikha von Guttena* [Ein Hutten-Autograph in Tashkent], *Zeitschrift für Kirchengeschichte*, XLVII, New Series X, 589.

1929

80. Hammerstein, Hans Freiherr von, *Der Waffenstillstand 1918–1919 und Polen* (Einzelschriften für Politik und Geschichte, 29) (Berlin, 1928), *Zeitschrift für Politik*, XIX, No. 6 (October 1929), 439–440.

1930

81. Grüning, Irene, *Die russische öffentliche Meinung und ihre Stellung zu den Grossmächten 1878–1894* (Berlin, Königsberg, 1929) (Osteuropäische Forschungen, III), *Zeitschrift für Politik*, XX, No. 2 (May 1930), 150–152.

1931

82. Pokrowski, M., *Geschichte Russlands* (Leipzig, 1929), *Zeitschrift für Politik*, XXI, No. 5 (August 1931), 360–363.

83. Preobrazhenskii, Nikolai O., *Krepostnoe khoziaistvo v Chekhii XV–XVI vekov* (Prague, 1928), *Vierteljahrschrift für Sozial- und Wirtschaftsgeschichte*, XXIV, 241.

84. Uspenskii, F. I., *Ocherki iz istorii Trapezuntskoi imperii* (Leningrad, 1929), *Byzantinische Zeitschrift*, XXXI, 101–102.

85. Petrushevskii, D. M., *Ocherki iz ekonomicheskoi istorii srednevekovoi Evropy* (Moscow, Leningrad, 1928), *Zeitschrift für die gesamte Staatswissenschaft*, XL, 617–620.

86. Schaeder, Hildegard, *Moskau, das Dritte Rom. Studien zur Geschichte der politischen Theorien in der slavischen Welt* (Hamburg, 1930) (Osteuropäische Studien, 1), *Zeitschrift für osteuropäische Geschichte*, V, 555–557.

87. Schlochauer, Hans Jürgen, *Der deutsch-russische Rückversicherungs-vertrag* (Leipzig, 1931) (Frankfurter Abhandlungen zum modernen Völkerrecht, 22), *Zeitschrift für osteuropäische Geschichte,* V, 630–631.

1932

88. Brandt, Otto, *Caspar von Saldern und die nordeuropäische Politik im Zeitalter Katharinas II* (Kiel, 1932), *Jahrbücher für Kultur und Geschichte der Slaven,* VIII, 83–85, 311.

1933

89. D'iakonov, Mikhail Mikhailovich, *Skizzen zur Gesellschafts- und Staatsordnung des alten Russland* (Breslau, 1931) [Bibliothek geschichtlicher Werke aus den Literaturen Osteuropas, 6], *Jahrbücher für Kultur und Geschichte der Slaven,* IX, No. 4, 627–628.

1934

90. Fleischhacker, Hedwig, *Russland zwischen zwei Dynastien* (Brünn, 1933) (Studien zur osteuropäischen Geschichte, New Series 1), *Jahrbücher für Kultur und Geschichte der Slaven,* X, 210–213.

91. Poltoratskii, A. V., and A. Glazyrev, trans., *Saksonskie snosheniia s pol'skim korolem kasatel'no posol'stva Chr. Shleinitsa* [Schleinitz] *v Moskve 1511–14 gg., Trudy Tul'skoi Gubernskoi Arkhivnoi Komissii, I* (Tula, 1914), 25 pp.; Blinov, I., and L. Sukhotskii, *Istoricheskie materialy izvlechennye iz Senatskago arkhiva. Iz istorii russko-niemetskikh otnoshenii, Zhurnal Ministerstva Iustitsii* (Petrograd, March 1915), 27 pp.; and Nikolai Mikhailovich, Grand duke, *Iz donesenii Bavarskago povierennago v dielakh Ol'ri* [Olry] *v pervye gody tsarstvovaniia (1802–1806) imperatora Aleksandra I, Istoricheskii Vestnik,* Nos. 1 and 2 (Petrograd, 1917), 69 pp., *Zeitschrift für osteuropäische Geschichte,* VIII, 148–150.

1935

92. *The Bolshevik Revolution,* James Bunyan and H. H. Fisher, eds., (Stanford, 1934) (Hoover War Library Publications, 3), *Slavonic and East European Review,* XIII, No. 39, 707–709.

1937

93. *The Testimony of Kolchak,* H. H. Fisher, ed. (Stanford, 1935) (Hoover War Library Publications, 10), *Slavonic and East European Review,* XV, No. 44, 472–473.

1940

94. Fleischhacker, Hedwig, *Die staats- und völkerrechtlichen Grundlagen der moskauischen Aussenpolitik, 14.–17. Jahrhundert* (*Jahrbücher für Geschichte Osteuropas,* Beiheft 1) (Breslau, 1938), *American Historical Review,* XLV, No. 3, 713.

1941

95. Levin, Alfred, *The Second Duma* (New Haven, 1940), *American Historical Review,* XLVI, No. 2, 403–405.

1944

96. Hagen, Paul [Pseud., Karl Borromäus Frank], *Germany after Hitler* (New York, Toronto, 1944), *Journal of Central European Affairs,* IV, No. 3, 331–334.

1946

97. Shanahan, William O., *Prussian Military Reforms, 1786–1813* (New York, 1945), *Military Affairs,* X, No. 3, 51–53.

1949

98. *Soviet Press Translations,* Ivar Spector, ed., *Russian Review,* VIII, No. 2, 167–168.

99. *Diplomaticheskii Slovar'* Vol. I. A. Ia. Vyshinskii, and S. A. Lozovskii, eds. (Moscow, 1948), *American Journal of International Law,* XLII, No. 2, 390–394.

1950

100. Kühlmann, Richard von, *Erinnerungen* (Heidelberg, 1948), *Journal of Central European Affairs,* X, No. 2, 183–186.

101. Hossbach, Friedrich, *Zwischen Wehrmacht und Hitler 1934–1938* (Wolfenbüttel, Hannover, 1949), *Journal of Central European Affairs,* X, No. 3, 312–313.

1951

102. Sokolnicki, Michael, *The Turkish Straits* (Beirut, 1950), *Journal of Modern History,* XXIII, 411.

1955

103. Lukacz, John A., *The Great Powers and Eastern Europe* (New York, 1953), *Western Political Quarterly*, VIII, No. 2, 301–303.

104. Ritter, Gerhard, *Staatskunst und Kriegshandwerk*. Vol. I: *Die altpreussische Tradition, 1740–1890* (Munich, 1954), *Western Political Quarterly*, VIII, No. 4, 644–645.

1957

105. Neumann, Rudolf, *Ostpreussen 1945–1955* (Frankfurt a.M., 1955), *Journal of Modern History*, XXIX, No. 4, 415–416.

1959

106. Zeman, Z. A. B., ed., *Germany and the Revolution in Russia, 1915–1918. Documents from the Archives of the German Foreign Ministry* (London, 1958), *Russian Review*, XVIII, No. 4, 342–344.

107. Mosse, Werner E., *The European Powers and the German Question, 1848–1871* (Cambridge, England, 1958), *Journal of Central European Affairs*, XIX, No. 3, 306–308.

108. Conze, Werner, *Polnische Nation und deutsche Politik im Ersten Weltkrieg* (Cologne, Graz, 1958), *Journal of Modern History*, XXXI, No. 4, 382–383.

1960

109. Slusser, Robert M., and Jan F. Triska, *A Calendar of Soviet Treaties, 1917–1957* (Stanford, 1959), *Russian Review*, XIX, No. 3, 296–297.

110. Spindler, Max, ed., *Electoralis Academiae Scientiarum Boicae Primordia. Briefe aus der Gründungszeit der Bayerischen Akademie der Wissenschaften* (Munich, 1959), *American Historical Review*, LXVI, No. 1, 151–153.

111. *Russian Thought and Politics. Essays in Honor of Michael Karpovich*, Hugh McLean, Martin I. Malia, and George Fischer, eds. ('s-Gravenhage, 1957) (Harvard Slavic Studies, 4), *Osteuropa*, X, No. 7/8, 570–571.

1961

112. Ritter, Gerhard, *Staatskunst und Kriegshandwerk*, Vol. II: *Die Hauptmächte Europas und das wilhelminische Reich (1890–1914)* (Munich, 1959), *Western Political Quarterly*, XIV, No. 3, 796–797.

113. Plötz, Karl, ed., *Geschichte des Zweiten Weltkrieges.* Second edition (Würzburg, 1960), *Jahrbücher für Geschichte Osteuropas,* IX, No. 3, 435–436.

114. Wagner, Wolfgang, *Die Teilung Europas. Geschichte der sowjetischen Expansion bis zur Spaltung Deutschlands 1918–1945,* Second edition (Stuttgart, 1960), *Jahrbücher für Geschichte Osteuropas,* IX, No. 4, 601–602.

115. Krusius-Ahrenberg, Lolo, Günther Stökl, Walter Schlesinger, and Reinhard Wittram, *Russland, Europa und der deutsche Osten* (Munich, 1960) (Beiträge zur europäischen Geschichte, 2), *Neue politische Literatur,* VI, No. 5, Col. 435–439.

1962

116. Ullman, Richard H., *Intervention and the War. Anglo-Soviet Relations 1917–1921.* Vol. I. (Princeton, 1961), *Historische Zeitschrift,* CLXXXXV, No. 3, 669–672.

*117. Fischer, Fritz, *Griff nach der Weltmacht* (Düsseldorf, 1961), *Jahrbücher für Geschichte Osteuropas,* X, No. 3, 381–394.

118. Denne, Ludwig, *Das Danziger Problem in der deutschen Aussenpolitik 1934–1939* (Bonn, 1959), *Jahrbuch für die Geschichte Mittel- und Ostdeutschlands,* XI, 474–475.

1963

119. Lederer, Ivo J., ed., *Russian Foreign Policy. Essays in Historical Perspective* (New Haven, 1962), *Historische Zeitschrift,* CLXXXVII, No. 2, 451–453.

120. Deuerlein, Ernst, *Die Einheit Deutschlands,* Vol. I. Second edition (Frankfurt a.M., 1961), *Jahrbücher für Geschichte Osteuropas,* XI, 129–131.

121. Fabry, Philipp W., *Der Hitler-Stalin-Pakt 1939–1941. Ein Beitrag zur Methode sowjetischer Aussenpolitik* (Darmstadt, 1962), *Neue politische Literatur,* VIII, No. 4, Col. 336–341.

122. Reitlinger, Gerald, *Ein Haus auf Sand gebaut. Hitlers Gewaltpolitik in Russland 1941–1944* (Hamburg, 1962), *Neue politische Literatur,* VIII, No. 4, Col. 341–343.

123. Epshtein, A. D., *Istoriia Germanii ot pozdnego srednekov'ia do revoliutsii 1848 goda* (Moscow, 1961), *American Historical Review,* LXVIII, No. 4, 1047–1048.

124. Feis, Herbert, *Between War and Peace. The Potsdam Conference* (Princeton, 1960), *Jahrbücher für Geschichte Osteuropas,* XI, No. 2, 286–287.

125. Armstrong, Anne, *Unconditional Surrender. The Impact of the Casablanca Policy upon World War II* (New Brunswick, 1961), *Jahrbücher für Geschichte Osteuropas*, XI, No. 2, 287–288.

126. Stern, Leo, ed., *Die russische Revolution 1905–1907 im Spiegel der deutschen Presse.* Five vols. (Berlin, 1961) (Dokumente und Materialien zur Geschichte der deutschen Arbeiterbewegung, 2 III–2 VII), *Historische Zeitschrift*, CLXXXXVII, No. 2, 423–424.

1964

127. Korbel, Josef, *Poland between East and West. Soviet and German Diplomacy toward Poland, 1919–1933* (Princeton, 1963), *Journal of Central European Affairs*, XXIII, No. 4, 518–522.

128. Ruge, Wolfgang, *Die Stellungnahme der Sowjetunion gegen die Besetzung des Ruhrgebietes. Zur Geschichte der deutsch-sowjetischen Beziehungen vom Januar bis September 1923*, *Jahrbücher für Geschichte Osteuropas*, XII, No. 1, 130–132.

129. Matossian, Mary Kilbourne, *The Impact of Soviet Policies in Armenia* (Leiden, 1962), *Historische Zeitschrift*, CLXXXXIX, No. 3, 704–706.

130. Triska, Jan F., and Robert M. Slusser, *The Theory, Law, and Policy of Soviet Treaties* (Stanford, 1962), *Russian Review*, XXIII, No. 3, 276–278.

1965

131. Zeman, Zbyněk A. B., *Nazi Propaganda* (London, 1964), *Jahrbücher für Geschichte Osteuropas*, XIII, No. 2, 247.

132. Markert, Werner, ed., *Deutsch-russische Beziehungen von Bismarck bis zur Gegenwart* (Stuttgart, 1964), *Jahrbücher für Geschichte Osteuropas*, XIII, No. 3, 446–448.

133. Janssen, Karl Heinz, *Macht und Verblendung. Kriegszielpolitik der deutschen Bundesstaaten 1914–18* (Göttingen, 1963), *Jahrbücher für Geschichte Osteuropas*, XIII, No. 2, 294.

134. Lutz, Heinrich, *Demokratie im Zwielicht. Der Weg der deutschen Katholiken aus dem Kaiserreich in die Republik, 1914–1925* (Munich, 1963), and Thieme, Hartwig, *Nationaler Liberalismus in der Krise. Die nationalliberale Fraktion des Preussischen Abgeordnetenhauses 1914–1918* (Schriften des Bundesarchivs, 11) (Boppard, 1963), *Jahrbücher für Geschichte Osteuropas*, XIII, No. 1, 108–109.

1966

*135. Fischer, Fritz, *Griff nach der Weltmacht.* Third edition (Düsseldorf, 1964), *Jahrbücher für Geschichte Osteuropas*, XIV, No. 1, 64–69.

*136. Ritter, Gerhard, *Staatskunst und Kriegshandwerk*. Vol. III. *Die Tragödie der Staatskunst. Bethmann Hollweg als Kriegskanzler (1914–1917)* (Munich, 1964), ibid., 69–77.

137. Steglich, Wolfgang, *Die Friedenspolitik der Mittelmächte 1917–1918* (Wiesbaden, 1964), ibid., 78–81.

138. Linde, Gerd, *Die deutsche Politik in Litauen im Ersten Weltkrieg* (Wiesbaden, 1965), ibid., 81–85.

139. Mann, Bernhard, *Die baltischen Länder in der deutschen Kriegsziel-publizistik 1914–1918* (Tübinger Studien zur Geschichte und Politik, 19) (Tübingen, 1965), ibid., 85–89.

*140. Röszler, Hellmuth, ed., *Weltwende 1917. Monarchie. Weltrevolution. Demokratie* (Göttingen, 1965), ibid., 89–91.

*141. Vietsch, Eberhard von, ed., *Gegen die Unvernunft. Der Briefwechsel zwischen Paul Graf Wolff Metternich und Wilhelm Solf 1915–1918 mit zwei Briefen Albert Ballins* (Bremen, 1964), ibid., 91–93.

1967

142. Ernst, Fritz, *The Germans and Their Modern History*. Translated from the German by Charles M. Prugh (New York, London, 1966), *Political Science Quarterly*, LXXXIII, No. 3, 482–483.

143. Geiss, Imanuel, *Der polnische Grenzstreifen 1914–1918. Ein Beitrag zur deutschen Kriegszielpolitik im Ersten Weltkrieg* (Hamburg, Lübeck, 1960), *Jahrbuch für die Geschichte Mittel- und Ostdeutschlands*, Ergän-zungsband zu XI, 240–242.

1968

144. *The Land and Government of Muscovy. A Sixteenth-Century Account*. Translated and edited by Thomas Esper (Stanford, 1967), *Renaissance Quarterly*, XXI, No. 2, 208–209.

145. Markert, Werner, *Osteuropa und die abendländische Welt. Aufsätze und Vorträge. Mit einem Geleitwort von Hans Rothfels* (Göttingen, 1966), *Jahrbücher für Geschichte Osteuropas*, XVI, No. 1, 121–122.

146. *Die deutsche Ostgrenze von 1937* (Studien zum Deutschtum im Osten, 4) (Cologne, 1967), *Jahrbücher für Geschichte Osteuropas*, XVI, No. 3, 460–461.

1969

147. Teske, Hermann, ed., *General Ernst Koestring. Der militärische Mittler zwischen dem Deutschen Reich und der Sowjetunion 1921–1941* (Frankfurt a.M., 1966), *Russian Review*, XXVIII, No. 1, 98–100.

148. Stökl, Günther, *Osteuropa und die Deutschen. Geschichte und Gegenwart einer spannungsreichen Nachbarschaft* (Oldenburg, Hamburg, 1967), *Historische Zeitschrift,* CCIX, No. 3, 634–35.

149. Wiegand, Günther, *Zum deutschen Russlandinteresse im 19. Jahrhundert. E. M. Arndt und Varnhagen von Ense* (Kieler historische Studien, 3) (Stuttgart, 1967), *Historische Zeitschrift,* CCIX, No. 3, 672–673.

1970

150. Ullman, Richard H., *Anglo-Soviet Relations, 1917–1921.* Vol. II. *Britain and the Russian Civil War, November 1918—February, 1920* (Princeton, 1968), *Historische Zeitschrift,* CCXI, No. 1, 170–173.

151. Dyck, Harvey L., *Weimar Germany and Soviet Russia, 1926–1933. A Study in Diplomatic Instability* (New York, London, 1966), *Journal of Modern History,* XLII, No. 3, 453–455.

IV. TRANSLATIONS

152. "Erklärung des Synods der Allrussischen Rechtgläubigen Kirche über das neue Verhältnis der Kirche zum Sowjetstaat," *Europäische Gespräche,* V (1927), 540–544.

153. "Abweichende Lesarten zu Litvinovs vierzehn Punkten," ibid., VI (1928), 22–27.

154. "Boris Stein und Michail Kol'cov. Nachruf für Graf Brockdorff-Rantzau," ibid., VII (1929), 18–29.

155. "Aufhebung der Extraterritorialität für die chinesischen Vertretungen in Russland," ibid., VII (1929), 321–324.

156. "Der russisch-chinesische Konflikt im Fernen Osten," ibid., VII (1929), 443–455.

157. "Manifest der russischen Wissenschaft an die Gelehrten aller Länder zum 1. August 1929," ibid., VII (1929), 562–565.

158. "Die Beilegung des russisch-chinesischen Konflikts," ibid., VIII (1930), 38–44.

159. "Das Protokoll von Angora vom 17. Dezember 1929," ibid., 46–47.

160. "Bekanntmachung des Tupan der Ostchinesischen Bahn," ibid., 110–112.

161. "Stalin und die Nationalitäten in der UdSSR," ibid., 116–118.

162. "Gruss Lenins an die bayrische Räterepublik," ibid., 395.

163. "Notenwechsel zwischen der Sowjetunion und Finnland," ibid., 578–586.

164. Busse, Gisela von, *West German Library Developments since 1945. With Special Emphasis on the Rebuilding of Research Libraries.* English

translation by Fritz T. Epstein and Barbara Krader (Washington, D.C.: Government Printing Office, 1962), 82 pp.

V. WORKS AS EDITOR

165. *Minerva. Jahrbuch der gelehrten Welt* ["Redaktioneller Leiter," with Gerhard Lüdtke, ed.], 27th year (Berlin, 1925), 28th year (Berlin, 1926).

166. Staden, Heinrich von, *Aufzeichnungen über den Moskauer Staat.* Nach der Handschrift des Preussischen Staatsarchivs in Hannover (Aus dem Osteuropäischen Seminar der Hamburgischen Universität. Hamburgische Universität. Abhandlungen aus dem Gebiet der Auslandskunde, 34 = Reihe A, Bd. 5) (Hamburg, 1930), "Selbstanzeige": *Zeitschrift für osteuropäische Geschichte,* V (1931), 264–272.

167. "Eine unbekannte Version der Beschreibung Nordrusslands durch Heinrich von Staden. Neue Staden-Dokumente aus dem Stockholmer Reichsarchiv. Her. von Fritz T. Epstein und Walther Kirchner unter Mitarbeit von Walther Niekerken," *Jahrbücher für Geschichte Osteuropas,* VIII, No. 2 (1960), 131–148. Reprinted in No. 168, 261–280.

168. Staden, Heinrich von, *Aufzeichnungen über den Moskauer Staat (Moscowiter Land und Regierung),* second, enlarged edition (Hamburg, 1964).

169. *Das nationalsozialistische Deutschland und die Sowjetunion 1939–1941. Akten aus dem Archiv des Deutschen Auswärtigen Amts.* Deutsche Ausgabe von Eber Malcolm Carroll und Fritz T. Epstein. Department of State, U.S.A. (Berlin, 1948). American edition: *Nazi-Soviet Relations, 1939–1941. Documents from the Archives of the German Foreign Office* (Washington, D.C.: Department of State, 1948). Edited by Raymond J. Sontag and James St. Beddie.

170. *Guide to Captured German Documents. Prepared by Gerhard L. Weinberg and the War Documentation Project Staff, under the Direction of Fritz T. Epstein* (Air University. Human Resources Research Institute, Research Memorandum, No. 2. HRRI War Documentation Project, Study No. 1) (The Bureau of Applied Social Research, Columbia University, Maxwell Air Force Base, Alabama, 1952), Supplement prepared by Gerhard L. Weinberg, 1959.

171. *Studien zur Geschichte Osteuropas (Studies in East European History; Etudes d'histoire de l'Europe orientale),* Werner Philipp and Peter Scheibert (editors), A. M. Ammann, F. T. Epstein (and others) (co-editors) (Leiden, 1954).

172. "Zwischen Compiègne und Versailles. Geheime amerikanische Militärdiplomatie in der Periode des Waffenstillstands 1918–19: Die Rolle des Obersten Arthur L. Conger" (Dokumentation), *Vierteljahrshefte für Zeitgeschichte,* III, No. 4 (1955), 412–445.

173. *Guides to German Records Microfilmed at Alexandria, Va.* (Washington, National Archives, 1958–   ). Initiated by Fritz T. Epstein and Gerhard L. Weinberg for the Committee for the Study of War Documents of the American Historical Association.

174. *Akten zur deutschen auswärtigen Politik 1918–1945.* Ser. D, IX: March–June 1940 (1962); X: June–August 1940 (1963) ("Geschäftsführender Leiter" [acting editor], together with Hans Rothfels, ed.).

175. *The American Bibliography of Russian and East European Studies* for 1963 (together with Albert C. Todd and Stephen Viederman) (Bloomington, Indiana, 1966); 1964 (1966); 1965 (1968); 1966 (1971).

VI. UNPUBLISHED WRITINGS AVAILABLE FOR PUBLIC USE

176. Die Hof- und Zentralverwaltung im Moskauer Staat und die Bedeutung von G. K. Kotoschichins Werk, *Über Russland unter der Herrschaft des Caren Aleksej Michajlovitsch für die russische Verwaltungsgeschichte.* Phil. diss., Berlin, 1924. Referees: Professor Karl Stählin, Professor Fritz Hartung. See *Jahrbuch der Dissertationen der Philosophischen Fakultät der Friedrich Wilhelms Universität zu Berlin, Dekanatsjahr* 1923–1924 (Berlin, 1925), 269–272. A copy of the typewritten thesis is available at the Osteuropa-Institut of the Freie Universität Berlin. Call No. Lr 241.

177. Russland und die Weltpolitik 1917–1920. Studien zur Geschichte der Intervention in Russland (mit einer Bibliographie). Six parts, typewritten [Frankfurt a.M., 1933]. Available in the Library of the British Museum, reproduced from typescript. Call No. 20087.b.34. Listed in Department of Printed Books, *General Catalogue,* LXVII (1960), Col 886.

178. Comparative Facilities for Slavic Studies in the Libraries of Germany and the United States. Memorandum, May 1939 (typewritten). 11 pp. Available at the Slavonic Division Desk of the New York Public Library.

179. European Military Influence in Latin America (1941). Washington, Library of Congress Photoduplication Service, 1961. Microfilm copy (negative) of typescript. Call No.: Microfilm 7104 F (Library of Congress Card Mic 62-7330).

VII. PRINTED CORRESPONDENCE

180. Discussion of the page proof (Library of Congress Microfilm D-18) of the unpublished Vol. XIV of the Official German History of the First World War Written by the German General Staff: Alexander Griebel, "Geschichte—Geheime Kommandosache," *Deutsche Rundschau,* 78th year, No. 10 (October 1952), 1024–1027 (pp. 1026–1027, Epstein letter of June 7, 1951); ibid., 79th year, No. 2 (February 1953), 187–197: letters to the Editor by Wolfgang Foerster, Alexander Griebel, and Fritz T. Epstein,

192–197; Hellmuth Greiner, "Der XIV. Band des Weltkriegswerks": *Wehrkunde,* 6th year, No. 3 (March 1957), 155–157; Alexander Griebel, "Geschichte—ohne Geheimschutz. Das Weltkriegsende und das Reichsarchiv," *Deutsche Rundschau,* 83rd year, No. 6 (June 1957), 587–595.

181. "Nazi Archives Rescue." Letter to the Editor, *The New York Times,* March 15, 1966.

VIII. WORK IN PROGRESS

182. "Aussenpolitik in Revolution und Bürgerkrieg (1917–1920)," *Osteuropa-Handbuch.* Band: Sowjetunion, Teil: Aussenpolitik 1917–1970. Dietrich Geyer, ed.